OVERCOMING THE DARK SIDE OF THE PRO-LIFE MOVEMENT

JOHN S. MICHENER

Copyright © 2024 by John S. Michener
All rights reserved.

ISBN: 9798879508420
Independently published

Cover Art: Kenneth B. Perkins

Cover Layout: Ken Wait

Editors: Jayne Michener, Polly Pat Michener, Lana Wooldridge, Thana Furr, Rusty Thomas

To my wife, Jayne, whose
friendship and profound influence has enabled
our ministry of saving lives and saving souls.

Contents

Preface — vii

Introduction — xi

1. A First Mistake: Assumptions — 1
2. The Offense of the Cross: A Graphic Display — 9
3. Earthly Kingdoms — 25
4. Do Not Ask for Permission — 37
5. Bad Arguments by Good People — 45
6. My Body, My Choice — 55
7. Elephants and Birth Control — 71
8. Starfish and Tractors — 83
9. 1984: Pro-choice Is Pro-life — 93
10. No Other Gods: The Judiciary — 105
11. Victims or Criminals? — 123
12. Pro-life v. Abolition — 139
13. Political Repentance: The Legislature — 149
14. Bearing the Sword: The Executive — 163
15. Grant Justice! — 177
16. Why Bother? — 201
17. Be Present at the Gates of Death — 205
18. What Can I Do? — 223

Appendix: Abortion Intervention Ministry — 237

About the Author — 241

Preface

This book is a story of growing up and maturing in faith and in wisdom. It is a book that asks us to consider how to match our works to our faith. If a proposition is true, then how should we change the way we live to accord with that truth?

Many anti-abortion activists have suffered the same trials, disappointments, back stabs, and burn-outs that I have, but that does not have to be the case for you, dear reader. With the help of this book, you can adjust your expectations and dodge many of the pitfalls and types of people that will give you grief. My recommendations will show you how best to use your time, energy, resources, relationship capital, and political capital so that you can thrive and be successful in saving lives and saving souls.

So, you want to get involved in saving lives? I did, too. Then I found myself wasting time and exhausting my resources with little to no return. Church leaders refused to help. Pro-life politicians refused to do what is right. Pro-life leaders were more interested in their next fundraising banquet than in the daily ministry of saving lives. Some pro-lifers gave everyone involved a bad name by using misguided tactics and bad arguments. Other pro-lifers criticized the way volunteers ministered, or called others heretics over theological differences—anything to avoid partnering with fellow believers to save lives. Over the years I have run into a lot of incorrect ideas, short-sighted strategies, and bad attitudes.

I also learned that the political pro-life movement is full of corruption. A large percentage of pro-life politicians and lobbyists are more interested in using abortion as an issue on which to raise money and win re-election than in actually abolishing it. Natural human tendencies, along with systematic corruption from within and strategic corruption from without, have weakened and undermined the pro-life movement.

In short, the pro-life movement has a dark side unknown to most believers. This book is about how to shine the light into those dark places, avoid them, and how to do the work of saving lives and saving souls despite the obstructions and opposition you will face within the pro-life movement.

In 2006, when I got started in earnest, I was full of enthusiasm, determination, and hope. I wanted to save as many lives as I could as quickly as possible. I dived into the deep end by volunteering with activists from Justice For All, Genocide Awareness Project, Operation Rescue, and Center for Bio-Ethical Reform.

Along the way I learned at the feet of thoughtful activists such as David Lee and Scott Klusendorf at Life Training Institute who served on our board at Justice For All. I brainstormed better teaching strategies with Stephanie Gray at Canadian Centre for Bio-Ethical Reform, and I studied the strategies of Mark Harrington at Created Equal. I spent thousands of hours in conversation with young people on college campuses across the United States.

Rejection by Christians and conflict with other pro-lifers came almost immediately. For various reasons that have been addressed in this book, it seemed no one wanted to join me in a passionate pursuit of saving lives. I immediately became accustomed to hearing *No*. No, I could not speak. No, I could not teach. No, I could not raise support. No, I could not share the truth from the pulpit or in the classroom.

But not everyone said no. I still found audiences in faith fellowships not my own, at conferences, at rallies, and especially among the homeschool community. And I kept seeking new ways to minister. I completed training to be a Forgiven and Set Free lay counselor. Using this twelve-step-like program, I have had the opportunity to minister to post-abortive men and women and help them find forgiveness and healing.

Later I met Mark Crutcher at Life Dynamics and learned the deeply racist history of the pro-abortion movement. I stormed the halls of political power with Matt Trewhella of Missionaries to The Preborn, and I interceded at death camps with Rusty Thomas of Operation Save America. I took to city streets and public spaces to reveal the horrors of the American abortion genocide.

One such project landed me in the home of former presidential candidate Dr. Alan Keyes who served as an ambassador under President Ronald Reagan. Keyes has hosted me on his podcast several times to discuss the new abolitionist movement—not the movement to abolish slavery, but to abolish abortion.

In 2014 I founded Oklahomans United for Life (now United for Life). Our mission is to train fellow servants to speak up for those who have no voice, to call on our magistrates to abolish abortion, and to rescue our preborn neighbors at the gates of death. I have been privileged to teach at Focus Leadership Institute, Charis Bible College, and at numerous private Christian schools and homeschool co-ops.

For four years I headed a political action committee that donated thousands of dollars to pro-life candidates and helped them get elected. Many of these legislators turned their backs on us once elected. I have shared many of the hard lessons I learned in this book. This led to helping "abolitionist" candidates get elected to office, and it also led to working on the gubernatorial campaign of the nation's first candidate to run on the platform of using executive authority to establish an abortion-free State.

In spite of severe and continual opposition from pro-lifers, we have found a way to train thousands of new activists to speak up for their preborn neighbors, to answer the toughest arguments of abortion advocates, and to share the gospel in the context of talking about abortion. Most Christians do not realize that pro-life work is a niche type of evangelism. It is virtually impossible to defend the preborn or call individuals and communities to repent for the sin of abortion without presenting the biblical good news of reconciliation.

Over the years we have saved untold lives and souls, and I have shared some of those stories in this book.

Even with measurable success, like knowing that a number of babies are alive because of our ministry, and that others have come to repentance, it is still easy to feel burned out. The stress of constant opposition, the strain of balancing ministry and family, and the lack of funding now and in the future all take their toll.

On top of it all, the Supreme Court of the United States issued its historic *Dobbs* opinion in 2022 which overturned forty-nine years of federally protected abortion policies and convinced many believers that abortion was instantly defeated in traditionally conservative States. I have explained the meaning and some of the unfortunate consequences of the *Dobbs* opinion in the chapter "No Other Gods."

Do not be put off by the doom and gloom. This book is about overcoming and so much more. I have also touched on reason, logic, language, religion, metaphysics, and law. I have considered the impact of serious theological, philosophical, and political questions on how and why we oppose or support abortion. I have looked at better ways to learn and to serve. I have explored issues and arguments that you will face and for which you must be prepared to give an answer.

There are hundreds of books about abortion already out there, but this one attempts to address some of the contentious issues overlooked or dodged by all the others. I hope that this book might encourage those already on the path to stay the course, because, although it is a road less traveled, it is the right path. I hope it might inspire others to start a similar journey, but with a better road map. In other words, keep on keeping on, or get off your duff and get to work.

J. Michener, Christmas 2023

Introduction

I grew up in a snow globe. Everything was perfect and beautiful. I had two parents who were, and still are, married to each other. They loved us kids. Mom prepared three meals a day and made sure we could read, write, and do our times tables. Dad worked to pay for everything and made sure we knew how to mow the grass and change the oil. They both took us to church every time the doors were open and modeled Christian living and service. Life growing up was idyllic.

In fact, I did not know any sinners. Sure, our congregation had a token alcoholic, but that was it. It was not until I left home for college that I began to understand the corruption of the human heart. Away from home, church, and a homogenous military community, I came face-to-face with racism, discrimination, envy, and petty Christian sectarianism. It was out in the real world that I began to see that each one of us is beset with sin. Finally, my own pride showed sharp and clear in the mirror.

My snow globe was shattered, and I needed to decide how I was going to respond to being confronted with the truth about the sin in myself and in the world. I determined that I would seek the truth in all things, even if it hurt, and I dedicated myself to authentic living in light of the truth. Faced with any newfound truth, I would ask myself, "Knowing what I know now, how should I reorder my life and work based on this truth?"

This question will provide the framework for this book. Each chapter will be a revelation of a truth that was learned at a price and gave me the opportunity to ask with Francis Schaefer and Chuck Colson, "How now shall we live?" How do I correct my course? Knowing what I know now, how should I reorder my life and work based on this truth?

The next story is not the beginning. I am sure this journey could be traced to the distant past, but for the sake of time and space, it is a sensible place to start.

In January 2007 I volunteered to help put up an eighteen-foot-tall graphic exhibit about abortion at the University of Arizona. As I walked around the erected exhibit that morning, I began discussing abortion with students who passed by. After only two hours of conversation, I broke down crying and wondering if I would be able to regroup. You see, I had talked with more than a dozen students, and each one had experience with abortion: *I had one… have one scheduled… my friend… my girlfriend…* Over and over came the stories and callous, casual references to abortion, sweeping over me like crushing waves.

For the first time I fully understood there was an American genocide taking place. To my knowledge I had never met anyone who had had an abortion. The million plus abortions performed in a year was just an abstract figure to me. Like a number from the federal budget, it meant nothing—zero emotional impact. But now the staggering number was finally real. *So, this is how it happens over three thousand times per day.* My snow globe was shattered all over again.

I walked away from that experience with another stunning revelation. The students desperately wanted to talk. They wanted someone to hear their thoughts and respond to them, to validate their ideas, or to challenge them. I was amazed that, incredibly, their minds were still open!

I asked myself, "Knowing what I know now, how should I reorder my life and work based on these truths?" For the next three years, I became a hyper-volunteer, spending all my free time and vacation time talking to others about abortion.

Then a friend at Justice For All pointed out that thousands of doctors and professionals work full time in the abortion industry. She asked, "Who is working full time to stop it?" Her question was not hypothetical. Justice For All had asked me to serve as their Regional Manager for Oklahoma and North Texas. In other words, I had been asked to prove that I could reorder my life based on newly discovered truth. If it was true that I was living in the midst of an American abortion genocide, and if it was true that college kids, at least, were open to changing their minds about abortion, then what was I going to do about it? Was I willing to dedicate myself full time to the work of saving the lives of preborn human beings by changing the minds of their parents and sharing the gospel with them? I had already made a habit of reordering my life based on truth, so, in the words of Isaiah the prophet, I said, "Here am I. Send me!"

Thus began my journey. Along the trail I initially had to fight through the brambles of others' bad attitudes, compromised tactics, and shortsighted strategies. I tripped over the obstacles of incorrect ideas and misguided arguments. But with time came trail toughness. What follows in this book are some of the most important truths revealed through my ministry adventures. Given these truths, I will discuss how you can perhaps avoid some of the pitfalls of heartache and burnout, and I will recommend ways you can better serve, teach, influence, campaign, and save along your path.

Before beginning any journey, one must prepare. If we are indeed in the midst of an American abortion genocide, how should we reorder our lives and work? Should we address the sin of abortion in church? Should we ask our governing officials to stop the bloodshed? Should we consider how to rescue our preborn neighbors from being led to the slaughter? Ask yourself: Should I become an activist? With whom should I volunteer? What should I be doing? When should I start doing it? Where and how should I minister?

I hope that in these pages you will find the answers to these questions. I hope that this book will become your map—a map that will help you decide how to dedicate your precious time, talent, and treasure.

Before we dive in, let me mention some conventions of this book. First, this book is written to and for those who believe in the one true God and who believe that abortion is morally wrong and that it ought to be legally prohibited. There is no attempt to reach non-believers or abortion advocates with this book. Reaching those individuals is our personal responsibility after properly equipping ourselves. Therefore, I will not use words that obfuscate the truth. My aim is not to lessen the impact of the subject matter, but if anything, to heighten the sense of gravity and injustice.

For example, rather than using the term *abortion facility*, the places where abortions take place will be called *death camps* or *altars of child sacrifice*. Rather than using the term *abortion* alone, which has lost much of its meaning after decades of political debate and acceptance, more accurate descriptions will be used such as *murder by abortion* or *child sacrifice*. Of course, I will take care not to needlessly offend people by how I share the truth, but neither will I sacrifice the truth to preserve people's feelings.

Second, real stories will be told to illustrate various points. Where you see a name enclosed in quotation marks, that name is a pseudonym to protect that person's identity for an important reason.

Third, some chapters end with one or more "Veritas Vignettes" that may or may not pertain to the chapter. *Veritas* means truth, and a *vignette* is a small illustration used at the beginning or end of a chapter. These illustrations of truth are stories about or from our ministry staff, students, and volunteers.

Next, we need to define some key terms used throughout this book.

Abolitionist: Someone who believes that elective abortion is an immoral choice equivalent to murder and that it ought to be treated as a criminal act under the law.

Abortion advocate: Someone who believes that elective abortion is morally permissible and ought to be legal, at least in certain circumstances. Who is against choice? Therefore the term *pro-choice* will not be used.

Blue State: A State in the United States of America that is considered politically progressive. Its branches of government are controlled by a majority of the Democratic Party.

Church: The New Testament Greek word *ekklésia* refers to a religious assembly or congregation of God's people. The word "Church" will be used as a proper noun referring to the whole body of believers, but we will not capitalize it when used as an adjective or when referring to competing concepts of church. Examples: She is a true believer, a member of the Church. He is a member of the church on Main Street; that church has good coffee, but very uncomfortable church pews.

Genocide: The deliberate and systematic killing or persecution of people from a particular group. The preborn are a specific people group that is being systematically killed through government-sanctioned and implemented policies in the United States. The definition fits.

Magistrate: Any civil officer with legal authority and jurisdiction concerned with the administration of the law. Some examples include, but are not limited to, justices of the peace, police officers, sheriffs, city and county officials, legislators, governors, district attorneys, presidents, judges, and even city dogcatchers.

Natural Law: God's law, law of God, moral law, universal law, objective standards, and universal morals.

Preborn: I like to refer to our fellow human beings who have not yet been born as the *preborn*. I find that the term *unborn* sounds too much like the undead or zombies.

Pro-life Movement (PLM): This is a collective term that refers generally to the majority opinions of well-established pro-life organizations, political activists, and politicians who wield influence.

Pro-lifer: Someone who adheres to the mainstream tenets of the Pro-life Movement.

Red State: A State in the United States of America that is considered politically conservative. Its branches of government are controlled by a majority of the Republican Party.

SCOTUS: Supreme Court of the United States and a modern god. Also referred to as "the Court."

State: A sovereign geopolitical jurisdiction that governs itself per its own charter, such as a constitution, through its own powers of law making, law enforcement, and dispute resolution. Note that in the Constitution of the United States the word State is capitalized. A similar convention will be followed when the word State is used as a noun. Examples: The State of Texas is home to many patriots. The state magistrates of a State have a duty to abolish abortion.

Yehovah: The personal name of the one true God. It means *The Existing One*. Although hidden in modern translations, it appears 6,874 times in scripture. Proper titles such as God and Father will also be used.

Yeshua: The contracted form of Yehoshua, the name of the only begotten son of Yehovah. His proper name is important because it shows his mission from his father. Note the name connection between Yehovah, which means *The Existing One*, and Yehoshua, which means *The Existing One Saves*. This intimate relationship and mission are obscured if we use only God and Jesus. Proper titles such as Lord, Son, and Anointed One will also be used.

To avoid a potential misunderstanding, I am not part of modern movements called "Messianic" or "Hebrew Roots." I am simply a worshiper and follower of the one true God and his Son.

Finally, I have chosen to write this book using a heavy dose of the royal we. *I* and *me* will be used where appropriate in personal stories or anecdotes, but beyond those contexts, this concerns all the people of God.

I was asked once about a newspaper article in which I used the royal we, when I alone was writing and involved in the particular story. The answer is twofold. First, our focus ought to be on the truth of the content, not the author. Second, we speak on behalf of all those who share a similar point of view, who agree with what we are saying—so much so that they are participating with prayer, time, talent, and treasure.

It is good for us all to feel that we are not alone and that our voices are heard. We need to share the truth. We need to recruit help, and we need to fight together. This is *our* work.

1

A First Mistake: Assumptions

When I was young, I had a serious problem with spelling. To be honest, I still do, but now I am old enough to listen to my Spidey sense and double-check words when I feel that doubt. Of course, having a mom who is a Grammar Nazi and who edits every manuscript makes a book like this turn out pretty clean. Back in the old days, we did not have spell-check, and in school we actually studied words and had spelling tests. We had to use memory devices to get tricky words to stick. My parents explained how to remember the correct spelling of *assume*: "If you assume, it will make an ASS out of U and ME." That is one word I never got wrong, but more importantly I got the life lesson.

Now just because we know to look out for a pit does not mean we do not fall into it. Ironically, those pits are often of our own digging. One would think he could remember where he dug a pit and what it looked like! On the contrary, life seems to be one endless process of digging holes, falling into them, and climbing out again. Pretty much every chapter of this book begins with a faulty assumption on my part.

When I started in ministry, I had a lot of basic assumptions. For example, I assumed that all believers know when human beings come into existence. What I learned is that many believers are ignorant of or confused about the basics. For example, my Christian friend Richard shocked me when he published an article in a conservative newspaper that displayed ignorance of basic biology concerning preborn human beings. He stated that when we become a human is a matter of belief. He also confused and used interchangeably the terms *life, a life, individual life, living cell, living human cell,* and *person.* He seemed to argue that since not every living human cell is a human being, then we need not concern ourselves with the youngest human beings who are merely clumps of cells. He rightly argued that the legal definition of an "individual life" cannot be based on anyone's belief but should come from a definition that is "rational, science-based, and consistent." However, he appeared to be unaware that we already have and operate on such a definition.

I have found that ignorance like Richard's is common among believers, so for the benefit of all, we should always attempt to correct and clarify the facts of basic biology.

When we become unique human individuals is not a matter of belief; it is a matter of settled science. We can prove that preborn human beings at every stage of development are (1) living, (2) human, (3) whole human beings, and (4) unique human beings.

Living. Once the fertilization process is complete, the preborn are clearly alive. They exhibit the three characteristics of living things: They are growing through cellular reproduction, reacting to stimuli, and metabolizing food for energy. There is no dispute about whether something that exhibits all of these characteristics is alive.

Human. The preborn are living cells, but what kind of cells are they? Obviously, since living things reproduce after their own kind, they are human cells. It is not possible that two human parents can produce offspring that are not human but later become human. A preborn human being, even as a zygote or blastocyst is still recognizable as a human according to its distinctly human DNA.

Whole. We have established that the preborn are at least living human cells, but so are the skin cells that we scrub off in the shower every day. Are we killing innocent human beings when we bathe? This question confuses parts and wholes. Even some pro-life people struggle because they have a vague impression in their minds of embryos developing like cars on an assembly line, constructed piece by piece. They have this notion that until the heart or some other functional part is attached, the preborn are not really whole individuals. But human beings are not constructed. The embryo does not have a heart added in week three. She develops it from within herself. The preborn, even at one cell old, is not a functional part of someone else's body; she is her own whole body with her own functional parts. She is unifying those parts for the good of the whole and developing herself to the next stage.

Unique. Again, human development is not like construction; it is more like the old Polaroid photos. Imagine I take a Polaroid photo of my daughter Nadia. The white, square photo paper is ejected from the camera, and I look in disappointment at the blank paper. Thinking I have somehow missed the shot, I tear up the paper and throw it away. In so doing, did I throw away an actual unique picture of Nadia? Yes! The picture is a metaphor, of course, for a unique human being. Exposure is like fertilization, and once the fertilization process is complete, a unique human being has come into existence. Once Nadia came into existence, she continued to develop the appearance of the girl we recognize today, but she could never have developed into Nick, no matter how much bad milk we fed her or how many manly toys we put in her crib. Nadia's unique DNA, which defines her individual physique and personality traits, ensures that Nadia has been, is, and always will be Nadia. Given adequate nutrition and a proper environment, every unique human being progresses through a lifetime of development.

Summarizing thus far, even atheists and agnostics admit that the preborn at every stage of development are human beings and that abortion kills a living, whole, unique member of the *Homo sapiens* community. No biology text disagrees. They cannot deny biological facts.

Biological Facts

Jerome Lejeune, M.D., Ph.D., is Professor for Fundamental Genetics at Hôpital des Enfants Malades in Paris, France. During a custody battle over embryos, Lejeune testified that "Science has a very simple conception of man; as soon as he has been conceived, a man is a man." ("Tennessee Judge Awards Custody of 7 Frozen Embryos to Woman," *The New York Times* 22 September 1989). Ralph P. Miech, M.D., Ph.D., Professor of Molecular

Pharmacology, Physiology, and Biotechnology at Brown University said, "Human embryos and human fetuses are human beings, each with their own unique genetic DNA" (brown.edu/academics/medical/about/faculty/1100924757). Similarly, C. Christopher Hook, M.D., Director of Ethics Education at the Mayo Clinic, said, "When fertilization is complete, a unique genetic human entity exists" (quoted by Richard Ostling in an AP news story 24 September 1999).

Steven Andrew Jacobs, J.D., Ph.D., published a 233-page study in *Issues in Law & Medicine* titled "The Scientific Consensus on When a Human's Life Begins." According to the study, "Biologists from 1,058 academic institutions around the world assessed survey items on when a human's life begins and, overall, 96% (5337 out of 5577) affirmed the fertilization view" (Volume 36, Number 2, 2021).

The most widely used university texts in the relevant fields agree:

> Although life is a continuous process, fertilization...is a critical landmark because, under ordinary circumstances, a new, genetically distinct human organism is formed when the chromosomes of the male and female pronuclei blend in the oocyte. (Ronan O'Rahilly and Fabiola Müller, *Human Embryology & Teratology*, 3rd ed. New York: Wiley-Liss, 2001, p. 8)

> The status of the fetus has been elevated to that of a patient who, in large measure, can be given the same meticulous care that obstetricians provide for the pregnant woman. (F. Gary Cunningham et al., *Williams Obstetrics*, 20th ed. Appleton & Lange, 1997, p. 151)

Where people differ is over the value of existing preborn humans. If Yehovah does not exist, then there is no basis for objective moral values and duties. They simply do not exist. If there is no God, then the idea that human beings are intrinsically valuable, the idea of equal rights, and the idea that murder is wrong and ought to be prevented, are all just interesting musings of our highly evolved meat computers. In a world without God, we might as well kill all the kids we want, preborn or otherwise.

However, Christian philosopher William Lane Craig argues, "Good and bad, right and wrong, do exist. Just as our sense experience convinces us that the physical world is objectively real, our moral experience convinces us that moral values are objectively real." Even the secular philosopher Michael Ruse admits, "The man who says that it is morally acceptable to rape little children is just as mistaken as the man who says 2+2=5." It is beyond reasonable doubt that objective moral values and duties exist. Therefore, it is highly likely that God exists.

When it comes to abortion, it is a biological fact that preborn human beings are innocent victims, which makes the act of abortion morally wrong. Abortion is not medical care; it is murder. The rationale is inescapable. Either there is no God, so we can rape, we can steal, and we can abort babies with impunity; or there is a God, and we are in big trouble for protecting murder by abortion in our States.

But What About...?

Abortion advocates try to convince opponents of abortion that if a State abolishes abortion, then some dramatic, life-or-death situation might kill a mother because a doctor could not perform an emergency, life-saving abortion. Abortion advocates have had great success selling this narrative. So much so that we have often heard opponents of abortion say things like, "I'm pro-life, but with exceptions," or "I'm pro-life, but what about...?"

We need to understand that even prior to the *Roe v. Wade* opinion, when all the States had laws against abortion, none of those laws prevented doctors from practicing medical triage, which is the practice of saving as many lives as possible in emergency situations. For example, an ectopic pregnancy is a pregnancy in an abnormal location, somewhere outside of the uterus, typically in the fallopian tube. At only one percent of pregnancies, ectopic pregnancies are rare. Typically, by the time the ectopic pregnancy is located, the baby has already died due to the lack of a life-sustaining environment.

The danger of an ectopic pregnancy is that the fallopian tube will rupture, causing internal bleeding and death of the mother without immediate intervention. Consequently, ectopic pregnancies should be monitored and treated through a hospital. When the doctor surgically removes the embryo or heterogenous mass to save the life of the mother, this is not murder by abortion; it is true healthcare. The doctor is practicing medical triage to save as many lives as possible in that situation.

Many proposed pieces of pro-life legislation include language that tells doctors they are permitted to kill a child by abortion in certain circumstances. This legal language is problematic because the politicians writing the bills are not medical professionals. By attempting to identify and describe specific medical situations in criminal statutes, they often inadvertently provide legal loopholes for abortionists to exploit. Examples of bad statutory language which abortionists can exploit are: "Abortion will be permitted in cases where the mother's health is at risk" and "A doctor may terminate the pregnancy of a woman with an ectopic pregnancy or when the unborn child has a lethal anomaly."

Rather than trying to identify and define in statute any imagined need for an abortion, legislators should simply offer protection from liability in cases where doctors attempted to treat and save both the mother and the preborn child. Anything else becomes a license to kill.

There is never a reason to murder a preborn person by abortion, and medical triage will continue to be practiced by doctors even when we return to a legal environment in which elective abortion is a criminal act. Understanding medical triage will help us prevent abortion advocates from successfully using medical emergencies as justification to keep elective abortion legal.

So how should we reorder our lives and work based on the truth that many people, including believers, are ignorant of basic biology? Personally, I teach heavily on this topic in presentations, workshops, and seminars, and try always to show pictures or videos of the victims of abortion at various stages of development—a practice, by the way, that has often caused some contention, as we will see in the next chapter. But we must constantly remind each other of the humanity of our preborn neighbors.

Veritas Vignette

In 1969 John Wayne starred in *True Grit*, one of his most famous films, and the role for which he won an Oscar for Best Actor, but the real hero is a fourteen-year-old girl who sets out on an arduous journey for justice.

The movie is rated "G" for General Audiences. In the opening scene of the film, we see gambling, drunkenness, and murder. In the second scene, we see an entire county gather in the town square to watch three guilty prisoners hanged by the neck until dead. Children are skipping and playing, and some are being pushed in swings as everyone watches the executions. There was a time in this country when we did not hide justice or injustice.

As we were setting up conversation starters at the University of Georgia, two educators approached our team. They inquired if there was a way we could move or turn our signs. They were afraid that their high school students who were visiting the campus might see the graphic images of abortion and get upset.

I grinned to myself at the ironies. Many of our volunteers who were helping to set up the signs were high school students. We used to let children witness public hangings, but these educators seemed to think that a modern teenage girl could not handle viewing pictures of a surgical procedure—a procedure that they likely considered a civil right. We used to execute civil justice in the public square, to openly display the death of the guilty, but now we hide the death of the innocent.

If we forever shelter kids from looking at death, then how can they ever fully appreciate and respect life? Like the young girl from the John Wayne film who witnessed death and evil but faced them head-on and bravely set out to set things right, our student evangelists can handle the truth, and they display *true grit*.

2

THE OFFENSE OF THE CROSS: A GRAPHIC DISPLAY

For Jews demand signs and Greeks look for wisdom, but we preach Christ crucified: a stumbling block to the Jews and foolishness to Gentiles. (1 Cor. 1:22-23)

Before your very eyes Jesus Christ was clearly displayed as crucified. (Gal. 3:1)

A Dirge

Venus, the bright and morning star, lit the way in the predawn haze. The lead vehicle turned into the deserted main street with its headlights on and cargo in tow. Dozens of cars filled with family members filed close behind, headlights glowing. The procession wound through the old part of town. As they arrived at the appointed place, they exited their cars and gathered in a circle to pray. Then, it was time. They carried the deceased onto the green grass and laid them down in a somber memorial.

This was not a traditional funeral. The lead vehicle was not a hearse; it was a truck towing a thirty-foot trailer containing The Exhibit. The Exhibit tells the story of preborn children who have been murdered by abortion. The cars carried activists who gathered to pray at sunrise for the day's work. We carried the eighteen-foot-tall exhibit panels out to the campus green and set them up in memorial, not to one particular victim, but to the tens of millions of preborn victims of America's ongoing abortion genocide.

We performed this ceremony dozens of times each year on college campuses, hoping to realize the benefits of a funeral. Funerals are not for the dead, but for the living, who must grieve and wrestle with haunting questions. Why were these killed? What impact and value did these lives have on our own? What does it ultimately mean? These questions are often painful and unwelcome, yet the struggle to answer them plays a significant role in the grieving process. It can result in a more meaningful life lived with greater depth and hope.

One of the things we experience at funerals is mourning. At the University of North Texas (UNT) we met young women who cried in the shadow of The Exhibit. I personally met two such women and was able to offer some words of comfort, but more importantly, I was able to connect them with an experienced local counselor.

Early Monday morning Pastor Bill noticed a female student writing on our Free Speech Board. Her hand shook as she wrote, and Bill felt called to talk to her. "Becky" had just found out that she was pregnant and had already decided she was going to abort. She was angry that we were "trying to tell her what to do." Bill signaled to me to come over, and together we asked her to consider that she was carrying a living human being. She seemed very hardened and jaded. Even after I offered to pay for her medical care if she would agree to give the child to me or my sister, she would not change her mind. We then invited our long-time friend and volunteer Shalene to join the conversation. Becky talked with her privately for hours as this experienced, godly woman listened. Shalene, who once aborted one of her own children, was in a position to persuade and warn Becky with the truth while offering help.

I met another special woman at UNT whose abortion many years ago still haunts her and drives her current ambition to volunteer and share the truth. She would admit that her tireless efforts are a type of penance for her past.

Deb, who works at the Woman to Woman pregnancy center in Denton, sent us the following email:

The second day of The Exhibit I had to leave at two o'clock to return to the clinic. Three students walked into the clinic just past three o'clock. One asked to talk to someone... I spoke with her, and she said she was pregnant and heard about our clinic from "the people who had those big signs of babies up on the campus." She made an appointment for the following day, and her friend asked about our Post Abortive services. They said they were glad to have seen The Exhibit. It helped bring them to the center.

Stuart stood under the stately oak trees and waited for his next divine appointment. A young lady approached The Exhibit, and like a stone statue, she stared at it. It was not raining, but a drop of moisture ran down this statue's face. Then the statue cracked and became human. Reacting to this sign, Stuart gently began a conversation. He learned that she had chosen to have an abortion earlier in the year. He asked if she would like to talk about it with someone who had made a similar decision. He then brought her to Lori and Angela, two volunteer missionaries. Lori and Angela sat with the young woman on a bench under the trees for over two hours. Besides providing her with immediate lay counseling and sharing the gospel, they were able to connect her with local professional counseling options and a local post-abortion women's Bible study.

What Might Not Have Been

Raising The Exhibit on a college campus does not just happen. It requires sponsorship from campus students and the volunteer support of the local Church. Going into this ministry, I had assumed that local churches would jump at the chance to participate in such a jaw-dropping and effective Christian outreach. I was completely shocked to find Christian leaders actively opposing us.

I remember that first morning of the outreach seeing a circle of Catholic students praying with rosaries in hand. After raising The Exhibit, I walked over to thank them for covering us in prayer and to invite them to participate in ministering to the student body. The leader of the group stared at me with cold, dark eyes and said, "We are praying against you and your group—that you will have to leave." I was so taken aback that I did not know how to respond.

I should not have been surprised, given the extreme opposition we had already faced from Gavin, an associate pastor of a large protestant church in the area. Upon receiving our early invitation to help us recruit and train local volunteers for the campus outreach, he had attacked our strategies vehemently and at length. Gavin argued that the use of large graphic displays in public was both immoral and ineffective. He claimed that our display argued only for the humanity of the preborn, which was not the actual problem. The real problem, he explained, was the love of freedom and personal autonomy. Finally, he claimed that we were just trying to refute logical fallacies, while our goal should be to change hearts.

How does one believer respond to another believer who disagrees? Our practice has always been to respond with courtesy and candor. It is one of our core beliefs that we should never sacrifice another person's feelings with how we share the truth, but neither should we sacrifice the truth for the sake of that person's feelings. So, I answered each of Gavin's points and his faulty assumptions. Below are excerpts from my correspondence with him. They have been lightly edited to fit the context of this chapter, and text in brackets is additional, current commentary.

> Thanks for allowing us some time to cogitate on all that you have said. You raise many tough questions, questions on which we reflect at regular intervals. It was time for us to do this again, so we welcomed your correspondence as an opportunity to review and question our beliefs once again as we move into our summer activities.
>
> One of the first things we must do is set the context for our use of graphic displays. Graphic displays serve multiple purposes. As you know, dialogue is what we teach, and the graphic displays function as a way to create ample opportunity for dialogue. Other purposes include revealing the injustice, shocking the audience out of complacency, bringing to light the daily violence,

and changing people's minds about the morality of abortion.

There is much disagreement across the pro-life community about graphic displays, but almost no one would say that using graphic displays is never appropriate. The debate centers around when and how to display them. One organization might focus on showing pictures to the pro-life community to motivate and energize them to action. Another group might show the pictures indiscriminately to as many people as possible. Other groups limit their use to private conversations or to classrooms. Our approach is a thoughtful hybrid. While we do not typically use large graphic displays in public parks or on overpasses, we do elect to use them on college campuses. We make no judgment about how different organizations use such displays; we are only illustrating that there is a wide range of beliefs regarding what is appropriate.

Gavin, your correspondence outlines your thoughts about the use of graphic displays in public and about our strategy. We will comment on your thoughts in the same order.

Large graphic displays in public are immoral.

You assert that using large graphic displays in public is immoral. Just to be clear, if something is immoral, that means it is wrong and sinful and should not be practiced. Your argument is that "Springing a grotesque picture on someone is analogous to shouting a profanity or springing a pornographic image on someone."

The problem with this argument is that graphic displays of abortion are not analogous to profanity or pornography. There is, however, some analogy to the "grotesque picture" that you referenced. For example, I drive by dead, mangled, gross, fly-ridden carcasses of possums every day. These are grotesque. Pointing them out to someone else might be in poor taste, but it would not be sinful. This might be somewhat like pointing out grotesque pictures of aborted babies, but again, it would not be sinful.

Profanity and pornography are a completely different matter. For example, were I to walk by pornography in a gas station, looking at it by accident might be unhealthy, but it would not be sinful. However, seeking it out and consuming it on purpose would be sinful. Furthermore, encouraging others to seek it out and consume it would also be sinful. Note how this is different from pointing out the dead possum or pictures of abortion. The sin in pornography is creating it and looking at it. The sin in abortion is not looking at the dead children; it is the murdering of the children. Asking someone to look at abortion, even if they would be uncomfortable looking at their own sin, would not be sinful. Yeshua calls us to examine the sin in our lives, both personally and communally. A quick search of the New Testament on "light and darkness" reveals that our Lord was never afraid to expose the darkness and evil motivations of men. Abortion is a sinful practice and a large-scale human rights violation. Looking at that injustice is not sinful, and pointing at the injustice is not immoral either.

Underlying the claim that displaying graphic images is immoral might be the assumption that it is immoral because it offends people. This begs another question: *Who is being offended?* My guess would be that your concern, like ours, is for the feelings of those who have had abortions. Rather than assume how they feel about these images, we have asked them directly. [Here I attached six personal testimonies from post-abortive volunteers who affirm the use of graphic displays.]

The feedback we received from these women is that viewing the pictures can be painful and hard, but facing the truth is a critical step in beginning the healing process and preventing future abortions. Facing the truth leads to repentance and forgiveness. Because we know that graphic displays can be hard to see for those who have experienced abortion, we prioritize training our volunteers how to interact compassionately with post-abortive people, and we typically have experienced lay counselors and/or professional counselors with us at these events.

That being said, are the graphic displays offensive? It is important to understand what is meant by "offensive." One kind of offense is a sin offense against God. For example, the killing of innocent human beings is a sin offense against God. Abortion, like slavery, racism, and murder, is a serious human rights violation and a sin offense against God. But when people say, "I'm offended," what they typically mean is that they find it hard to look at, it makes them uncomfortable, or they feel emotionally upset. This is not the same thing as a sin offense. This type of offense is in the eye of the beholder and is not subject to an objective moral standard such as, "You shall not murder." We don't find any commandments like, "You shall not make people feel uncomfortable."

[It is not a sin to hold up a mirror so that others can see themselves plainly. As my fellow ministry leader Steve Wagner once said, "If…women who have had abortions are troubled by the pictures, isn't it the abortion itself that is causing the women grief or distress? Showing the pictures either clarifies the facts for the woman…or brings to the surface feelings the woman already had about her abortion. We believe that both of these effects, while difficult, are ultimately positive because they help her move from denial or ignorance to the next stage of a healing process." Recognizing guilt is the first step in the redemptive process. If others look in the mirror, but then turn away and forget, that is on them (Jas. 1:22-24).]

There may be instances when it is more proper not to needlessly offend someone, but matters of life and death and genocide are in a totally different category. We can not and must not hide the injustice. The horrors of

Auschwitz were hidden behind a wall, and the German people were able to pretend that they did not know what was happening. Would the Holocaust have continued if all the citizens were given regular tours of the camps with front row seats to watch live executions?

So, will some people feel disturbed when they see the pictures? Yes. When people are offended by seeing the truth and facing injustice, does that mean that *showing* the truth and *revealing* injustice is immoral? Is showing the truth a sin? Did the Lord ever offend or upset anyone by revealing the truth and shedding light on injustice? There is no scriptural or moral argument to be made that using graphic displays in public is sinful. In fact, there is more scriptural basis to conclude that Yeshua was in favor of offending people over matters of grievous sin.

The real question is how and when to use them. There will always be disagreement on this point based on individual preferences, sensitivities, and missions. The question of how and when to use graphic displays is best viewed as a matter of conscience in which we should choose to work with those with whom we agree and are comfortable without condemning those with whom we disagree.

Large graphic displays in public are not effective.

You assert that using large graphic displays in public has several deleterious effects such as distancing abortion advocates, causing division among pro-life advocates, stifling activism, and desensitizing people to the images.

We believe that everything you say here is true to some extent. These are logical consequences of the actions we take, and we do not disagree. They are serious concerns, and we must weigh the costs against the benefits. You have accurately mentioned some of the costs, but what are the benefits?

1) Graphic displays prevent some abortions. Is it worth making some people emotionally uncomfortable if it saves even one life? We know of dozens of lives saved.

2) Graphic displays help some women begin a healing process from past abortions.

3) Graphic displays inspire Christians by the thousands each year to get involved in pro-life work of all types. [I was one.] Our training program, which includes the graphic outreaches, teaches Christians to speak up for preborn human beings with grace and truth. We have thousands of written reflections from training participants which detail how working around such displays helped them personally develop their faith and how they convinced passersby that abortion was wrong and should end.

4) Graphic displays are effective at creating a lot of dialogue, and dialogue is the scriptural method of evangelism, which is a major purpose. [This is confirmed by our photos and reflections of volunteers in action.]

The effectiveness of using the graphic displays on campus comes down to a cost-benefit analysis, and we believe that the benefits are worth the costs. While some will be offended and alienated, we believe many more will be convicted, convinced, and emboldened. The graphic displays are a key ingredient in triggering repentance and healing, rescuing babies in imminent danger, saving moms and dads from pain and guilt, emboldening Christians to be salt and light, and providing a venue to share the good news.

It is a heart problem, not a head problem.

[Here, Gavin claimed that we were not addressing the real problem. He assumed that we only exposed the logical fallacies in the arguments of abortion advocates, without ever sharing the gospel.]

We believe that you are correct about the real issue being a heart problem. It all comes down to humans putting their own selfish desires ahead of other people's needs. We believe that the strategy is not an *either or*; it is a *but also*. We concur that it is not enough to simply focus on the humanity of the preborn. We must *also* focus on putting ideals like freedom and autonomy in their proper order among God's values so that we live in proper relationship with our neighbors. I believe we are doing that in our seminars and in our campus outreaches.

I agree that our goal is to change hearts, but keep in mind that in our culture that often entails refuting logical fallacies. Paul said, "We demolish arguments and every pretension that sets itself up against the knowledge of God, and we take captive every thought to make it obedient to Christ" (2 Cor. 10:5). That sounds a lot like refuting logical fallacies.

Gavin, we take this work very seriously, and we want others to as well. It is valuable to be clear in our own minds about what we think is right, what we think God expects, and what things are a matter left to our own consciences.

We believe that graphic displays may offend some, but it is not offensive in the sense that it is immoral to display such pictures. They are also an effective tool for training pro-life advocates, creating dialogue, triggering the healing/repentance process, changing hearts, and saving lives.

I hope that these points are convincing to you, because we value your partnership on the mission field and want to be able to continue working with you and your students. Even if you decide that you cannot work near graphic displays in clean conscience, we hope that you will still be able to work near one of our non-graphic dialogue tools on outreach day.

Even after the two-day outreach, we received a similar letter of criticism from another local ministry leader named Alexis. Most of her complaints were the same as Gavin's, but there were a few variations, to which I responded with the same courtesy and candor. Again, here are the pertinent excerpts from my response:

You are doing more harm than good.

[Here I again explained the difference between emotional discomfort and sin.] We do know that we are doing good at UNT. Each year we are able to connect young people who are hurting from abortion to local counseling, and in some cases, we know of babies whose lives were saved because their mothers saw our graphic displays or interacted with our volunteers. We also share the good news of reconciliation with our heavenly Father.

No one will talk to me because of you.

Our experience with activism for almost twenty years is that certain abortion advocates will not engage in real dialogue, no matter what. They use one excuse after another to avoid actually sharing and discussing ideas. We saw this in a dramatic fashion at UNT when several student clubs banded together to chant, yell, rant, cuss at us, and call us names—anything to avoid real dialogue. Blaming us was just a convenient excuse not to talk to you. They would find a different excuse if it were someone else. Do not lose heart, though. For every one with that attitude, we find a thousand others whose minds are open and whose hearts are receptive to the truth. Find the fertile soil.

You do not get enough responses to justify the event.

On the contrary, we engage in literally thousands of conversations over a typical two-day outreach, and those conversations continue across the campus community for days, if not weeks, afterwards. We typically train dozens of local volunteers before an outreach. Not only do those volunteers engage in productive conversations during the outreach, that experience gives them the confidence to continue defending their preborn neighbors in their everyday lives. We have thousands of volunteer reflections about their conversations and how they changed people's minds.

Jesus calls us to plant seeds of love.

"Do not suppose that I have come to bring peace to the earth. I did not come to bring peace, but a sword" (Mat. 10:34). Certainly, we agree that Christians should try to live in peace and love, but we are also to be salt and light in a lost and dying world. Yeshua preached repentance everywhere he went. The world has no idea that it needs to repent unless they first face and are convicted of sin and guilt.

Do you believe that Yehovah would ever use a graphic display to get his message across? The answer is, *he already has*: "You foolish Galatians! Who has bewitched you? Before your very eyes Jesus Christ was clearly **displayed as crucified**" (Gal. 3:1). He was literally lifted up like a billboard. Now that is a graphic display! One intended to teach us how God sees sin—like the sin of abortion.

You should use other tactics.

My first question is, *tactics for what?* We are training believers to speak up for their preborn neighbors. Our training tactic is a two-part program. The first part is an interactive training seminar, and the second part is a campus outreach. The experience of both parts put together teaches believers how to engage in productive evangelism from the starting point of abortion.

I presume that you mean, *have you considered using anything other than graphic displays as an outreach tactic?* We actually use many tactics concurrently so that we can reach as many people as possible. Besides the graphic displays, which we use only in select venues like large college campuses, we also use poll tables, free speech boards, open-mic sessions, non-graphic kiosks, and surveys. In short, we employ any tactic that helps us engage in dialogue and which will also have a passive teaching aspect. Not everyone will stop to engage, whether it is a sign or a cupcake, so we like to use tools which teach people who pause to take a look or listen but do not want to have a conversation.

Is There a Better Way?

Another church leader said, "I'm just not convinced the methods of [using graphic displays] are the best way: they seem to me to be more 'shock and awe.'"

Dr. Martin Luther King, Jr. wrestled with this very question while fighting the battle against racism. Pastors and leaders of churches called his leadership of marches, sit-ins, and other demonstrations "unwise and untimely." In fact, the naysayers became so loud that he eventually answered them at length in his "Letter from Birmingham Jail." Of particular note is paragraph ten in which King argues:

> Nonviolent direct action seeks to create such a crisis and foster such a tension that a community...is forced to confront the issue... There is a type of constructive, nonviolent tension which is necessary for growth... We must see the need...to create the kind of tension in society that will help men rise from the dark depths of prejudice and racism to the majestic heights of understanding and brotherhood.

Dr. King was by no means the only revolutionary who brought about change by the methods he used. In fact, Yeshua often created tension on purpose. Take the example of his healing on the Sabbath. There were six other days of the week on which he could have worked, yet he made it a habit to heal and engage in other worthy activities that might be construed as "work" on the Sabbath. It was important for him to make sure the Jewish leaders were uncomfortable about his ministry so that they might see how they had incorrectly ordered their own priorities. Many of them had elevated Sabbath keeping, a sacred act of worship, above caring for the sick and poor. Similarly, many church leaders today have prioritized church worship and other worthy religious activities over the needs of defenseless preborn children.

The entire biblical account indicates that Yehovah takes sin quite seriously. In conclusion, we reiterate the rhetorical question: Would Yehovah ever use a graphic display to get his message aCROSS?

It is in this spirit that many believers choose to use graphic displays and other means to create the type of tension that demands a response. Our objective is not to unduly shock and awe the audience; rather it is to create a constructive tension that leads to growth. Without tension, without a catalyst, no one examines himself, and collectively we leave public policy alone.

We hope that those wondering if there is a better way will not let the hypothetical better become the enemy of the actual good we can be doing. We have lives to save right now, every day.

The antipathy over graphic displays was my baptism into the contention, division, and closed doors of the pro-life movement. There were many other obstacles to putting up graphic displays, from counter-protestors, to leftist campus officials, to bureaucratic red tape, and politburo-like restrictions, but nothing as disheartening as the opposition from other believers.

Based on this experience, what should we do? How should we reorder our lives and work? The answer is to not let the naysayers get us down. We must constantly remind ourselves not to let someone who is doing nothing keep us from doing the something that we know to do.

Veritas Vignette

It was a sunny afternoon in April on the first day of our outreach at Metropolitan State University of Denver in Colorado. A petite, dark-eyed, raven-haired Hispanic girl stood staring at The Exhibit. "Gloria" had recently learned that she was eight weeks pregnant. She shared that she was trying to decide what to do and felt that God had been sending her signs not to abort. She said that she never walked through the area where The Exhibit was stationed. Gloria thought our eighteen-foot-tall exhibit was definitely the biggest sign that God would send her way.

We talked about the development of her baby and how God expects us to treat innocent human beings. Then I invited Bubba, my good friend and fellow missionary from Alabama, to join us. He put one hand on Gloria's shoulder and his other one on mine. We stood in a triangle as Bubba prayed one of the most touching prayers I have ever heard, asking for God's grace and courage to be upon Gloria. The next day Gloria sought me out and introduced her boyfriend "Josh." They had stayed up all night excitedly talking about their future. They said God wanted them to keep their baby. After encouraging them further and exchanging contact information, they left to go visit Alternatives Pregnancy Center to get free help and support.

I continued to encourage Gloria throughout the year by email. Just after Thanksgiving I sat by the fireplace basking in the radiance of our freshly adorned Christmas tree when I heard the familiar email notification. It was a message from Gloria:

> I am happy to announce that…our son was born on Monday… He is beautiful and healthy and vivacious. Josh and I are very proud and very much in love with our son…
>
> I wanted to let you know that…you and your team made a huge contribution to the quality of my life: You indirectly helped birth my son, and…this one life you did touch is breathing today because of the selflessness, love, and devotion your team has for the beauty of LIFE.
>
> Your efforts are never in vain.

3

Earthly Kingdoms

Imagine a church congregation in which ten percent of the members are alcoholics. Members never talk about alcohol abuse when they gather, the congregation never hosts an A.A. meeting, and there is never a public address on the topic. No one individually does anything, and collectively there is no program to help members sober up. This is exactly what is happening in most American churches when it comes to abortion.

As of this writing, every State, including the more conservative ones, still permits abortion. Women are still demanding abortion, and self-induced chemical abortions are skyrocketing. Our churchgoing teens are sexually active, and we are silent. Our silence teaches them to accept the cultural norm and view abortion as a viable option for themselves when they "get into trouble." In the absence of clear teaching, they also support their friends' choices to murder their babies by abortion.

So, why do most churches not officially and systematically address abortion? Many reasons they give are not reasonable and are actually excuses. Let us examine some of those before looking at the real reasons. Here is what we often hear from church pastors, preachers, priests, and elders.

Separation of Church and State

Church leaders fear talking about anything remotely political, hiding behind the bogeyman of possible legal entanglements. There is a myth that churches registered as 501(c)3 nonprofits risk losing their tax-exempt status if they appear to endorse or oppose candidates from the pulpit. It is true that any organization incorporated under the laws of the U.S. subjects itself to additional laws and regulations that it would otherwise not be under, but the reality is that no corporate church has lost its tax-exempt status for talking about politics. Every year thousands of preachers record their electioneering sermons and send them to the IRS just to prove this point. The Church is not tax-exempt, it is tax-immune in the U.S. For more information, research Pulpit Freedom Sunday, sponsored by the Alliance Defending Freedom.

Abortion is Too Divisive

Church leaders fear that talking about abortion will only cause tension, division, and infighting in the congregation. One preacher told me directly, "John, we have Democrats here, and I don't want to offend them or drive them away."

Guess what? Churches are already full of tension and infighting, usually over petty stuff like whether or not doughnuts and coffee should be allowed in classrooms or the sanctuary. If there is going to be tension anyway, let it be over the big questions of justice and mercy.

Yeshua did not seem too concerned about the tension he caused in the temple when "he made a whip out of cords, and drove all from the temple area, both sheep and cattle; he scattered the coins of the money changers and overturned their tables. To those who sold doves he said, 'Get these out of here! How dare you turn my Father's house into a business!'" (John 2:13-17). He even warned his followers that his movement would bring severe division among family members like that prophesied by Micah (Matt. 10:34-39). If the Son of God anticipated the conflict he would bring about between blood relatives, do we honestly think he would soften his message to avoid a bit of tension between members of opposing political parties?

We Might Hurt Members

Church leaders fear that addressing the sin of abortion from the pulpit might trigger those who have participated in the sin of abortion, causing psychological harm. These leaders typically have not thought through their reasoning. They tend simply to feel that it would be wrong to emotionally upset congregants. But if we could force them to defend their feeling logically, it might look something like this. They equate emotional distress, such as feeling guilt, with physical pain. Then they assume that all types of pain are inherently bad or evil. Then they conclude that causing others pain is a sin, or at least always to be avoided. The logical syllogism goes something like this:

1. Feeling emotional discomfort is pain.
2. Pain is the result of sin in the world.
3. Sin is to be avoided.
4. Therefore, causing someone to feel pain is a sin.

As you can see, this line of reasoning stacks multiple equivocation fallacies. This is similar to the argument we addressed in the context of using graphic displays in the chapter "The Offense of the Cross." Again, causing tension over sin is like holding up a mirror. We are called to face the truth that we are sinners, and then we must make a choice. We can walk away and forget about it, or we can humble ourselves in repentance (Jas. 1:23-25). If we humble ourselves, Yehovah is faithful to forgive and restore us to fellowship.

There is a parallel situation in the life of Paul. Some grievous sin infected the Church in Corinth. It was serious enough that Paul wrote to them about it, even though he knew it would cause emotional distress and tension. This is how he summarized what happened:

> Even if my letter hurt your feelings, I do not regret it. I was sorry that my letter hurt you, but it was only for a little while. Now I rejoice, not because of your hurt feelings, but because your grief led you to repentance. For you became grieved as God intended, and so we caused you no harm. Godly sorrow brings repentance that leads to salvation and leaves no regret, but worldly sorrow produces death. See what this godly sorrow has produced in you: what earnestness, what eagerness to clear yourselves, what indignation, what alarm, what

longing, what concern, what readiness to see justice done. (2 Cor. 7:8-11)

We have seen this pattern repeated countless times, year after year in our ministry. Our abortion presentations sometimes catch congregants by surprise. Had they known the topic, they might have chosen to stay away that day. Faced with the reality of current or past sin in their lives, they squirm with discomfort, emotional pain, and guilt. But after the fact come cleansing and healing, and then a renewed sense of purpose, an eager longing for justice, and a willingness to help fight abortion.

My friend Sheila is a classic case in point. She has told me that she hated me the day that I came to preach at her church. For decades she had lived a self-destructive lifestyle resulting from her past. She stubbornly refused to think about her abortions and she had never even confessed them to her children or closest friends.

Her church at that time met in what we jokingly referred to as a "gymnatorium." Imagine a big steel building that can be a gym, a fellowship hall, or a sanctuary. That Sunday morning, over four hundred people crammed into a space designed for about two hundred. The rows were long and the seats were tight together. Sheila found herself stuck in the middle of a long row, packed in on both sides by dozens of people. She told me that if she could have gotten out, she would have run away and skipped the service. But she was forced—providentially, she would say now—to sit there and confront the sin in her past.

That day became a turning point in her life, and since that time Sheila has become an amazing teacher, lay counselor, and healer of those in similar situations as she was. I do hurt for the people I hurt in my presentations, but I rejoice over their journeys to healing and joyfully anticipate their future passion and ministry.

We Do Not Need to Talk About It

Church leaders often claim that talking about abortion is not necessary because they have literature and resources available and because their church supports the local pregnancy center. They might claim they already did enough by talking about abortion that one time…on the anniversary of something…way back when.

"Besides," they reason, "our members know what is right. This is not a problem in our congregation."

This response is to bury one's head in the sand, to pretend there is no problem by refusing to look at it. Studies have shown that abortion affects at least a quarter of those sitting in churches, but does the percentage really matter? Even if the percentage were low, we know it is a major issue in our culture. Silence on abortion communicates that it is neither worthy of discussion nor important enough to address. Do we also ignore divorce, lying, and gluttony? Maybe we do. Are we afraid to look at the divorce and addiction rates in churches?

We already said that we believe these reasons are excuses, but if that is true, then what are the real reasons?

A False Gospel

We have found that a false gospel that misunderstands grace is prevalent in American churches. The explanation goes something like this: God loves me just the way I am. We even have gay marriage and gay ministers in churches now. God's grace is boundless, and because I am a Christian, I can get an abortion if I want, and God will forgive me. Elizabeth, a self-professed Christian I met at the University of Texas San Antonio, told me that she agreed abortion was wrong, but also identified as pro-choice and would even abort her own baby "if I thought it was necessary."

"How could you do that as a Christian?" I asked.

"Because God will forgive me," she said.

Of course, God can extend mercy to whomever he chooses, but to those believers who arrogantly presumed a license to sin, Paul responded, "What then? Shall we continue to sin that grace may abound? Absolutely not!" (Rom. 6:1-2). Scripture also teaches that Yehovah opposes the proud but gives grace to the humble (Prov. 3:32-35).

Abortion Is Not Really a Sin

Some church leaders have made their peace with abortion or have adopted our culture's version of social justice. For them, abortion is no longer a sin causing spiritual death. Perhaps you are unaware that many mainline denominations have officially sanctioned abortion:

The Book of Discipline of the Methodist Church states, "We support the legal option of abortion..."

The Lutheran Church published *A Social Statement on Abortion*, which states, "This church opposes...legislation that would outlaw abortion..."

The 2006 General Assembly of the Presbyterian Church said, "Those well-developed enough to survive outside the womb...ought...not [to be] aborted." Meaning, of course, that all the rest—over ninety percent—may be murdered by abortion.

At its 1994 General Convention, the Episcopal Church resolved, "That this...Church express its unequivocal opposition to any...action on the part of...governments...that would limit the access of a woman to safe means of acting on her decision [for abortion]."

Those congregations that teach against abortion and actively fight to legally abolish it are few and far between. The growing number of churches that accept abortion, combined with the silence of the rest, has filled pews across America with Christians who have made their peace with legal abortion.

While church leaders are silent, the secular world relentlessly teaches the next generation through school, social media, and popular news and entertainment programming that abortion is acceptable. Churches that refuse to take a strong, public stance against abortion are filled with members who, when questioned, will defend abortion just like the average secular person.

American churches have been corrupted right along with secular culture. The arguments sound a little different; the phrases and jargon sound more compassionate, but the results are the same: preborn children are murdered by abortion, which is now sanctioned by Christians.

We must fight this trend in our churches. Do you know the official position of your church denomination or congregation on abortion? Do you know the beliefs of your pastors and ministers, and more to the point, what they are teaching or not teaching your children and grandchildren? Keep in mind that teaching nothing is no better than teaching false doctrine. We must teach, reprove, and exhort one another (2 Tim. 4:2).

Not every local church has embraced the views of popular culture. Some want to speak out against abortion and equip their members for the task, but they do not know where to begin. This is where we must step forward.

The Big Reason

We sat on a deck, surrounded by a carefully landscaped garden. The tables around us were elegant, and the patio furniture was comfortable. We sipped lattes from the adjoining bistro as we watched hundreds of people scurry from shop to shop. Through open French doors we saw customers perusing the shelves in the bookstore. Under raised glass garage doors, kids swallowed up in oversized leather couches played video games on giant projection screens. A group of grownups hailed each other from down the way and met up to enter the theatre together for the next show. In the midst of it all, children climbed on playground equipment. The thought occurred to me that this was one of the most relaxing and pleasant shopping malls I had ever visited.

Just to be clear, it was not really a shopping mall. It was a megachurch campus. My friends and I decided to attend the next show in the "theatre," which they called a *service* in the *sanctuary*. After the band entertained us for a long time, a full-time staff person began a presentation that ran over twenty minutes. The main point was that the "mall" needed to install video surveillance equipment around certain shops because someone was stealing printer paper, toner, and miscellaneous office supplies. The cost of the surveillance equipment was going to be over thirty thousand dollars. I casually wondered just how much paper and toner was being stolen. The staffer asked the patrons to foot the bill, and when she came to the hard sell at the end, I will never forget her words: **"Think of it as a Kingdom Investment."** Slowly I turned to observe my friends' reactions. Their mouths, too, hung open in stunned amazement.

Now, I am not opposed to megachurches, campuses, or local congregations owning great stuff. That is not the point at all. Large groups with pooled resources can do some amazing things that individuals and small groups cannot do alone. But let us not deceive ourselves. Owning stuff comes at a price greater than the salary of the full-time corporate fundraiser who secures the pledges and cash to buy and maintain the stuff. Stuff is a corrupting force. Those who own nice houses, boats, and cars know the proverb: *Do you own the stuff or does the stuff own you?* Whether it is a little or a lot, any amount of stuff can be a corrupting force.

Perhaps this story illustrates in a microcosm the tension between the earthly and heavenly kingdoms. Here was an opportunity for this church to address sin in its midst, to preach the biblical good news of reconciliation and to secure souls. Instead, they chose to prioritize securing office supplies. They were more interested in protecting the earthly property than the heavenly treasure.

In addition, American churches have been convinced that in order to own stuff collectively, they must register themselves as a corporation with the Internal Revenue Service, in other words, as a business entity.

The corporation then owns property, hires staff, and begins to protect itself and grow. The lifeblood of the corporation is cash flow, which is needed to perpetuate property, programs, and payrolls, all of which come with large and ever-growing maintenance costs. Think of the property insurance, liability insurance, utilities, benefits, and toilet paper. And now they need security cameras to spy on the toilet paper thieves.

You might be familiar with the terms Military-Industrial Complex, Big Oil, or Big Pharma. These are powerful conglomerates that are driven to protect and grow their business interests. Thanks to having overlain a corporate business model onto American churches, a Religious-Industrial Complex has emerged.

In the words of my long-time friend Charlie Meadows, it comes down to "numbers, nickels, and noses." It is not uncommon in American churches for more than 97% of the budget to be allocated to areas other than evangelism. Anything that might disrupt the cash flow gets categorized as too divisive, too political, or too fill-in-the-blank. While the hired pastors and corporate elder boards can typically point to a corporate vision or mission statement that gives lip service to the kingdom of God, their goals and daily to-do lists are overrun by tasks centered on protecting and growing their earthly kingdoms.

In the first century, the Church focused on preaching repentance unto salvation. They strengthened and prepared their generation for persecution and tough times while encouraging each other with the Lord's message of hope and resurrection. Today, churches function more like a business that is providing the services of a social club, which is not inherently bad. We desperately need social clubs. They are places that satisfy fundamental urges and needs. We all want a place to belong. We live in a culture made up of broken families, so we long for family, a place to be comfortable and accepted, a place to drink coffee with friends, a place to play basketball and pickleball, a place to raise our kids together in a safer environment.

We just need to have clear understandings and expectations of our organizations. What are they really, and what are their purposes? We should not get mad when our social clubs do not fight abortion. That is not what social clubs do. That is what the Church does, which begs the question, what is the Church?

Let us begin with an individual member of the Church. Today we use the term Christian, which arrived rather late on the scene, as explained in Acts 11:26, but early on they were called disciples (Acts 1:15), saints (Acts 9:13), believers (Acts 5:14), brothers (Acts 6:3), witnesses (Acts 5:32), followers of the Way (Acts 9:2), and Nazarenes (Acts 24:5). But what does one call a collection or meeting of believers?

Several descriptors in the New Testament refer to the people of God. Most are metaphorical literary devices to communicate the relationship between Yehovah and his followers. Some examples are:

- Body of Christ – Eph. 1:22-23, 5:22-23; Col. 1:24
- Bride of Christ – Rev. 21:9
- Church of God – Acts 20:28; 1 Cor. 1:2; 1Tim. 3:15
- House of God – Eph. 2:19; 1 Tim. 3:15; Heb. 10:21
- Letter of Christ – 2 Cor. 3:3
- People of God – 1 Pet. 2:10

- Temple of God – 1 Cor. 3:16-17; 2 Cor. 6:16
- Flock of God – 1 Pet. 5:2; John 10:16

In the New Testament, the Greek word *ekklésia*, translated church, refers to a religious assembly or congregation of God's people. The preeminent point is that when the biblical writers speak of a church, they are talking about people and relationships, not property and programs. Therefore it is important for us to clearly differentiate what we mean when we use the word church. Are we referring to the people of God, or to the earthly stuff and programs that primarily serve our legitimate social needs and only sometimes support direct outreach and evangelism? There is a place for both, but understanding which is which and having no illusions about how stuff and programs function can save us a world of frustration.

We must learn to differentiate between corporate churches and the true Church, between earthly kingdoms and the kingdom of God. Paraphrasing what the Lord said, "My kingdom is not of this world. If it were, my servants would pave parking lots and hire associate pastors of pizza procurement" (John 18:36).

I am frequently asked after presentations, "Where do you go to church?" To which I answer, "We don't go to a church, we are the Church!" Remember, fellow believer, you are the Church!

So, there are the excuses that leaders of earthly kingdoms give for not getting involved in anti-abortion ministry, and then there are the real reasons. If the keepers of church corporations will not get involved or help, what should we do? How should we reorder our lives and work? Remember Yeshua's instruction to "kick the dust off your feet." There are others out there willing to partner in any good work, and it is to them that we turn next.

Veritas Vignettes

One day we received an email as follows:

> When you were here at the University of Central Oklahoma...one of the girls had taken your pamphlet to school and shown it around. Several months later she received a note that said, "Karen, you don't know me,

but those pictures you passed around at school about abortion saved my baby's life."

This note came from a student in Colorado:

I've always said that I'm pro-life, but I never knew what that entailed... I now know what abortion does to a child. This exhibit shows that even a pro-lifer can be changed. I always kept abortion in my mind as a backup plan if I got a girl outside wedlock pregnant. After The Exhibit I could never, ever consider it again. Thank you...for showing me the error in my way and revealing to me what it really means to be pro-life.

A trained volunteer in Georgia wrote this:

They were walking past when I asked them if they had had a chance to look at the display yet... I took them to the first side while asking them what they thought about abortion... Andy told me he hadn't thought about it much, but he was pro-choice because he thought the woman should have the right to choose. As soon as we rounded the corner and he saw the very first picture of a baby at eight weeks, I could see his mind explode... After only about five minutes he said, "I don't think I can be pro-choice anymore. I just had no idea."

4

Do Not Ask for Permission

I had been contacted by Jenny, a student at Oklahoma State University, to help her train pro-life students and conduct a massive campus outreach. We discussed the dates, the strategy, and the logistics. After hours of planning and list-making, she said, "Okay, this looks great. Now let me go ask my priest."

It was a no-go. We could not officially promote or recruit on Sunday morning, and we could not use the parish property for training. Jenny, still young and idealistic, never saw it coming. It would have been great to have had our training sessions right in the parish where believing students were already hanging out and comfortable on a Sunday, but we ended up using a campus hall at an odd time, and we had a hard time getting anyone to come.

This was not the first time, and it was far from the last, that we witnessed a local church leader quench the spirit of one of his fellow church members. Too many believers start out with a fire to do something about the abortion genocide, only to hear from those in authority all the reasons their church should not get involved. Feeling that they have a duty to submit to these leaders, they accept their fate and allow their fire to go out. Sadly, the spirit is quenched (1 Thess. 5:19).

Knowing what we know now about how corporate churches protect their kingdoms from controversy, from losing numbers, nickels, and noses, how must we reorder our lives and work? Three keys to success are: (1) do not ask for permission to do good; (2) build on a solid network; and (3) use personal invitations.

Do Not Ask for Permission

Imagine you want to start an abortion-related ministry at your church. It could be campus outreach, distributing literature, holding signs, interposing at a local death camp, lobbying state magistrates, etc. You need time and space to train volunteers, to teach them why they should do something, what to do, and how to do it, a place to equip the saints for a good work (Eph. 4:12). How will you go about starting this ministry, and what might be the response of those in leadership positions?

First, I do not recommend asking for permission to participate in or to lead regular anti-abortion activities. Why not? Because: "Permission Denied!" Now you have to decide if you want to fight this new battle on top of the one you set out to fight. Do you want to fight for the lives of preborn children, or do you want to fight your own church? I recommend that you simply fill out the facilities use form and move along with your events. Big churches usually have an official process for securing a room for you to use.

Remember what we said about the Church in the chapter "Earthly Kingdoms." Ideally, the Church would follow a family model based on relationships, not a business-based corporate model. In a family, members are entitled to a place to eat, sleep, and work. Even if others do not like your ministry, they ought to find a way to let you do it behind closed doors, just as we do with our messy children. In a family we might not always like the clothes our kids wear or the music they listen to, but unless they are indecent, we let them carry on and express themselves. Unfortunately, when church leaders think like a business, with supervisors, managers, and directors, instead of a family with brothers and sisters, they might try to shut you down.

Aside from the practical need to avoid friendly fire, you morally do not need permission. You can minister according to your own conscience as part of a chosen people and a royal priesthood. Consider these passages:

- You are a chosen people, a royal priesthood, a holy nation, God's special possession, that you may declare the praises of him who called you out of darkness into his wonderful light. (1 Pet. 2:9)
- Since we have a great high priest who has ascended into heaven, Jesus the Son of God, let us hold firmly to the faith we profess. For we do not have a high priest who is unable to empathize with our weaknesses, but we have one who has been tempted in every way, just as we are, yet he did not sin. Let us then approach God's throne of grace boldly, so that we may receive mercy and find grace to help us in our time of need. (Heb. 4:14-16)
- For there is one God and one mediator between God and mankind, the man Jesus the Anointed One. (1 Tim. 2:5)
- My brothers and sisters, do not grow tired of doing what is right. (2 Thess. 3:13)

Remember, your authority is from your heavenly Father. We ourselves are already priests, and we may approach God's throne boldly and directly. You may have to enter the pastor's parlor, the elders' board room, or the deacons' doughnut hall to ask how to use the facilities, but do not let them tell you *No*. You do not need their permission to do good.

There are direct parallels in the ministry of Yeshua. Remember when he cleansed the temple of its business aspects and then began teaching his interpretation of the scriptures in the temple courts. The executive pastor, pulpit minister, church staff, and elders of his day challenged him with this question: "Who gave you the authority to do these things?" (Mark 11:28; Luke 20:2). Neither did the Lord ask permission from the Pharisees to heal on the Sabbath. Rather, he listened to his Father's voice.

Earthly pastors, priests, and staff often function as the gatekeepers of earthly kingdoms, but as members of the Church, we have a moral right to use earthly parking lots and classrooms in our obedience to the Higher Authority, who has said we should speak for those who have no voice (Prov. 31:8), rescue those being led to the slaughter (Prov. 24:11), and look after orphans and widows (Jas. 1:27). What about orphans and widows, you say? Is not an unwanted child who is scheduled for execution by his parents an orphan? Where are his parents? Is not a pregnant woman who has been abandoned without any male support in her life a widow? Where is her husband?

Keep in mind, most worthy church ministries started out as the effort of a grassroots activist fulfilling his vision. Long before the corporate church had a "Pants and Pancakes" ministry complete with budget, leadership, oversight, and advertising, someone in that congregation was moving ahead with clothing the homeless. The ecumenical ministry known as "Feed His Sheep" began as the service of one couple, along with a few friends, feeding the homeless downtown every Sunday.

Be forewarned, if you ask, you may hear *No*, and when you go ahead, you may hear *Hey, what are you doing over there? Who told you you could do that? You can't do that.* We have learned that the mentality that says *Now let me go ask* typically gets quashed by management.

Be prepared, like your big brother Yeshua, not to take no for an answer. What is your backup plan? Be ready and willing to move off campus. When they try to shut you down, move to your own sphere of control. Are you a Sunday school teacher with a classroom? Is your living room big enough? Is there a homeschool co-op location available to you? In the worst case you could rent a library or hotel conference room. Even the Lord often had to go down by the lake, across the river, or out into the wilderness.

Build on a Solid Network

In the movie *Field of Dreams,* a voice tells the main character, "If you build it, he will come." While not always an absolute given, we have found that if you select a time and place, and get started, others will see and hear what you are doing and join in. Just get started. Provide some occasions and opportunities for others to join you in service. If the work is fulfilling in any way or bears any kind of fruit, others will join.

Do not waste your time trying to get anybody and everybody to come. Look for an anchor group to hold the ministry event in place. Work with your Sunday school class, men's prayer breakfast, ladies' book club, home group, life group, personal friends from your inner circle, or your homeschool co-op. Focus on a small band of faithful friends. What matters is the kind of people you work with, people who are dedicated to one another and who want to do things together. Then from among those, consider who is fearless, who does not take no for an answer, and who has a reputation for always doing good.

Invite Personally

Another time we had a passionate volunteer at a large protestant church with over six hundred members who actually did get permission to promote training and use church facilities. A promotional slide rotated on the big screens, details were printed in the weekly order of worship, and announcements were made from the pulpit for several consecutive weeks. When the morning of the seminar arrived, not a single soul from that congregation attended. Not the preacher, not an elder, not an associate minister, and no one from the pews. The training session did have attendees, but they came from other churches because they had been personally invited by our staff and volunteers.

We have learned from years of trial and failure that an invitation to everyone is an invitation to no one. When your friend sees that you invited forty-nine or two hundred forty-nine other people, he will choose not to participate because he assumes that, surely, many of those others will. Consider these following two styles of invitation to a close friend or church colleague.

The first invitation is a group email and/or Facebook event to everyone at church. The verbiage is something like: "Dear Mr. Smith, Our church is hosting a training workshop next Saturday for those who are interested in anti-abortion activism. All are invited to attend."

The second invitation comes from you personally as the organizer of or participant in an event. You pick up the phone and call John Smith. When John answers the phone, you say something like:

> John, I could really use your help. I agreed to participate in the upcoming abortion apologetics workshop, but I'm second-guessing my decision. My

Saturday mornings are precious to me. There is so much I need to get done, but I'm also passionate about doing something about all the babies being killed by abortion. It just seems like we could do more, but I'm not sure what. That's why I'm attending this workshop. But I'm also concerned that the material might be uncomfortable and challenging to process. I really don't want to go alone. Would you go with me so that we can experience it together and talk about what to do with what we learn? It's a huge commitment, I know, but I think it's important, and your support would be a big help.

Which approach is more likely to secure at least one participant? To ensure a successful event you must partner with at least one or more host families. Then each member of each host family personally invites a number of friends and secures their commitment to attend. We want to encourage you not to measure success by the number of people you recruit. Yeshua did not start out with even twelve. It took him some effort and momentum to get there, and even then, the number would ebb and flow with the ministry seasons.

Remember, sending a blanket invitation to do something that does not involve pizza and fun will not get anyone involved, especially when it looks like scary, hard work. Be sensitive to your audience and realistic in your expectations. Who is going to give up a major part of their weekend or a workday to go talk about one of the scariest, most controversial topics in our culture? Typical adults are away from their homes fifty to sixty hours per week for work. The remaining time goes to taking kids to a million different activities. They barely have time to mow the grass, fix the plumbing, or cook a decent meal. No wonder anything beyond the official church service is a distant priority.

A Picture of it All

I grew up in the church tradition of *a capella* music. I delighted in the soaring sopranos, the harmonization of the altos and tenors, and my dad's rich bass. To this day, we still love to sing the old hymns with four-part harmony.

One famous group who made a living by performing this type of music for Christian audiences called itself *Acapella*, after the form of music they performed. One song that has stuck with me through the years in an instructive way was called "Everybody Said." Here are some of the lyrics:

> *Everybody said that anybody could do*
> *The important things somebody should do.*
>
> *Everybody knows that anybody could do*
> *All the good things that nobody did.*

Paula and two of her homeschooled daughters, Renee and Stormie (then ages sixteen and seventeen), understood that they were the "anybody," and that it was up to them to do all the good things that nobody would do if they did not. They decided to lead a dedicated group of individuals to do mission work in their town. What followed was remarkable. Over thirty students attended a Saturday training seminar, and almost every trainee participated in taking the truth about abortion and the biblical good news of reconciliation to their local university during a two-day outreach event.

They did not use their church's bulletin or pastor to get the word out. In fact, no one in church leadership was involved or attended. They did use the church fellowship hall, but those who attended were there because Paula invited the other homeschool moms she knew and because Renee and Stormie invited their friends.

The impact of that mission project reached far beyond the activities of those three days. Kathryn, who was a student at the university, took it upon herself to start a campus club that would continue the evangelistic conversations on campus for semesters to come. Kathryn wrote: "We are extremely grateful to you...for taking your time to come train us. It was absolutely awesome getting the chance to use our training Monday and Tuesday, and I could easily say it was one of the best experiences in my life."

Another volunteer, Rebecca, wrote:

> I told myself that I would just listen the first day and not say anything, but when I saw people saying [abortion]

should remain legal, I couldn't let them get away without asking why and talking about the pictures in the brochure. This amazing power came to me, and I was bold! I surprised myself and my friends. I'm usually a shy person, but here I was stepping out in front of people, being the first to speak and make the case for the [pre]born.

Siera, another volunteer at the outreach, wrote:

I don't think I have ever done anything as amazing as the...event here at [the university]. I really felt like I actually made a difference. Just being out there trying to save the lives of those who can't stand up for themselves has made me realize just how important this is in the world—how important it is for me.

Typically, when all is said and done, more is said than done. May it be said of us that plenty was said *and done*.

5

BAD ARGUMENTS BY GOOD PEOPLE

Ever notice on TV news shows that no one is allowed to say more than a sound bite? Even in what passes for debate these days, the commentators just take turns throwing platitudes at one another—nothing more than shallow, thoughtless, counterproductive responses. When it comes to abortion, it sounds something like this: "I'm pro-choice because it's my body, and you should stay out of my womb," says one talking head. "Well, you're wrong because abortion stops a beating heart," says the other talking head. Cut to commercial.

Perhaps more culturally relevant and pervasive these days are memes posted on various social media platforms. In a cartoon-like image and phrase, memes communicate the same kind of pithy one-liners as the talking heads on TV. Memes, sound bites, billboards, and bumper stickers do serve a purpose, but we are mistaken if we think they will save lives all by themselves. In some cases, they may do more harm than good.

I made the assumption that believers generally have the best answers and make the best arguments by virtue of being believers. Unfortunately, many anti-abortion posts on social media are harmful and make believers look bad because they make a faulty argument or create a straw man fallacy. After reading hundreds of debates on Facebook, I finally realized that pro-lifers often insult and offend abortion advocates with their flawed approaches to defending the preborn. In the process they shut down productive dialogue that could change minds and hearts. Here are three of the top offenders: (1) Abortion Stops a Beating Heart, (2) Before You Were Born, and (3) Killing the Curer of Cancer.

Abortion Stops a Beating Heart

My first car was a gray Oldsmobile Cutlass Ciera. In 1993 I purchased its one and only bumper sticker. It showed the heartbeat as an EKG line with one normal blip and then a flatline. It read, "ABORTION STOPS A BEATING HEART."

We all have probably encountered this catchphrase somewhere—if not on a bumper sticker, then on someone's sign at a March for Life, or posted on Facebook. The whole country has been internalizing this message since the mid-1980s. Since we born people have beating hearts, it is designed to make the reader think about the common humanity of the preborn, but the trouble with the message is that it implies a faulty argument. It inadvertently communicates that a beating heart is the key requisite to being classified as a valuable human being worthy of protection. It dehumanizes young human beings whose heartbeats are not yet present or detectable. An argument can be made that decades of spreading this catchphrase has led to pro-life legislators running heartbeat legislation which directly discriminates against our youngest preborn neighbors.

We need to think more critically and carefully about our messaging, because the incidental messaging could be undermining our cause. We are not valuable for having attained a particular developmental benchmark; we are valuable because we are human beings, made in the image of God.

Before You Were Born

The Hebrew prophet Jeremiah introduces himself and his credentials by recording what Yehovah said to him: "Before I formed you in the womb I knew you, before you were born I set you apart; I appointed you as a prophet to the nations" (Jer. 1:5). This verse is quoted ubiquitously by pro-lifers as a proof text that abortion is wrong, but to do so is to misuse this text in several ways.

First, it treats prophetic poetry as if it communicated literal science. Take note that this passage in context is part of Hebrew poetic verse. Our modern English translations have maintained this fact by stylistically setting the verses apart from the narrative text. The passage communicates in poetic language that Yehovah had a plan in his mind for a powerful prophetic voice to his people. The need was there, and God would raise someone up to fulfill that need. Jeremiah says that he is that prophet. It is not appropriate to use a poetic passage to make metaphysical claims about preexisting souls entering the universe. Which is the more reasonable meaning of the verse, given the time, place, and purpose of the author's poetic writing: (1) that Yehovah had a plan for a powerful prophetic voice that he worked out through Jeremiah, or (2) that all human beings are somehow, somewhere preexisting and that these souls later enter the universe through wombs?

Second, many pro-lifers make an illogical leap that what may have been true for Jeremiah in his case, in a particular time and place, somehow applies to all human beings. This completely ignores the context. We are not Moses, Elijah, or Jonah. So until we witness a burning bush that does not char or get barfed up on a beach by a big bass, we should be careful not to apply the poetic descriptors of one historical prophet to ourselves and others.

The other big mistake in using Jeremiah 1:5 as a proof text is the assertion that Yehovah has a specific, preordained plan for each individual human being. Again, just because Jeremiah had a very specific and important calling from God does not mean that we each do. True, we all are called to live righteous lives, at peace with God and man, but is there a singular path laid out for you from before the beginning of time? This seems to be the argument, assumption, or implication of many believers. There is a tendency to read the biblical stories of God's particular plans and then make the illogical leap that there must be a specific plan for every human being. But this is a debatable point among believers.

Some Christians believe that the eternal destination of every human being is predetermined by God's will. If this is accepted as true, then it would not be a leap too far to conclude that every aspect of our lives is predetermined. If it is true that each of us has a pre-scripted destiny, then is it God's will that millions of babies be murdered by abortion? Following this line of logic makes it look as if God is the author of evil on earth. This is a huge stumbling block to many believers and nonbelievers alike.

The purpose of this book is not to enter a deep doctrinal debate, but to illustrate how some lines of logic are problematic when it comes to defending the preborn. Debatable doctrines that are hard-fought between factions of believers ought not to be the basis of our leading arguments to abortion advocates and nonbelievers. Such arguments will not be convincing to skeptics and agnostics when believers themselves cannot agree.

Killing the Curer of Cancer

Pro-lifers often argue along these lines: "Abortion is bad because it might kill the next President of the United States or the person who was going to cure cancer." The argument is that because we might kill a future hero, then abortion is bad.

This is not an argument that we should use. Notice that it cuts both ways. Using the same logic, we could make the case that abortion is good because we might preemptively kill the next Stalin or Jabba the Hutt, thus saving the universe from massive amounts of pain, death, and evil.

Whether the argument is made from the pro-abortion or the anti-abortion position, it is still a form of arguing from the greater good which is problematic. Each side is arguing that abortion is either permissible or impermissible based on the circumstances.

The pro-abortion side argues that actual or potential circumstances are so difficult that it would constitute a greater good, or better outcome, for the child not to be born. For example, they might point to unwanted children raised in orphanages or foster care who end up in jail. Or they might point to cases of extreme poverty, arguing that some pregnant women are too poor to care for a child. They believe that it would be better all-around if these babies simply were never born; therefore, abortion should be legal and available. To illustrate this type of thinking, let us relate two true stories.

A crowd had gathered around "Tom," a sandy brown-haired young student, and me at the University of Arizona. They were listening to him make a greater good argument to support abortion.

"What about all these disabled and handicapped people? Wouldn't it be better for them not to have been born?" Tom said.

"Perhaps *she* would like to comment on that question," said my student Lukas, pointing behind Tom.

Tom turned around. The blood drained from his face as he beheld a fellow student in a wheelchair. She did have something to say. In fact, Bethany Benedict responded eloquently and instructed the whole crowd that had gathered.

"I was born ten weeks early, twenty-five years ago, and when I think about how hard my parents worked and how hard they prayed to keep me alive, it just sickens me when I think about babies who are aborted at the stage I was when I was born. It just hurts inside."

"Bethany, what do you say to people who argue that abortion is justified in the case that this child might have a challenging life due to disability?" I said.

"Honestly? You need to get your head on straight! That's bullshit! Just because a life is not what you want to live doesn't mean it's not a life worth living. Yeah, it's hard; it's not easy, but you get used to it, frankly. You learn to adapt. You learn to find joy. You learn to find peace...

"I mean, it's just sad. It's like I can't imagine not being here. I can imagine being here differently, you know, walking or running or whatever, but I can't imagine not being here. I really can't."

It is one thing for us to make the case that every life is precious, but it is so much more powerful coming from Bethany who has precisely the set of challenges people commonly use to justify abortion.

J.B. did not believe in God, but then his daughter was born. While his conversion was a lengthy process, he points to when he held his daughter for the first time as a significant moment in which he realized that he believed in miracles. Given J.B.'s faith in God, Sheila and I were surprised when he revealed his view that abortion should remain legal.

"I would never want anyone in my family to choose that," he said, "but you never know the circumstances. Sometimes it would be better if they weren't born."

We asked J.B. to tell us more about his view. He talked about not wanting any child to be unwanted, to be abused, or to suffer the lifelong consequences of abuse. We listened carefully, letting J.B. know that we understood his concerns and wanted to help children in those circumstances. Then I turned to Sheila.

"Sheila, I think you should unload on him for about two minutes, if you don't mind," I said. She took over.

"J.B., I can't remember a time when my parents didn't hate me, and my dad even told me so. It started when I was just a little girl. They abused me verbally, physically, and emotionally. My father molested me.

"Before I was even a teenager, that hatred and abuse led me into a lifestyle of sexual promiscuity and drug addiction. When I was pregnant at only fourteen, my parents threatened me and coerced me into getting an abortion. I watched at the clinic as my baby, who was twenty-two weeks and four days old, was murdered by my own decision.

"Years later when I was pregnant again and decided to keep my baby, the voices in my head kept telling me, 'You're a murderer. You'll never be a mom. Just kill him.' Somehow, I made it through, and my son was born, but something was wrong...with me. I felt nothing. No love for him. No joy. Nothing that a mother is supposed to feel.

"J.B., you experienced a miracle when you held your beautiful baby girl. I never have—and I never will—be able to feel what you felt."

"That's enough, Sheila," I interrupted. J.B. was shaking his head in dismay.

"I'm so sorry that happened to you," he said. "That's terrible."

"Sheila," I said, "let me ask you a question about your story. Let's wind back the clock to the time when your mother was pregnant with you. Let's assume that your mom and others had foreknowledge of the abuse that you would suffer for two decades and beyond. Imagine that friends of your mother counseled her to abort you so that you would not suffer. Would it be right or wrong for your mom to abort you?"

"It would be wrong," she said.

"Here's a tougher question. At the time your parents were coercing you to abort your own baby, did you believe it was right or wrong for you to choose abortion?"

"It was absolutely wrong, and I knew it." We looked at J.B. to see if he was getting the message.

"Okay," he said, "you've convinced me it's wrong... You've given me a lot to think about."

J.B.'s point of view is pretty typical of many Christians and agnostics. They are uncomfortable with the killing of innocent humans, or admit that it is wrong, but they still hold that abortion may be allowed for the greater good. Here are three major problems with arguing from the greater good.

First, making a case for the greater good confuses an explanation with justification. To explain why someone contemplates evil or commits evil is not to justify it. When news stories attempt to explain why a mass shooting occurred, it may become tempting to accept the explanation as justification. "Oh! The young man was depressed, abused, and on medication. I guess his behavior was justified." No, his behavior was merely explained. Similarly, not wanting to live in poverty does not justify stealing other people's property. These situations explain why someone may be motivated to act immorally, but they do not justify the immoral act or make it moral.

Second, making a case for the greater good can confuse hardship with evil actions. Is it a sin to live in poverty or to depend on foster care? Of course not. These are hardships. But is it a sin to murder or steal? Yes. We all want to prevent and alleviate poverty, but sometimes our desire to avoid suffering clouds our judgment. To remove poverty by killing an innocent child is to compare hardship with murder, to treat them as if they were the same kind of thing, or to claim that hardship is worse.

Finally, making a case from the greater good assumes that we know the future. In the movie *Minority Report*, Tom Cruise plays a police officer in the future. In the intense opening sequence, he breaks down the door of a suspect just before it appears that the man is going to kill his wife and her lover. Cruise's character handcuffs the man, telling him, "Mr. Marks, by mandate of the District of Columbia Precrime Division, I'm placing you under arrest for the future murder of Sarah Marks and Donald Doobin that was to take place today April 22 at zero eight hundred hours and four minutes." As they drag him off to jail, Mr. Marks pleads, "No. I didn't do anything. I wasn't going to do anything!"

Pretending for the moment that Marks is a real person in the real world, was he or was he not going to kill the lovers? We cannot know absolutely because he was not given the chance to fully realize the choice. The point is that humans cannot know the future if free will is real. Free will precludes knowing the future.

Will every child born into poverty or foster care become a criminal and menace to society? Proponents of abortion talk as if they know for certain that unwanted children will cause untold mayhem in our streets. While some will undoubtedly grow up to hurt themselves and society, others will lead healthy, happy lives. Some might even grow up to be amazing researchers or leaders who bless others. Who are we to condemn innocent preborn children to death today for future unknown hardship, or for crimes that they may or may not commit some day? This line of reasoning is both arrogant and deadly. We do not know the future.

Arguing from the greater good is another way to claim that the end justifies the means. Because the advocate of abortion is focused so heavily on the good outcome of preventing future poverty, abuse, and crime, he fails to see that these goals cannot be morally attained by killing innocent people.

We who oppose abortion should guard against accidentally affirming that the ends justify the means by making the argument ourselves. Let us not assign life or death today based on tomorrow's heroes and villains.

There is one more huge, prevalent mistake that believers make when answering the toughest pro-abortion argument, but it will require its own chapter.

Veritas Vignette

The apostle Peter told believers throughout the Roman empire to "always be prepared...to give the reason for the hope that you have, but with gentleness and respect" (1 Pet. 3:15). I often ask Christians whom I meet why they are pro-life. Many are more than ready to give an answer. In fact, they are excited to wield their words like weapons, without gentleness or respect.

On the other hand, some are gentle and respectful, but ill-prepared to give an answer. They begin, but they quickly lose their way or become defensive when confronted with the questions posed by serious abortion advocates. We must put both of Peter's admonitions into practice: the rational and the relational, the reason and the respect.

Ron waited patiently for me to finish my previous conversation. As the other student walked away, he stepped forward as if he had been waiting in line at a checkout counter. He looked more mature and relaxed than most college students. Turns out that was because he was a graduate student in his thirties. His question surprised me.

"Do you know of any pro-life organizations that come from a non-religious point of view?" he asked.

I didn't know where he was going. Typically, secularists are skeptical of organizations driven by religious motivation, so I felt defensive and reacted by asking if he saw any religious references on our signs. He explained that he was pro-life and might even consider doing pro-life work after graduation if he could find a group that would let an atheist work with them.

Rather than grilling him about why he was an atheist, I tried to find common ground by inviting him to tell me about his pro-life views. He explained that he had been involved in two abortions when he was younger and that they continued to cause him immeasurable guilt. He said he was very pro-life because he wanted people to live well and not suffer from their mistakes. He did not want anyone to suffer the way he had.

"So, where do you think that feeling of guilt comes from?" I asked.

"I believe it is a product of the way our frontal lobe has evolved," he said.

"It seems as though we both must use faith in forming our worldview. You have chosen to believe by faith that all of the universe came into existence from nothing, or that it has always been here. I have chosen to believe by faith that a being of intelligence far beyond our ability to comprehend designed and created everything we know. So, we both live by faith, but which of us has a more reasonable view given the evidence?"

We then took some time to further explore the evidence and the reasonableness of the views at hand. At the end of our conversation, I said, "Ron, you seem really intelligent and clear-thinking. These abortions obviously affected you deeply. Are you open to the idea that you may have chosen atheism as a self-defense mechanism because you fear facing a Creator and giving an answer for the choices you made in this life?"

A look of bemused sadness spread across his face as he slowly nodded his head.

"Yes, I am open to that possibility. Maybe it's even true," he said.

Challenge given. Challenge accepted.

I reached over the barricade to shake his hand, but he just looked at me for an awkward second. Then he reached past my hand to my shoulder. We executed a perfect man hug—a casual, back-slapping sign of encouragement. As he walked away, I was already hoping to see him again.

6

MY BODY, MY CHOICE

"It's my body, so it's my choice!"

"It's a part of the woman's body."

"It's in her body."

"She should be able to do what she wants with her body."

"It's totally dependent on her body."

"She has a right to her body!"

We hear these soundbites everywhere. Even in the Church. But these are mere slogans, not explanations. What do these abortion advocates really mean? What are they truly claiming?

The Right to Refuse Argument

The toughest pro-abortion argument, which we will call the "Right to Refuse" argument, can be summarized this way:

> *Even though the preborn are human, a woman can abort because she has the right to refuse the use of her body to anyone who needs to use it, especially in the case of rape.*

This argument was made famous by Judith Jarvis Thomson, Doctor of Philosophy, in her essay "A Defense of Abortion," first published in 1971. It has subsequently been republished more times than any other paper in the history of modern philosophy. It is currently taught in multiple academic tracks of every major university across the U.S. It is arguably the most influential writing on the subject of abortion, and her ideas have taken deep root throughout our culture. Thomson's most famous expression of the Right to Refuse is referred to as "The Violinist," after one of her thought experiments. Quoting from her essay:

> You wake up in the morning and find yourself back to back in bed with...a famous unconscious violinist. He has been found to have a fatal kidney ailment, and the Society of Music Lovers has canvassed all the available medical records and found that you alone have the right blood type to help. They have therefore kidnapped you, and last night the violinist's circulatory system was plugged into yours, so that your kidneys can be used to extract poisons from his blood as well as your own... To unplug you would be to kill him.

Thomson then asks if you have the moral right to unplug from the violinist and go your own way, or do you have to stay plugged in? "No doubt it would be very nice of you if you did, a great kindness. But do you have to accede to it?" she asks. Then she puts these sarcastic words in the mouth of the hospital director:

> Because remember this. All persons have a right to life, and violinists are persons. Granted you have a right to decide what happens in and to your body, but a person's right to life outweighs your right to decide what happens in and to your body. So you cannot ever be unplugged from him.

Thomson then says, "I imagine you would regard this as outrageous..." and she is right. Most people do find it outrageous. We have informally surveyed thousands of our Christian students over the years and found that more than ninety percent of them agree that you can morally unplug in these circumstances.

Thomson, of course, argues that this scenario is like pregnancy in the case of rape. She concludes that in aborting her preborn child, a pregnant woman does not violate the child's right to life, but merely withdraws the nonconsensual use of her own body.

This becomes a real problem for believers who affirm the right to refuse the use of your body against your will. In fact, the Right to Refuse is the underlying principle and argument against slavery and why Christians led the movement to abolish slavery. So how can we affirm that slavery is wrong, based on the Right to Refuse, but then demand that women stay enslaved to unwanted children?

Before we answer that question, let us make a few salient observations about the argument and its strength. Note that those who hold the Right to Refuse view acknowledge the preborn person's right to life and that at least two persons are involved, i.e. the mother and her preborn son or daughter. One abortion advocate posted on Facebook, "I'm fine with calling them babies; the terminology doesn't bother me. Either way they can't survive without my body, and it's my choice whether or not they get to use my body for survival or not. I'll kill any baby that I don't want inside of me."

We also need to be aware that the Right to Refuse argument in the context of abortion is so dominant in our culture that many Christians believe in it and adhere to it, even when they do not like abortion and call themselves "pro-life." My faulty assumption was that no serious believers would actually affirm the argument, but reality slapped me in the face. In reality, many Christians fully understand the argument and embrace it wholly and on purpose, and others have passively absorbed it from the cultural water in which we swim. They may not fully understand it, but they have accepted it operationally. The argument is that powerful, persuasive, and pervasive.

To illustrate how the Right to Refuse has infiltrated sacred communities, let me tell you about my friend Rick. In the 1990s Rick and I often had lunch and played games on Sunday afternoons after church services. He was a fellow student at Oklahoma Christian University and was pursuing a degree in Biblical Studies. Not long ago he posted on Facebook:

> Even if I am a perfect match to donate a kidney, I am in no way obligated to do so… What gives anyone, then, the right to force a woman to carry a pregnancy to term? Maybe she has a good reason to terminate a pregnancy;

maybe her reason isn't good enough for you. But it's her decision, not yours. Your opinion doesn't matter. Ever.

The Wrong Response

Before getting into how to respond appropriately to the Right to Refuse argument, let us take a look at some of the really poor responses fielded by well-meaning activists.

One popular meme posted on Facebook began with this header: "For the logic-impaired." Below was a picture of a pregnant woman. The label "Your body" pointed to the woman, while the label "Someone else's body" pointed to the baby in the woman. The footer concluded, "NOT your body. NOT your choice."

Another one said, "BABIES ARE NOT BODY PARTS," with a graphic that differentiated between a baby and the uterus.

An abolitionist group promoted a T-shirt with this slogan: "THE BODY INSIDE YOUR BODY IS NOT YOUR BODY."

The approach of these memes and materials is not good for several reasons. First, this approach is rude. It begins with name-calling, which is offensive and shuts down dialogue. And of course, using all capital letters means you are YELLING at the audience! If we want anyone to listen to us, we should not start by verbally punching them in the nose.

Second, it insults the intelligence of those on the other side. Thoughtful abortion advocates know there are two bodies. They have had high school biology. They may be wrong, misguided, deluded, or wicked in their reasoning, but they are not stupid.

An email marketing piece we received from an anti-abortion group stated, "Pro-choice nonsense is fairly easily dismantled... *My body, my choice* is perhaps the favorite slogan of pro-choice activists, but it conveniently ignores—like always—the existence of another human being within the body of the mother." Actually, they do not ignore the preborn body, and their argument makes perfect sense if we listen and understand it properly. It even has merit when applied appropriately, as we saw in the case of slavery. Once again, this campaign calls names, insults, and is factually false.

Third, these responses completely miss the actual argument. That is to say, they fight a straw man. When a fighter wants to intimidate his challengers and make himself look tough and undefeatable, he sets up fights against weak opponents that he can knock out easily. It would be as if the fighter were punching a scarecrow dressed up to look like a fighter. College football is popular in my State, and all the fans get excited when their favorite team starts the season 4-0. They talk about how great the team is and how it will make the college football playoff. But wait, what does that 4-0 record mean? Sure, they played against what looked like other football teams. Those opponents had uniforms and coaches, and they lined up on the field, but did anyone mention they were Podunk junior varsity squads, not real competition?

Anti-abortion activists who share memes and materials like the ones noted are not fighting the real opponent. That is, they are not actually countering the strong, persuasive argument that we outlined above. Abortion advocates have come at us with a strong argument. It is hard to handle, especially since we agree with it. So what do we do? We set up a different version of it that is not actually their argument, one that is easy for us to defeat, and then we attack it instead of the real deal. That is what these memes do. They do not accurately portray the Right to Refuse bodily rights argument. Our opponents are not saying that the preborn are a part of the woman's body or are not human, or even that the preborn do not have a right to life. They make none of these claims, yet pro-lifers pretend they do and attack only these false versions of the Right to Refuse argument.

Fourth, responding along these lines communicates either that we are not listening, or that we are not capable of following the argument. Ironically, while these responses insult the intelligence of the Right to Refuse advocates, those who use them are the ones demonstrating a seeming lack of intelligence to their intended audience.

Finally, when one believer issues a poor response like the examples we just shared, those responses become associated with all other believers. If you have been one of those activists posting these memes, wearing the T-shirt, or distributing the literature, we get it. You are a fellow believer who hates abortion and wants to abolish it. You want to make a difference. We ask that you take a step back and examine just what kind of difference you might be making. You may not have meant to, but you can accidentally make all of us look bad. One more question: Why would a nonbeliever or abortion advocate want to join our club if this is how we treat potential members?

The Right Response

I saw Claire and Abby laughing at comments on the Free Speech Board we had set up at Georgia Tech. I started a conversation with them and found out that although they were personally uncomfortable with abortion, they believed it should stay legal and identified as pro-choice. So, I asked them to clarify their positions.

"Well, it's *her* body, so it's *her* choice," Claire said.

"Do you believe the baby also has a body, but has no choice?" I asked.

"Yeah, I guess. I know it sounds bad, but it's *her* body, so it's *her* choice, right? I mean, what about rape?"

"Okay," I said, "I think I understand what you are saying, but let me make sure. Abby, let's say that someone kidnaps you and then surgically connects your kidneys to someone else's failing kidneys. After you are rescued, you have a choice to make. Abby, do you believe you have the moral right to disconnect from this stranger who needs to use your body to survive?"

"Yes," said Abby.

"So, is your view that this story is like pregnancy? Are you saying that no one should be forced to use her body against her will, to include supporting the life of another human being like in the case of pregnancy?"

"Yes," they both said.

"I agree with you that your body is yours and that no one should force you to do something with it. This is a very high value that we all share. I want to support that right. However, I do not think it is always the highest moral principle that applies in a given situation. There may be times when another moral principle takes a higher priority than your bodily autonomy.

"Ladies, I heard you say earlier that you are not personally comfortable with abortion. I also do not believe that the story we just told about Abby and her kidneys is really analogous to pregnancy. Do you have time for me to share a different story that might be helpful in putting bodily rights into perspective?"

"Sure," they said.

"Did y'all ever see the Pixar movie *Up*?"

"Oh, yes, we loved that movie."

For those who have not seen it, here is the relevant part of the story. Carl, an elderly widower, had promised his wife that they would go to Paradise Falls in South America. Even though she is now gone, he decides to keep that promise. He ties thousands of balloons to his house and lifts off for adventure. Once Carl is hundreds of feet in the air, he hears a knock at the door. He opens the door to find Russell, an eight-year-old Wilderness Explorer, clinging to the front porch. "Please let me in," Russell says. "No," Carl says, and he shuts the door. Of course, upon a moment's reflection, he lets Russell come in. After reminding Claire and Abby of this scene, I asked them a question.

"Can Carl kick Russell off the porch to his death?"

"Of course not!" they said.

"So, Carl must use *his* house to shelter Russell and use *his* food to keep Russell alive until someone else can take over Russell's care. This sounds a lot like pregnancy. What if someone had tied Russell up and put him on Carl's porch? That would be a lot like rape, but would it change Carl's moral obligation?"

"No, it wouldn't."

I went on to ask Claire and Abby if they believed parents had a moral obligation to feed and house their children, to provide them with basic care. They agreed with this and admitted that *Up* actually illustrated that point.

"I never heard it explained like that before. That's really helpful to me," Claire said.

"I agree. Thanks a lot," Abby said.

Both girls said that they could no longer identify as pro-choice and that they were excited to try convincing others that abortion should not be legal.

Breaking it Down

Now let us examine the components of this real-life, good response to the Right to Refuse argument.

First, *listen and understand.* Demonstrate that you grasp the argument. Help make the argument stronger if necessary. Do not fight a straw man. Make sure that both they and you fully understand the argument, that a pregnant woman is no more obligated to donate the use of her body to sustain a preborn human than she is obligated to donate one of her kidneys to help a stranger live. She has the right to refuse the use of her body to someone else.

Second, *point out the differences* between the violinist scenario and pregnancy. Is the comparison parallel and justified? It turns out that Thomson's thought experiment is not truly analogous. The key to refuting the Right to Refuse argument is to show that there are moral differences between being hooked up to a strange violinist and being pregnant. Because the scenarios are morally different, there is no equivalent right for pregnant women to "unplug" from their children. You might say, "It sounds like you are saying that the decisions to donate an organ and choosing to continue a pregnancy are equivalent. Would you consider these differences significant?" Then highlight these differences:

Violinist Scenario	Pregnancy
indefinite	temporary
surgical connection	natural connection
stranger	parent
dying patient	healthy baby
kidney	uterus
unplugging	dismembering
death by disease	death by murder
not responsible	parental/guardianship duty

All of these differences are morally significant, but the moral responsibility or duty that parents and guardians have toward their children might be the strongest objection to the Right to Refuse argument. Parental duty is the winning counterargument. It is strong, compelling, and resonates with our natural moral intuition.

When parents have a child, they have a duty to keep him alive. They must at least feed and house him. They do not owe him a car, a cell phone, or a college education, but they must keep him alive until someone else can take over the job. In fact, were we to see a neighborhood kid kept in a dog house and thrown a bag of Funyuns or Twinkies once a week, we would all cry *child abuse!* and rally to rescue the child from those wicked parents. You might ask the abortion advocate, "Don't parents have an obligation to provide their children with food and shelter? Why should this duty not apply during the first forty weeks of a child's life?"

Even in the case of rape, parental duty still applies. We have a parent-child relationship, biologically at least. Sometimes, circumstances beyond our control can place us in the position of being a guardian, of having to care for a child until someone else can take over the duty. We believe that pregnancy in the case of rape is a situation like that. Through a horrible circumstance, a woman has been forced to become a guardian of a child that she did not sign up to care for. She is the responsible party on the scene, and as the temporary guardian of a child, she has a duty to keep that child alive. She is responsible for food and shelter for about forty weeks until someone else can take over the job. We do not see this as slavery. We agree that it may constitute a severe temporary hardship, but it is not tyranny.

Finally, *share a better thought experiment* such as *Up* to show that parental-type responsibility can apply in situations where the responsibility was not sought and the child is not even biologically related.

Yeshua addressed misunderstandings about moral questions in his day using a similar strategy. He told stories, which we call parables, to test people's moral intuitions and help them see the Father's moral principles. Parables are a lot like thought experiments.

For example, the Hebrew people in the first century were strict keepers of the Sabbath. After all, it was one of the Ten Commandments: "Remember the Sabbath, to keep it holy" (Exod.

20:8). But the Lord put this value in its proper place by telling a story: "Which one of you will have a son or an ox fall into a well, and will not immediately pull him out on a Sabbath day?" (Luke 14:5). The story taught that helping those in need was of higher importance than resting on the Sabbath. Both principles were true, but many civil and religious leaders of the day had prioritized them incorrectly.

After Yeshua told a parable, the disciples would often say, "Explain the parable to us." So, let us explain *Up*.

Explaining the Parable

God programmed the moral compass in each one of us, and it starts out pointing north. Our moral intuition is an accurate guide for telling us what is basically right or wrong until it gets messed up by our culture or by our own sinfulness. The messages of our culture can act like metal objects near our moral compass which interfere with its reading, causing us to go in the wrong direction.

Sometimes, moral principles come into conflict, and we must decide which principle comes first. If we allow our culture to influence our compass, then a message like "my body, my choice" can influence us to choose the wrong heading.

Consider these two moral principles:

1) You should not be forced to use your body to do something against your will.
2) You should provide food and shelter to another human being who is completely dependent upon you for those things.

The second principle is higher than the first when they are competing for application. Claire and Abby's moral compasses still wanted to point north, but our culture was interfering with them. In our culture we highly value autonomy, freedom, and choice; but your right to your own body is not absolute. It is subject to other moral principles. This is the lesson of the parable *Up*. (I want to thank my friend Tim for giving me the idea of using *Up* to help clarify bodily rights.)

Does it Work?

Listen and understand, point out the differences, and share a better thought experiment. Sounds doable, but does it work? Well, it worked with Claire and Abby, and here are three more stories to answer that question.

For the first, we return to my friend Rick. I spent a week corresponding with him. I was kind and courteous. I agreed with him that slavery and oppression are wrong based on the Right to Refuse argument. I demonstrated that I heard him, cared about what he cared about, and fully understood what he was saying. I gently suggested that there were other scenarios more analogous to pregnancy than slavery that would yield a different answer on the question of abortion. With his permission I shared *Up*, articles, essays, and quotes from noted philosophers and scientists.

Here is his response at the end of it all:

> I've read them. They have not changed my mind. It is still up to a matter of Individual choice... If I attempt to force someone to do what I would do, I become a tyrant... I will stand with the oppressed every time. Every. Time. The hijacker scenarios, as well as the *Up* scenario, are simply ridiculous.

I had invited him to come and reason together (Isa. 1:18), but he could not answer the objections and arguments shared with him, so he resorted to an ad hominem attack: *Ridiculous!*

This was a very hard experience for me. I have cried and prayed much over Rick. This story demonstrates that you can have every good, right argument in the book, but still feel like you lost because they do not admit that they were wrong and you were right—because they do not humble themselves in repentance—because they do not convert—because they do not believe. We have been looking at the hardest argument to overcome, and now we see the worst possible outcome—a friend and fellow believer rejects you and your message.

This story also demonstrates that our reason follows our will. We decide what we want, then we use our reason to justify getting what we want. We choose what we will do, and then we use our reason to create justifications for our actions. We must ask ourselves, am I willing to humble myself and follow God's way to live, to be a responsible human being who loves other people's lives, liberty, and property as much as my own? Or have I decided that life is just about me, my wants, my perceived needs, my prosperity, my time, my resources, my comfort, my security, and what makes me feel good? Do I want the holy life that God wants for me, or do I want what I want regardless of any rational, moral arguments against it? It is a hard lesson to learn, but reason is just another God-given tool. We can use it to build physical and spiritual houses upon rock or upon sand (Matt. 7:24-27). And we are experts at deceiving ourselves. We can convince ourselves that sand is rock. I told me so, and I believe me.

We are left to conjecture why Rick would reject the truth. Obviously, he is passionate about the issue. Perhaps it is less painful for him to believe the lie than to accept the personal responsibility for some deeply painful experience that has gone unspoken. Trauma, emotional pain, abuse, rejection, and loss are strong ingredients in the human psyche that can influence decision making and worldview formation, though these are not always the case. Sadly, sometimes the heart is just that hard.

Of course, not everyone is like this. There are those who are truly open-minded, who are willing to follow the truth wherever it leads. Remember, when the Lord sent the disciples out two by two throughout the land of Judea, he warned them that they would experience rejection, scorn, mocking, and beatings. When that happened, they were instructed to kick the dust off their sandals and go on to the next town (Matt. 10:14). There are those out there who will hear and respond to our message.

You will have your own conversations like this one. They will break your heart. Pray for them, and do not let them discourage you from talking to the next person. Remember, their relationship with God is between them and the Father. Your responsibility is just to plant the seed. You put that pebble in their shoe, and they are going to have to walk around on it. Eventually, that pebble might get so uncomfortable that they have to stop and take it out.

Here is story number two. "Susan," who received this bodily rights training in her senior philosophy class at Christian Heritage Academy, wrote:

> Coming into class Monday, I was a little hesitant… I came in with the conviction that abortion was wrong, but I didn't have the right to take that option away from another woman… I was operating on a bodily rights basis, but I can safely say that after this week I can no longer hold to that claim.
>
> Is it wrong to kill innocent human beings? This was the question I had never really pondered in link to abortion… I see now that although the situation may be uncomfortable…murder is murder. It doesn't matter how you dress it up…
>
> This [bodily rights] argument is really just an…ignorant philosophy… If it weren't for this class, I would probably have functioned under that philosophy for much longer than I would have liked.

To conclude, here is the last story. Kayla and I were walking alongside the pond at the University of Central Oklahoma. We were literally connected at the hip by three feet of swimming pool vacuum hose, which we had lashed around our waists. Coming towards us was a pale-faced, raven-haired coed wearing black yoga pants. Her massive backpack slowed her walk. When she looked up at us, she halted, mouth agape.

"Would you like to meet my kidney?" I asked.

"Okay, you got me. What's all this about?" "Molly" asked.

"Well, I'm his kidney," Kayla began. "I know that sounds weird, but let me explain. I'm going to tell you a short story about our connection, and then I want to ask your advice."

"All right. Go ahead."

"Last night I was walking home from class in the dark. Someone attacked me from behind and knocked me unconscious. When I came to, I found that my kidney was attached to John. You see, John is suffering from kidney failure, and now my kidney is filtering

John's blood so that he can live. Here's the question: Do I have the right to disconnect myself from John and go my own way?"

"I think so," said Molly.

"Are you sure? I will die," I said.

"Um, well... You could get help some other way, and Kayla didn't ask to be put in this position. She was attacked."

"I totally agree with you," Kayla said. "I wouldn't want to stay connected to John, and I think I have the right to go my own way."

"Yeah, that sounds right. So, why are you out here?" Molly inquired.

"This scenario is often given by supporters of abortion as a justification for abortion. They claim that this story is just like a woman who does not want to be connected to her fetus. She wants to disconnect and go her own way. Do you think the kidney story justifies abortion?" I asked Molly.

"Well, I'm not sure. It doesn't seem like the same thing, but I don't know."

"I think your instinct is right; it's not the same thing," Kayla picked up the thread. "Pregnancy is only a temporary way of providing food and shelter to a healthy individual, but in the kidney story, John will need special medical assistance for an indefinite period of time. When I disconnect from John, I'm not killing him. He will die as a result of his failing kidneys if he does not obtain extraordinary medical care."

"Yeah, I can see the differences, but I still feel like it's her body, so it's her choice," Molly said.

"Well, let me tell you a different story about our connection. Now imagine I'm a mother, and John is my fetus. It doesn't matter how we got connected. Perhaps I was raped. Here's the question: Do I have a right to stab John with a knife and use pliers to pull him apart? Do I have a right to burn him to death or poison him to death with chemicals before disconnecting and going my own way?"

"Oh my gosh! No!" Molly exclaimed.

"See, that's what happens with abortion. An innocent child who only needs food and shelter for forty weeks is murdered. It's not at all like disconnecting from someone with kidney failure. We expect parents to feed and house their children. If not, we consider it child abuse and we seek to rescue those children. That's why I'm out here being his kidney," Kayla concluded.

"And that's why I'm her fetus," I said. "We're explaining that we support bodily rights, but that those rights do not take away the right to life or justify killing children. Do you still believe *It's her body, so it's her choice?*"

"That's a very compelling case," Molly said.

For a deeper dive into the nuances of the Right to Refuse argument, I highly recommend the essay "De Facto Guardian and Abortion: A Response to the Strongest Violinist," which is available at www.jfaweb.org/DFG.

7

ELEPHANTS AND BIRTH CONTROL

There is an elephant in the room. In fact, there are two. We do not see them because they are in the dark—the dark side of the pro-life movement. What we cannot see are the twin pachyderms of birth control and in vitro fertilization (IVF). Neither topic is adequately addressed from pulpits, and innumerable Christian pastors and doctors have encouraged and enabled Christian couples to use chemical birth control pills and IVF. But should they have?

The Pill

In 2008 Jayne and I were sitting around the chiminea with our newlywed friends. Somehow the conversation turned to birth control and what we used, so we shared our experience. Here is the flashback.

The first few years after Jayne and I were married I became super unhealthy. We had received a bread maker as a wedding gift and used it constantly. Jayne's home cooking was amazing and healthy, but I had zero self-control and added on top of that ramen noodles, Little Debbie snack cakes, and pizza buffets. At work it was always someone's birthday, so I had huge piles of Crisco and sugar icing daily. I had gained over twenty pounds, I had bags under my eyes, and worst of all, my mind was always in a fog.

Around that same time we began noticing how many older people are decrepit at the end of life. Diabetes, dementia, and

Alzheimer's are common among the elderly. So many have a general loss of vitality and mobility. We decided that we wanted to feel good and be in our right minds when we reached old age. So, Jayne, especially, started researching. It did not take long to make the connections from these old-age diseases to the lifestyle choices I had been making. I needed to make some changes. Sadly, all-you-can-eat pizza buffets were right out, and Little Debbies had to be limited to high holy days.

We started paying closer attention to anything that went into our bodies. Jayne had used the birth control drugs Ortho Tri-Cyclen and then Depo-Provera for a combined total of five years, so we researched those, too. We pulled out a magnifying glass and began to read the fine print on the drug inserts. Imagine my anxiety when I came across this: "Although the primary mechanism of this action is inhibition of ovulation, other alterations include…changes in the endometrium which reduce the likelihood of implantation."

You see, every pill manufacturer, whether it is Ortho, Syntex, or Wyeth, admits that their drugs "reduce the likelihood of implantation." Implantation of what? Implantation of a living human being. If that human being cannot implant in the womb, then he or she gets flushed away.

The immediate question almost everyone asks is, how often does breakthrough ovulation occur? How often could there be a whole, unique, living human being present who wants to snuggle up next to mom in her uterus? If we listen to the pill manufacturers, it hardly ever happens, but to listen to those few voices on the other side, the pill acts as an abortifacient most of the time.

Research by Dr. Nine Van der Vange, State University of Utrecht, The Netherlands, Dept. of Obstetrics and Gynecology, in 1984, determined a breakthrough ovulation rate of 17% by using a high resolution ultrasound which visually showed that women sometimes ovulated on popularly prescribed low-dose pills. He also confirmed ovulation via blood test. Subsequent researchers pegged an even higher ovulation rate of 27%. While the specific rate is inconclusive, it is true beyond reasonable doubt that breakthrough ovulation absolutely does occur. This is admitted and acknowledged in every birth control drug insert. And every couple will admit that they especially like to have sex when the woman is ovulating. You can do the math.

In fact, I did do the math. For the sake of the argument, I assumed a low breakthrough ovulation rate of only 10%. Based on the length of time we were on birth control, the math told me that I was responsible for possibly killing as many as eight of my own children. This revelation was not easy to process. I had to go through all the stages of grief. I was already past denial. The numbers do not lie. I was on to anger. Why were we not told about this? Why were church leaders silent? Why were Christian counselors and doctors recommending these drugs? Finally, I humbled myself in repentance. I had to ask for forgiveness, maybe not for murder, but certainly for manslaughter. And knowing what I knew now, how would I reorder my life around the truth? Obviously, we had to stop using chemical forms of birth control.

In May 2009 we were again sitting around a fire in our back yard with our now not-as-newlywed friends. They had a big announcement.

"We're pregnant!" they said. "And it's all because of that talk we had last year."

This has been an introductory and primarily personal treatment of the subject. Others have researched deeply and written entire books, and I have not added anything new or better than what they have written. I highly recommend Randy Alcorn's book *Does the Birth Control Pill Cause Abortions?* It was first published in 1997 and is now in its tenth edition. You can purchase paper copies for only three dollars or download a free PDF file at his website: store.epm.org.

If I did not add anything new, then why write this chapter? Knowing what I know now, that the pill flushes innocent children, is it not my moral duty to tell others? I would be guilty of a sin of omission if I did not at least briefly point out the need to closely examine an issue that involves life and death. I cannot leave it to chance that readers of this book will stumble upon all the better materials that are out there.

74 OVERCOMING THE DARK SIDE

Christian Objections

One of our students had an exchange with a professional sonographer at church who wrote:

> There is some thinning of the uterine wall, but the primary purpose of the pill is to increase hormone levels to the point of stopping ovulation. I was on the pill for years... [My doctor] was a surgeon and primary care physician for decades [and] he prescribed tens of thousands of birth control pills throughout his career. He was a good, godly man, who served many years as an elder in the church. He was by no means an abortionist.

Many Christians believe that ovulation simply cannot occur while on the pill. This is widely taught and repeated by secular sources, but also by Christian doctors who have not carefully researched the drugs. Remember, studies have shown, and the manufacturers readily admit, that ovulation can occur even when birth control pills are used as directed. Does it really matter the exact number of times ovulation occurs per one thousand cycles when all it takes is one? That one person would have been killed because her mother took a synthetic hormone that flushed her away. Are we comfortable with the argument that her avoidable death was justified because the total number of deaths over the years on the pill was relatively few? The number of deaths per one thousand does not affect the morality of the choice that caused them. That is the point of the famous saying that "a single death is a tragedy; a million deaths is a statistic." We should not allow these deaths to become a statistic that justifies our choices.

The sonographer's second argument is that an elder in the Church prescribed tens of thousands of birth control pills throughout his career, and since he is not an abortionist, then those pills could not have caused abortions. In no way does a Christian doctor's lack of knowledge change the facts. Pill manufacturers admit right in the insert that their pills prevent implantation. It is a black-and-white statistical fact that a certain number of innocent human beings are flushed by these products. This fact is precisely why we want to educate Christian parents and church leaders—so that views like these will be corrected in the faith community.

I have found that intelligent people who work in scientific and medical fields can be the worst at claiming they know things and using poor logic. Sometimes they have fooled themselves into believing their own faulty claims, and other times they just assume you will not catch them at it. Perhaps they just know a lot of impressive scientific words but are not clear, orderly thinkers.

It should be noted that this believer admits to having been on birth control pills for many years, so it is personal for her. It is a statistical certainty that her actions caused the miscarriage of a certain number of her own children. To admit such to one's self, much less to others, would be extremely painful and hard to do. She is, perhaps, making a faulty argument to avoid the pain of guilt. Therefore, we should approach these conversations with discernment, humility, and respect. We should not sacrifice the truth to preserve people's feelings, but also, we should not trample on people's feelings as we share the truth. Both are moral requirements. It demands a sensitive, relational approach.

I teach a class on this topic annually to nontraditional adult college students. It is always difficult emotionally, because many of them have to face the reality of what they have done or encouraged others to do. We do a lot of crying and repenting, but the beauty of it is we support each other as we do it together. It is easier in a community of believers who understand that Yehovah is a gracious father who loves us and forgives us when we humble ourselves. If you find yourself feeling guilty because you have been there and done that, remember your heavenly Father will not hold you accountable for what you did in ignorance and for which you have repented. Read Paul's letter to the Romans for encouragement, and remember Yehovah gives grace to the humble (Prov. 3:34) and "There is now no condemnation for those who are in Jesus the Anointed One" (Rom. 8:1).

Is Every Sperm Sacred?

After such classes I typically get the same question. The young married men ask me, "If not the pill, then how do we avoid getting pregnant? We're not ready yet." I must admit that there is a huge theological debate preceding this question. The question itself assumes that avoiding pregnancy is morally acceptable, but not all believers share this view.

In Monty Python's musical *The Meaning of Life*, we see a poor, dejected Yorkshire laborer enter his home. He is greeted by hundreds of his children as he breaks the news that he is out of work and will have to sell them all for scientific experiments. Wondering why there were so many children in the first place, one of the boys asks his dad why Mum could not have used birth control. The Yorkshireman answers by breaking out into song:

> *I'm a Roman Catholic,*
> *And have been since before I was born.*
> *And the one thing they say about Catholics is:*
> *"They'll take you as soon as you're warm."*
>
> *You don't have to be a six-footer.*
> *You don't have to have a great brain.*
> *You don't have to have any clothes on.*
> *You're a Catholic the moment Dad came,*
> *Because*
>
> *Every sperm is sacred.*
> *Every sperm is great.*
> *If a sperm is wasted,*
> *God gets quite irate.*

Traditionally, Roman Catholics and some Protestant denominations have argued that using birth control is immoral because God commanded Adam and Eve to be fruitful and multiply. There is also a misunderstanding over the story of Onan refusing to impregnate his brother's widow. This was about Onan's arrogance and selfishness. He was unwilling to provide social security to the needy widow and was obsessed with making sure his own household would stay dominant over his deceased brother's. Nevertheless, the argument from Genesis does bear consideration. The fault I see in the argument is in the way proponents define the command to be fruitful and multiply. They see it as an all-encompassing, all-the-time priority that can never be set aside for any reason. If we follow their logic, a couple must multiply at every conceivable opportunity from marriage to menopause.

Furthermore, it would follow that any time a couple chose not to have intercourse during ovulation, they would be sinning. We begin to see why Monty Python chose to poke fun at this view.

On the other hand, we know that "Children are a blessing from Yehovah," (Ps. 127:3) and we see repeatedly in scripture that God wants families to be blessed by children and that he has compassion on the childless. So, while I do not personally believe it is immoral to avoid pregnancy, I respect those on the other side and understand their position.

The solution that works with God's design has come to be known as "natural family planning." It entails learning when the wife is ovulating to avoid intercourse during those times. When practiced carefully, it is highly reliable. Obviously, no health risks or side effects are associated with fertility awareness. The drawbacks are that it requires diligence, self-control, periods of abstinence for up to a third of the month, consistent and accurate recordkeeping, and it can be more challenging for women with irregular cycles.

That being said, for those who still want to use a birth control product of some sort, my answer to that question is, "Every sperm is *not* sacred." You may kill them. They are not human beings; they are functional cells in a man's body. You might look into using spermicide. Encare makes a spermicide that I call the "Silver Bullet," because each foil-wrapped product looks like a silver forty-caliber round. It has no hormonal side effects, and of course it does not kill innocent children trying to implant. As soon as you are ready to grow your family, you can stop loading ammunition.

In Vitro Fertilization

In vitro fertilization is the process of joining a woman's egg and a man's sperm in a laboratory dish, rather than inside the woman's body. Once the egg is fertilized by the sperm, the result is a whole, living, unique, human individual, called a zygote, then blastocyst, and then embryo, as he progresses through the very early stages of development. This little human needs a proper environment to survive, needs food and shelter to continue developing, so he is then implanted in the woman's womb in the hope that he will continue to develop like any other baby.

Believers across faith traditions differ on the moral acceptability of using IVF. Some argue that it could always be acceptable, some that it is right under certain circumstances, and some that it is always wrong. I am not completely sure where the truth lies myself, but let me outline some of the key concepts and ethical questions.

If we view IVF as nothing more than a medical procedure to help married couples overcome their infertility and receive the blessings of children, then what could be the problem? None, if that is all there was to it. The Son of God was very compassionate and had a thriving ministry of healing. Is it reasonable to believe that Yehovah desires healing for his people, and that IVF could be that kind of healing? Perhaps, but we have to look more closely at the IVF process.

One problem that immediately presents itself is that IVF doctors routinely help couples create more than one child to increase the chances of getting one to survive the process. A doctor might facilitate the creation of little Johnny, little Suzie, little Timmy, and little Margaret in the lab. Then, he might place the two healthiest-looking youngsters in the womb and either freeze or discard the other siblings. Sometimes all the embryos are inserted, and then later the doctor culls the weaker-looking ones to make room for the healthiest one, kind of like when a farmer drowns the runt of the litter. These processes are obviously morally wrong.

Why not fertilize and implant only one egg? That would avoid the problem of murder, right? Right, but that is not the rest of the IVF story. There is another troubling ethical question. What if a couple knew that there was a fifty-fifty chance that little Suzie, who was conceived in the lab, would not successfully implant and that she would be flushed away? Would it still be morally right to create her under those circumstances? What if the odds were better? How certain of success would the couple have to be to play Russian roulette with little Suzie? Would a two-shot revolver be good enough? What is the best-case scenario? According to the Society of Assisted Reproductive Technologies (sartcorsonline.com), in 2020 the singleton birth rate per IVF cycle with women using their own eggs is 50.8% among women younger than thirty-five, 37.5% for those aged thirty-five to thirty-seven, 24.7% for those aged thirty-eight to forty, and the success rate drops to 12.7% in those aged forty-one to forty-two. Thereafter, it drops to 3.9%. It is important to note that the procedures reflected in this data typically attempted to implant two or more embryos per cycle. So, although fifty-fifty is about the best rate being reported with a young woman using her own eggs, hidden in that success rate is the fact that many more embryos died than survived the procedure. This brings us back to the question of playing Russian roulette; there are not even two whole chambers in the revolver.

In light of IVF's low success rate, something to consider is the possibility that infertility is not itself the problem, but a symptom of some other problem. Why is the couple suffering from infertility in the first place? The womb might already be a hostile place for some unidentified reasons such as environmental toxins, hormonal imbalances, poor diet and exercise, or genetic anomalies. If a child is created and then placed in a hostile environment, she is not likely to make it. I mentioned this example in an earlier chapter, but it might be like putting your toddler out in the doghouse for the winter with no door, no blanket, and nothing but a bag of Funyuns. She is going to die.

In conclusion, we know that children are a blessing from God and that he wants us to be healed. From that perspective, IVF could be seen as a morally good choice, as long as the procedure does not destroy embryos, which are innocent human beings. However, we cannot overlook the fact that infertility is present for a reason that may or may not be curable and that IVF doctors may not be addressing. Even under the best circumstances of modern medicine, where only a few children are created at a time, the best success rates are fifty-fifty. Is it moral to flip a coin for a child's life?

Many good articles and research papers are available online for follow-up. And while I cannot endorse every position in every chapter, John and Paul Feinberg's *Ethics for a Brave New World* provides a thorough and scholarly treatment of IVF.

This has been a hard chapter to write, and I know it may have been a hard one to read and process. If there be truth in these concerns about birth control and IVF, how should we reorder our lives? Our desire would be for the Church to turn on the lights and talk about these elephants. We want individual believers to find the peace of the Father's forgiveness for their decisions and to lead other believers on their own journeys of understanding and informed decision making.

Veritas Vignette

Hongxia looked horrified. Although Chinese was her first language, a picture of an aborted child reads the same in any language. "This legal in your country?" she asked.

"I'm afraid it is. Do you think it is right or wrong?" I said.

"It wrong. It kill a life."

"Why do you think it is wrong to kill humans, Hongxia?"

"I don't know."

"What is your religion, Hongxia?"

"Umm...no religion."

"Have you heard about Christianity?"

"Umm...is maybe one you can live again after you die?"

"Ah, so you have heard something. Christianity is very simple. Let me tell you some of the basic things about it."

Just then she noticed Dongmei, a fellow Chinese classmate, walking by. "Come, come," she said, beckoning with her hand. Dongmei stood beside Hongxia.

"We were just talking about religion," I said. "I was about to go over a few simple principles of Christianity. First, we believe that one loving God created everything, and he made humans to be special. Second, we believe that you should treat other people the way you want to be treated. Third, we believe that God is willing to forgive you when you fail to meet that rule I just mentioned, if you are willing to repent and ask God's forgiveness. Finally, we believe that because Jesus was raised from the dead, his resurrection confirms these things and proves that we can live again after death if we believe."

Hongxia turned to Dongmei with a questioning look. "Is this true?" she said. Dongmei nodded vigorously.

"And who is your God, Dongmei?" I said.

"My God Jesus. I go Chinese church."

I could not believe it. Before me were two Chinese acquaintances who had apparently never discussed their faith with each other.

I looked intently at Dongmei. Then I asked if she would be able to read the New Testament with Hongxia. She said that she would.

As they were about to leave together, Hongxia turned back to me.

"Umm…almost I have confidence to be Christian."

8

STARFISH AND TRACTORS

> One day a man was walking along the beach when he noticed a boy picking something up and gently throwing it into the ocean. Approaching the boy, he asked, "What are you doing?" The youth replied, "Throwing starfish back into the ocean. The sun is up and the tide is going out. If I don't throw them back, they'll die." "Son," the man said, "don't you realize there are miles of beach and hundreds of starfish? You can't make a difference!" At this, the boy bent down, picked up another starfish, and threw it back into the ocean. As it met the water, he said, "I made a difference for that one."

The Star Thrower by Loren Eisley is well-known and oft referenced, and for good reason. It makes a great metaphor for the work we ought to be doing as believers. It poignantly illustrates that in the face of overwhelming odds, and knowing that "broad is the path that leads to destruction" (Matt. 7:13), we still ought to go about the work of saving lives and saving souls.

This paradigm guided the totality of my ministry in its early years. My work focused on recruiting ministry partners, training students and volunteers in anti-abortion apologetics, and teaching them how to be good ambassadors and evangelists. I conducted outreach events on university campuses where our trained volunteers found starfish that had been left high and dry on a corrupt cultural strand and needed to be put back in their proper environment, a reconciled relationship with God. Our mission on those days was to change hearts and minds as we worked our way down the beach sharing the truth with as many students as we could.

Loren Eisley did not tell us what happened to the young idealistic star thrower when he grew up, but to illustrate my own paradigm at this time, here is how I imagined the rest of the story. Later in life we find him again on the beach, but this time he is not alone. He has brought with him his old schoolmates, his family, his friends, and his church family. Together they are a throng. They work their way down the beach, some in pairs, some in small groups, and some alone. At the end of the day they congregate for a celebration meal. They talk of the joyful day of work together, and they share stories of the beautiful and unique creatures they found and rescued along the strand. As the sun sets, our star thrower looks down the beach and hails his comrades. "Look, everyone! We did it. We saved every starfish on this stretch of sand."

Applying this metaphor directly to my ministry, I believed that if we shared the truth about abortion with one person at a time to make "a difference for that one," and engaged other believers in doing the same with us, we would eventually turn the tide. I imagined that if we taught enough people the truth about abortion, it would change the culture, and thus the law. After all, public policy reflects the will of the people. My view on stopping abortion was echoed in the words of Mark Harrington, founder and president of Created Equal, when he said, "We must change the culture before we can change public policy."

How idealistic and naïve I was. Since those early days, I have watched our culture slide deeper and deeper into the abyss of depravity. We can never overcome the sheer numbers produced by the popular culture machine through its total control of mass media and the educational system. It churns out millions upon millions of godless, secular citizens annually, and the best we can hope for is to rescue a few starfish here and there.

In 2011 Jayne and I spent our fifteen-year anniversary on the beaches of Florida, from Fort Lauderdale to the Keys. You might be imagining pristine white sands, but that is not the natural state of Atlantic beaches before the sun rises. Every night the surf washes up piles of dead seaweed along the shore. It stinks, and it attracts swarming flies. So, when you show up later, why is it pristine? Where is all the refuse? Early in the morning, a tractor rakes it all up, and that is when I had the *Aha!* moment. We *can* save all those stranded starfish, but we will need a tractor.

The tractor, in this continuing metaphor, represents proper law and law enforcement. Consider this example. Why do people not speed across city highways at over one hundred miles per hour? The reason is because people generally follow the law. The speed limit is posted and enforced, so people choose to obey. Civil laws strongly influence behavior, even when people disagree with those laws.

People basically thought abortion was wrong prior to 1973. It was generally against the law in every State. When the Supreme Court of the United States (SCOTUS) said everyone must accept child sacrifice, it became the new policy of the land. As a result people started making different choices, and the abortion rate escalated. The culture transformed from one of life to one of death at the issuing of a single opinion. An entire industry sprang up where there had been none—all because of a public policy change. It was as if the tractor that had kept our culture cleared of abortion got parked for fifty years.

Over the years I have come to believe that we cannot abolish abortion simply by converting one person at a time. While it is theoretically possible to shift public policy by transforming the broader culture, it is self-evident that the culture is directed by public policy, much like a rudder directs a ship. If we want more people making righteous decisions, then we need to set up righteous boundaries through the law. To reiterate, while culture can affect some public policy, we must recognize that public policy largely directs and determines the culture. The law is a teacher.

We have seen leaders come to power and radically change things for the worse. The practice of modern-day child sacrifice became accepted public policy overnight. But on the flip side, righteous leaders could come to power and radically implement justice and make things right. Imagine what would happen to the culture, to the aggregate behavior of the individuals in our society, if righteous leaders reversed current abortion policy. Officials occupy what Teddy Roosevelt called the "bully pulpit." When someone with a lapel pin, a badge, or a gavel speaks, people listen. It is the duty of our civic leaders to establish and enforce laws that are boundaries for a civilized society, to say, "Thou shalt not" where it concerns protecting property and murder. Righteous leaders of today could abolish abortion just as fast as it was originally permitted. The people would follow the law.

Faced with the realization that it would take the force of law to abolish abortion, I wondered how I should reorder my life and work. My paradigm was shifting. How do we fire up the tractor of just law to save preborn babies from murder by abortion? Clearly there was a need to work not only from the grassroots level, but also from the top down.

I decided to get more involved in the political process, which is the method by which we choose our officials and make and administer public policy. In a representative republic like ours, we can have some influence over whether or not our leaders and public policy will be righteous. Righteous public policy is about protecting people's property and protecting innocent lives. If elective abortion takes the lives of innocent human beings, then in God's eyes it is murder and should be against the law. Legislators are the ones who codify our laws, and getting laws through the legislative process requires the exercise of politics. So in this sense, Christians need to be engaged in the political process, the process of selecting their elected representatives and encouraging them to make righteous public policy. "When the righteous rule, the people rejoice, but when the wicked rule, the people groan" (Prov. 29:2).

I had already been politically active in the sense that I paid attention to issues and voted in every election, even those with low voter turnout. I was also a volunteer in a local organization called the Oklahoma Conservative Political Action Committee (OC-PAC). The mission of OC-PAC was to "promote and support public servants who oppose expansive government while at the same time promoting liberty, free markets, and Judeo-Christian standards." I stepped up my involvement with OC-PAC and became a vice president. I began examining how to influence pro-life legislation. I learned how it is written and advanced. I began to be more intimately involved in meeting and vetting political candidates. I was looking for righteous leaders who would help stop the bloodshed, and I was looking for pro-life legislation to support.

In 2014, while still working to rescue individual starfish at the grassroots level, I founded Oklahomans United for Life (now United for Life) with the intent to provide clear communication regarding abortion policy to the people of Oklahoma and our magistrates. This new ministry brought me face-to-face with pro-life politicians and pro-life politics. I did not like what I found, but more on that in the next chapter.

In 2015, after a few years of learning the political ropes, an interesting opportunity presented itself. After nearly twenty-five years of service, Charlie Meadows, the founder of OC-PAC, stepped down, and I became the next president. We had grown the organization's contact list into the thousands, and we regularly attained more than five thousand newsletter reads per week. We contributed tens of thousands of dollars to conservative candidates each election cycle, and our members further helped good candidates get elected by providing manual labor, endorsements, and media coverage. In the small State of Oklahoma with a population of less than four million, where only a fraction are registered to vote, we had amassed at least a little influence. Candidates and sitting legislators were willing to listen to our advice and recommendations. They attended our meetings and interacted with our members. This was a huge opportunity to advance the cause of life, and I could not wait to get started.

There was just one catch. How could I, as a full-time minister of the biblical good news, justify spending so much time involved in the dirty, secular world of politics?

Mission to Magistrates

My grandfather, called "Papa Dear" by the family, was raised in a church tradition that taught Christians ought to have nothing to do with politics. For most of his life, he believed that he was a member of the kingdom of heaven only, and that this earth was not his home; he was "just a-passin' through." These beliefs did not stop him from grumbling and complaining about politicians and their rotten public policies. He routinely called them a "bunch of crooks." But after a lifetime of suffering at the hands of the crooks, he finally looked back and realized that this earth had been his home for quite a long time and that it would continue to be the home of his children and grandchildren. He decided that he wanted to be part of the solution and earn the right to gripe; so, at age eighty-six he registered to vote and began to speak the truth about local magistrates and their policies with more authority and clarity.

Many believers have a worldview similar to the one Papa Dear had for most of his life. It keeps them from speaking to their magistrates in any meaningful way, but as the people of God, we are his prophetic voice on the earth to everyone, including our magistrates. In fact, we have a mission to magistrates. To support this view, I want to explore the following scriptural themes: the Ten Commandments, the proximity principle, the prophetic role, and the prophetic role of Yeshua the Anointed One.

The Ten Commandments

First, consider the Ten Commandments. Commandments one through four speak to how we are to live in relationship with Yehovah our God:

1) You shall have no other gods before me.
2) You shall not make for yourself any idols or worship them or serve them; for I, Yehovah your God, am a jealous God, bringing the consequences of your idolatry upon your next three generations, but showing lovingkindness to generations of those who love me and keep my commandments.
3) You shall not use the name of Yehovah your God deceitfully, for Yehovah will not hold anyone guiltless who uses his name for a false purpose.
4) Remember the Sabbath day by keeping it holy.

Commandment five speaks to how we are to live in relationship with immediate family. Parents care for children when children are young, and then children take care of parents when parents are old. This is Yehovah's plan for proper social security:

5) Honor your father and your mother, so that you may live long in the land Yehovah your God is giving you.

Commandments six through ten speak to how we are to live in relationship with one another in civil society:

6) You shall not murder.
7) You shall not commit adultery.
8) You shall not steal.
9) You shall not give false testimony.
10) You shall not covet any of your neighbor's property or possessions.

Also consider that there must be a political system of some sort with magistrates who have been delegated authority to administer the civil laws. In the Ten Commandments, then, we find the sacred and the secular, the oneness of religion and politics. Only in recent western civilization has mankind tried to divorce the two, but it was never so in God's economy.

Proximity Principle

Second, consider the principle of proximity, which means that our first responsibility is to those closest to us. If we take good care of our families, our neighborhoods, and our communities using godly principles, then society as a whole will take care of itself.

Two biblical stories illustrate this principle well. The first is the rebuilding of Jerusalem's city wall, found in Nehemiah. Each family took responsibility for the section of wall closest to their home. In this way, the whole wall was rebuilt, even though no one had to work on every part of the wall.

When it comes to abortion, maybe some of you have passively followed abortion-related news with some level of interest but have not seen the problem of abortion as proximate to you. I urge you to reconsider. You may not believe you know the people involved in child sacrifice, but they are certainly in your family, your church, and your community. Furthermore, those abortions are permitted because so many people in your local community either believe that choosing abortion is a fundamental right or they stay quiet about it. Like it or not, your neighbors' and your magistrates' attitudes towards abortion are your part of the city wall that needs to be rebuilt.

Another example, which is less well-known, is found in Deuteronomy 21:

> If someone is found slain, lying in a field...and it is not known who the killer was, your elders and judges shall go out and measure the distance from the body to the neighboring towns... Then all the elders of the town nearest the body shall wash their hands over the heifer whose neck was broken in the valley, and they shall declare: "Our hands did not shed this blood, nor did our eyes see it done. Accept this atonement for your people...and do not hold your people guilty of the blood of an innocent person." Then...you will have purged from yourselves the guilt of shedding innocent blood, since you have done what is right in the eyes of Yehovah.

Notice that the city magistrates were responsible for evil acts that occurred near their town, whether they knew who did the evil act or not. They took responsibility because the blood was shed in their proximity or jurisdiction. While we no longer sacrifice heifers to make atonement these days, Romans 12:1 teaches that we do offer the righteous actions of our lives as spiritual sacrifices.

We passively follow the news from around the States and the world, but most of it does not fall within our circle of proximity. There is not much we can do about it. Abortion is actually a big problem globally, but the proximity principle says that our local magistrates must take responsibility for the innocent blood shed in their jurisdictions. There are slain preborn babies lying in a field near you. Will you encourage your local magistrates to take responsibility? Will you, too, offer a living sacrifice of service?

The Prophetic Role

Third, Yehovah expects every nation-state to follow his moral law. He expects the civil law of any jurisdiction to rest within his moral law and be based upon it. Laws which violate God's moral law are no law at all and should be overturned and ignored by magistrates. Those magistrates who administer immoral laws, God calls to repent or be replaced.

As evidence of this, we see biblical examples of Yehovah calling magistrates to repent, and not only those of Israel. He sent Moses, Jeremiah, and Ezekiel to Pharaoh of Egypt. He sent Daniel and Jeremiah to Nebuchadnezzar of Babylon, and he sent Jonah to the king of Nineveh, just to name a few. At one point or another, all the kings of the region heard from one of God's prophets concerning their pride, deceit, and destruction.

The Prophetic Role of Yeshua

If those examples were not enough, Yehovah sent his son Yehoshua, the Anointed One, who served in multiple roles. One of those roles was to continue the prophetic voice to the political leaders of Israel, exposing the corruption that would lead to judgment, and calling for repentance. Yeshua took up that prophetic role with boldness and sometimes with righteous anger. Proverbs 28 begins, "The righteous are as bold as a lion," and Proverbs 8:13 says, "To fear Yehovah is to hate evil; I hate pride and arrogance, evil behavior and perverse speech." The Lord was bold, and he hated evil. His righteous anger burned and impelled him to action.

We find one example in the way he cleaned out the temple with a whip. He loudly and violently drove out cattle and kicked over tables. He confronted the crooked businessmen who were stealing from people as they tried to carry out their religious duties. That was bold!

Yeshua also publicly confronted the magistrates of his day. The Pharisees, the "teachers of the law," were not simply religious leaders; they were the civil body politic. Local government was handled by these civil magistrates who had the power to bind law on the people and the power to prosecute people for breaking the law.

When we read about these magistrates, we can imagine our own polished politicians in silk ties. If we applied the words of the Lord to our leaders, it might sound something like this:

> Everything they do is for people to see: They sport American flag pins on their sharp suits. They love to be honored at banquets and in churches. They love to be

greeted with respect and called "Senator," "Governor," or "Congressman." (Matt. 23:5-7, a loose paraphrase)

Notice how the Son of God addressed these local magistrates in Matthew 23. In front of all the people, where everyone could hear (think *60 Minutes*, Fox News, and CNN), he called them hypocrites, children of hell, wicked, blind guides, fools, rotten flesh, snakes, and murderers. Note that he did not confront them over worship styles in the synagogue. He was angry because they were tyrants, because they used the cover of law to allow murder and theft and to advance their own interests. Maybe one of his trusted advisors, perhaps the politically rebellious Zealot or one of the "sons of thunder," should have whispered something in his ear about political correctness or separation of church and State.

Does our righteous anger impel us to bold political action? In the same way that God sent prophets and his son to civil authorities to call them to repent, today he sends us to our civil magistrates to demand justice and equal protection for every human being. Do we make our political leaders uncomfortable by calling out their hypocrisy and failure to uphold the highest laws? Maybe we should do a better job of following the example of Yeshua our Lord when it comes to calling magistrates to repent. Remember, to fear Yehovah is to hate evil, and the righteous are as bold as a lion.

Although political involvement would cost our ministry the financial and relational support of some churches and individuals, I was still convinced that we had a higher calling and duty, a mission to magistrates. We turn now to our attempts to reorder our lives and work in light of that mission.

9

1984:
Pro-choice Is Pro-life

George Orwell's *1984* describes a dystopian world in which "the Party" maintains its governmental power and control by creating an environment of constant fear through propaganda. The atmosphere of fear and abject reliance on government for a sense of security breaks down the people's ability to think rationally. They believe and accept anything they are told, even when it is entirely illogical. The Party's campaign of psychological mind control is so effective that the citizens have been taught to believe such things as "two and two make five." The Party controls everything and everybody through its official governing ministries. For example, the Ministry of Truth produces news, entertainment, history, education, and art that agree with the Party, and its motto is "IGNORANCE IS STRENGTH." The Ministry of Peace wages war for the Party, and its motto is "WAR IS PEACE." I was stunned when I finally realized that in our own day, the Ministry of Pro-Life Politics protects abortion for the Party, and its motto might be "PRO-CHOICE IS PRO-LIFE."

In *1984* the citizens practice "doublethink," the act of simultaneously holding two mutually exclusive ideas and believing both absolutely. The pro-life versus pro-choice false dichotomy has been a reality in the United States for many years, but it has now approached perfect dystopia. We have arrived at doublethink in the

PLM. This will be hard for many readers to accept, so let me walk you through my journey of discovery.

Role of the Legislature

Let me begin with my assumptions. First, I called myself pro-life, and as a pro-life political activist, I assumed that I had been supporting pro-life policies and politicians who were attempting to enact just law, which is, after all, the job of legislators. To enact just law concerning abortion would require legislators to remove the contradictions, ambiguity, and inequality in state abortion statutes and establish equal protection for preborn humans. Just law requires equal protection for the following reasons:

Consistency. Abortion is murder; therefore, it should be equally unlawful for everyone—no exceptions for parents and doctors.

Protection. We should provide equal protection for all victims. Why should the laws of a State protect one preborn human while sanctioning the murder by abortion of another one? When it comes to moms, the law should allow us to distinguish those who are truly under coercion from those without excuse. Justice requires equal protection for all victims.

Teaching. The law is a teacher, and we must teach that murder is a crime. To criminalize all abortion is to agree with God and reinforce our consciences, which already tell us that abortion is sin requiring repentance. Criminalizing all abortion will promote the truth, quickly and effectively exposing the lies and indoctrination that have supported abortion for decades.

Equal Value. Human beings are intrinsically valuable because we are made in the image of God. We are different from opossums and cockroaches. Because we are all equally human and equally precious to God, we should be valued equally under the law.

Deterrence. People naturally respect authoritative boundaries. To criminalize abortion is to provide a boundary beyond which the average person will not go.

Impartiality. We are created in God's image, and we are called to be like him. God does not show partiality or favoritism; therefore, our laws should not show partiality or favoritism. Consider these verses:

- Do not pervert justice; do not show partiality to the poor or favoritism to the great, but judge your neighbor fairly. (Lev. 19:15)
- For Yehovah your God is God of gods and Lord of lords, the great God, mighty and awesome, who shows no partiality and accepts no bribes. (Deut. 10:17-18)
- For God does not show favoritism. (Rom. 2:11)

Second, I assumed that I was informed, but I was wrong. I thought I knew what my elected officials were doing and why because I listened to trusted sources such as conservative, pro-life politicians and online pro-life news agencies. But now I was the trusted source. As the president of OC-PAC, others looked to me to find out what their elected officials were doing. I realized almost immediately that media reports omitted the most important facts and data in their stories. Rather than report accurate happenings, they more often told us what to think about what they said was happening. I realized that I would have to personally attend important meetings and read source documents such as minutes of meetings, transcripts, and, most importantly, the actual policy proposals of our legislators. For years I had been listening to legislators tell me what their bills would do if enacted, and I had always taken their word for it. No longer.

In 2015, right after I became president and started seriously to pay attention, I got my first clue that something was rotten in the PLM. The National Right to Life was promoting a piece of legislation called the Oklahoma Unborn Child Protection from Dismemberment Abortion Act. Sounds great, right? Who would not want to protect preborn babies from being torn apart? So I did what I had never done in previous years; I read the bill. Following are two excerpts (emphasis added):

> "Dismemberment abortion" means...purposely to *dismember a living unborn child*...through use of...instruments that, through the convergence of two rigid levers, slice, crush, and/or grasp a portion of the unborn child's body to cut or rip it off. This definition *does not include an abortion which uses suction to dismember* the body of the developing unborn child by

sucking fetal parts into a collection container; (Okla. Stat. tit. 63, § 1-737.8)

[I]t shall be unlawful for any person to purposely perform or attempt to perform a dismemberment abortion *and thereby kill an unborn child* unless necessary to prevent serious health risk to the unborn child's mother. (Okla. Stat. tit. 63, § 1-737.9)

First, note that the law specifically defines dismemberment abortion as the purposeful killing of a preborn child by dismembering him with pliers. With this definition in place, an abortion doctor need only to kill the preborn child first by some other means. Then his dismemberment procedure would not be breaking the law. Also note that dismemberment by sharp vacuum tubing is specifically protected.

Second, how would this law be enforced practically? Would we have medically trained police officers stationed bedside at each procedure to make sure the doctor murdered his victim with something other than pliers prior to extracting the corpse in pieces?

This bill passed the State House 84-2, the State Senate 37-4, and was signed into law by Governor Mary Fallin. Out of one hundred forty-nine legislators, every Republican who voted cast a Yea vote, and thirty out of thirty-six Democrats voted for it. The sheer number of Democrats who voted for it should have been a tip-off that it would not bring about any meaningful change.

In case this has not been clear, let me spell it out. We cannot prove that this law has saved a single life. Yet National Right to Life paid a full-time lobbyist to support it, and countless hours were spent by pro-life legislators shepherding it through the daunting political approval process. Once passed, it was heralded by National Right to Life as a huge victory. In fact, Oklahoma is touted among national pro-life organizations as the most pro-life State in the union because it has passed so many pro-life laws.

Why all this political theatre, I wondered, over legislation that will save zero lives? I began digging into the past, reading the language of highly-touted pro-life legislation from previous years. I found the same pattern year after year. Enormous amounts of pro-life political capital were spent to pass legislation that could not be shown to have saved any lives.

Here is one more example from the following year. Pro-life legislators, again at the request and support of a national pro-life lobbyist, ran a bill they called the Prenatal Nondiscrimination Act of 2016. It said (emphasis added):

> No person may intentionally perform or attempt to perform an abortion *with knowledge* that the pregnant woman is seeking the abortion *solely* because the unborn child has been diagnosed with either Down syndrome or a potential for Down syndrome.

Once again, the abortion doctor need only be ignorant of the reasons for the abortion, or the woman's reason could also include she simply does not want a child. Like the previous example, the law would be completely unenforceable, and once again, it passed with overwhelming support across political parties. It was all symbolism over substance. I have been using examples from Oklahoma, but my contacts in other States tell me it is the same there, too.

The Cozy Arrangement

This kind of repeated political posturing showed me the cozy arrangement between pro-life lobbyists and Republican Party leaders on the one side, and pro-choice lobbyists and Democratic Party leaders on the other side. Together they use preborn human beings as political footballs to score points in the never-ending game that SCOTUS kicked off with *Roe v. Wade*. You might have thought the *Dobbs* opinion in 2022 finally ended the game, but not so fast; we are still in a seemingly endless series of overtimes, but more on that in the chapter "No Other Gods."

Only two teams have been allowed to compete in the game: the Pro-life team and the Pro-choice team. These two teams have highly paid promoters, advertisers, owners, players, coaches, political analysts, politicians, and referees. No matter which side appears to have momentum, the game never ends, and murder by abortion continues.

Politicians and lobbyists on both sides trade endless scores for dollars and votes. Here is how the game is played:

1) Lobbyists arrange for donations to friendly politicians.
2) Politicians are elected and support bills or fight bills as recommended by lobbyists.
3) Lobbyists ask for more donations to fight for or against bills.
4) You donate.
5) Bills are passed, defeated, or stayed.
6) Lobbyists report victory or defeat and ask for more donations to further the fight.
7) You donate.
8) Politicians claim victory and report high marks from lobbyists and ask for donations and votes to further the fight.
9) You donate and vote.
10) Lobbyists and politicians show up next year to do it all over again. The meaningless game continues to be played.

You may be wondering who these players are. Individual politicians come and go, but the organizations that support them are entrenched. The Republican Party and Democratic Party are obvious, but here are some of the most highly-paid coaches and support staff, along with 2021 reported annual revenues:

On the Pro-choice team:

- Center for Reproductive Rights $31.9 MM
- NARAL Pro-Choice America $25.5 MM
- National Institute for Reproductive Health $5.5 MM

On the Pro-life team:

- Susan B. Anthony List $56 MM
- Students for Life of America $12.2 MM
- Priests for Life $10.6 MM
- National Right to Life $5.5 MM

To summarize, lobbyists on both sides "fight" every year to get status quo politicians and regulations passed or defeated. No matter what happens, they expertly use victory or defeat to keep the donations flowing, and they use the money to keep the game going. Similarly, politicians "fight" every year and claim success to keep the donations and votes going their way so they can stay in office and keep playing the game—a cozy arrangement. All the while, murder by abortion continues unabated.

Ten Corrupt Commandments

Why are pro-life legislators content to pass symbolic regulations of abortion? Why do they ignore or kill any legislation that might abolish abortion? We suggest that there are several possible reasons which we will address as the legislature's Ten Corrupt Commandments:

I	Thou shalt have no other gods before the judiciary.
II	Thou shalt not punish the woman.
III	Thou shalt fit in.
IV	Thou shalt follow the will of the people.
V	Thou shalt follow the leader.
VI	Thou shalt fear bad press.
VII	Thou shalt stay anonymous.
VIII	Thou shalt stay on the bench.
IX	Thou shalt fear leadership.
X	Thou shalt not lose office.

Wrong thinking, sinful hearts, ignorance, naiveté, justification, rationalization, and self-preservation all play a part. We will address Corrupt Commandments III through X here, but numbers I and II will require their own chapters.

III. *Thou shalt fit in.* Keep in mind that our legislators are a cross section and reflection of the culture. They believe what everyone else believes about abortion. They have made their peace with it. Even if they do not like it personally, they do not want to tell others what to do, or they have bought into "my body, my choice." In short, many pro-life legislators simply do not want to abolish abortion. Of course, they know what to say to get elected, but what they say and what they believe are often quite different.

For example, when my personal State Senator Paul Rosino, who proudly professes his Catholicism, campaigned as a pro-life Republican in 2017, he sent me numerous postcards in the mail with pictures of little babies and hearts and precious feet proclaiming his 100% pro-life stance. But when I interviewed him about his specific policy plans and positions, he stated that he approved of aborting babies conceived in rape or incest, and also approved of aborting "a Down syndrome child or something worse than that." He concluded that the State was "pretty restrictive right now already." Through meeting and working with legislators over the years, we have found that Rosino is not the exception; he is the rule among establishment pro-life politicians. He was elected in a proverbial landslide by more than twice the number of votes for his opponent.

IV. *Thou shalt follow the will of the people.* Legislators do not understand "representation." They keep using that word, but it does not mean what they think it means. Too many of them believe we live in a democracy and that their job is to author and pass whatever the majority of their constituents want. This is nothing more than mob rule and tyranny of the majority.

We live in a representative republic, and the job of our magistrates is to represent us in administering the limited constitutional duties which we have delegated to them. They are supposed to defend the lives, liberty, and property of everyone in their jurisdictions. In short, some legislators fail in their duty because they misunderstand their job descriptions.

V. *Thou shalt follow the leader.* There are no qualifying tests or serious job requirements to become a legislator. Generally, whoever has the most money and the prettiest face to put on campaign propaganda gets elected. Most do not know what their job is (see Commandment IV) or how to do it when they start. Their on-the-job training comes from established politicians who have been there and play the game.

VI. *Thou shalt fear bad press.* Another motivating factor is fear of organized opposition, whether from opposing organizations or candidates. Few like a messy, emotional fight, yet that is what legislators get almost every time they take a meaningful position. Any principled stance is going to draw nasty voicemails, hateful emails, and ugly names posted on Facebook. Many legislators would rather avoid ugly opposition altogether than sponsor a bill even remotely controversial. If the legislator were to do something meaningful, it might draw attention to him and give opponents something to criticize and use against him.

VII. *Thou shalt stay anonymous.* Legislators know they can get away with doing nothing meaningful because the average voter has no idea who his State legislator is, much less what he is doing. The average voter waits until the day before an election to pay attention and then chooses a candidate from the pile of campaign literature in the mailbox. I once polled a class of forty adult Christian college students. I asked them to name one of the following: a personal legislator from their State, a personal Congressman, a city council member from their own city, a county commissioner from their own county, or their own county sheriff. Not one student could give a correct answer. Then I asked them to name a basketball player on their hometown NBA team. More than half the class could name one.

VIII. *Thou shalt stay on the bench.* Many legislators hide behind the presumption that they know the future. "It'll never work anyway, so why try?" they say. Some leaders even argue that it would damage the cause to vote on a bill and have it defeated. Many at the capitol hold the view that they should only run a bill when it has support from leadership and is likely to pass. This attitude begs the question, why do sports teams bother to play any game? Why not simply look up the Vegas odds and declare a winner? How many times have we watched our favorite team beat the odds? We must field our team and try. We must expect and demand hearings and votes, so we can cheer for the good players and know the score. There is never a wrong time to do the right thing.

IX. *Thou shalt fear leadership.* Legislators also fear reprisals from leadership. Legislators know that if they go against leadership, then other bills they care about will not be allowed to advance. The average citizen believes his legislator has the right to have any of his bills heard. While that ought to be any legislator's right, it is not reality. According to legislative rules, all power rests with the kings of the capitol. The Senate President pro tempore is the king of the Senate, and the Speaker of the House of Representatives is the king of the House. These leaders appoint all committee chairs, they make all committee assignments, and they assign all bills to committees. Therefore, they exercise complete sovereignty over their fellow legislators and all proposed legislation. They meet in secret caucuses to decide which bills to hear and which bills to kill. Your legislator is forced to buy, sell, or trade favors with leadership to get any bill heard.

For example, one year we asked one of the State's most conservative representatives to sponsor a bill to criminalize all abortion. That legislator said, "I feel like it would be doing the right thing at the wrong time." What he really meant was, "Leadership won't like it, so I don't want to jeopardize my other important bills." Even after explaining that there is never a wrong time to do right, and pointing out that he should not gamble on there being a better time later, he still refused.

Or consider this example of being tempted into the cozy arrangement and what happened to Oklahoma State Senator Joseph Silk. In 2015 he authored a bill that in the eyes of leadership attempted to criminalize too many abortions. His bill threatened to upset the cozy arrangement, so he was pressured by the PLM. The National Right to Life wrote to him expressing concerns over "serious problems we believe are associated with the bill as currently drafted." They asked him to delete the language making abortion unlawful. Senator Silk responded:

> For the past forty-two years, this type of legislation [you recommend] has actually hindered people from attacking the issue by offering a false sense of success...
> I will not be a part of legislation that only prolongs the actual fight against abortion...

A brave and noble response. He understood that good leadership is not knowing when to compromise, but knowing when *not* to compromise. He followed up in 2016, 2017, and 2018 with a bill to include abortion in the homicide code. For that, leadership stripped him of his committee positions, moved his office to an obscure corner of the capitol building, and denied a hearing of all his proposed bills. Consequently, he was not allowed to represent or speak for the more than 82,000 residents of his district during his last two years in office. Silk continued his valiant efforts in 2019 and 2020 with the Abolition of Abortion in Oklahoma Act, but the frustration and disillusionment eventually influenced his decision not to seek re-election.

Senator Silk was right. By "offering a false sense of success," the PLM, with its cozy arrangement, was putting off the real conflict that needed to come in the abortion battle. Dead bodies were piling up year after year as the PLM refused to attack abortion head-on and abolish it once and for all.

X. *Thou shalt not lose office.* The greatest threat to good legislation might be the fear of losing office. There is tremendous incentive in most States to become a career politician. Most States offer some kind of pension plan or other retirement benefit after one reaches a certain number of years of service. Legislators desperately want to get re-elected, so they do what is easiest and least controversial. They aim to placate the most voters while upsetting the fewest. This approach leads to the proliferation of what my friend Charlie Meadows calls "Pink Puff and Piffle," which is legislation that looks pretty and sounds nice but does nothing. Given the choice of a controversial bill to abolish abortion, or a noncontroversial, do-nothing pro-life bill, legislators choose Pink Puff and Piffle every time. Essentially, they trade meaningless victories for votes. They create a never-ending fight, where there is always another skirmish, never a lasting victory or permanent peace. Everyone settles into the cozy arrangement.

In conclusion, 2015 was a year of rude awakenings. I discovered that the political PLM was corrupt and idolatrous and that there was no local legislation worthy of support. During this year I began to think in terms of political repentance. Once again I asked, how should we reorder our lives and work? How do we stop repeating the same mistakes? How do we break up the cozy arrangement between PLM lobbyists and politicians? How do we change direction so that we return to an abortion-free State?

We could not continue supporting the Orwellian bills of the PLM. We needed official action of some sort to end the football game once and for all. We had to do something that would actually abolish abortion. So, in the summer of 2015 we began laying the groundwork for a new approach, and in 2016 we began to repent politically. That story is coming, but first we have two more Corrupt Commandments.

10

NO OTHER GODS: THE JUDICIARY

The most pernicious Corrupt Commandment of all, the one that keeps magistrates in every office in every branch of state and federal government from lifting a finger to fight for the abolition of abortion is: "Thou shalt have no other gods before the judiciary." This Corrupt Commandment is embodied in a number of false doctrines such as:

- Court opinions are the law of the land.
- Magistrates must unconditionally obey all court opinions.
- SCOTUS is the final arbiter of what is constitutional.

Before looking more closely at these false doctrines and revealing a proper response and political strategy, we need to recap the very real consequences of believing and acting as if the judiciary were a god.

The Hydra: From *Roe* to *Dobbs*

The Hydra, from Greek mythology, was a multi-headed, serpent-like creature whose lair was the lake of Lerna, thought to be a passage to the underworld. It had poisonous breath and toxic blood. Those who tried to kill the creature by cutting off its heads found that for each head cut off, two new ones grew from the stump. According to the Greek lyric poet Alcaeus writing in about 600 BC, the Hydra had nine heads. Simonides, writing a century later, increased the number to fifty.

In its infamous *Roe v. Wade* opinion in 1973, the Supreme Court of the United States (the Court) said that the preborn are merely "the potentiality of human life," and that abortion is "primarily, a medical decision, and basic responsibility for it must rest with the physician."

I was born in 1975, so I grew up being taught that *Roe* was "the law of the land," handed down to us by the Court. When I was old enough to get involved in the PLM, it was simply understood that the Court was our primary enemy and should be the focus of our activism. Therefore, the most important mission of every pro-lifer was to see that a pro-life Republican was always elected President of the United States so that he would appoint pro-life justices to the Court who would eventually overturn *Roe v. Wade*, thus ending abortion. This is how we would slay the Court Dragon, that serpent of old.

So that is what we all did. In fact, this political strategy of the PLM was so successful that in the first two decades after *Roe*, six new justices were appointed by three different pro-life Republican presidents. As a result, eight of the nine justices on the Court had been appointed by pro-life Republicans. In 1992, in *Planned Parenthood v. Casey*, these pro-life justices had an opportunity to overturn *Roe v. Wade*, but instead they went even further into the dark side by barring a State from placing "a substantial obstacle in the path of a woman seeking an abortion."

Although the strategy of changing the Court was proven an abject failure, the PLM refused to give it up and doggedly stuck with it for another thirty years as the bodies of dead babies piled higher and the blood of tens of millions of innocents, the worst genocide in human history, stained the hands of magistrates and lobbyists in the PLM. In an 8 October 2018 interview on *Truth & Liberty*, Marjorie Dannenfelser, president of the Susan B. Anthony List, said, "Our whole strategy has been to make sure that the Senate and the President can work together to change the Court to overturn *Roe* so that we can finally start passing laws... What they need is smart political strategy, and we try to help them with that."

Christian conservatives thought that Donald Trump and the Republican Party were going to stop abortion, but the Republican-led Congress and White House never even managed to cut public funding to Planned Parenthood, the number one perpetrator. As Kentucky Senator Rand Paul said to the media on 23 August 2018:

> Many voters think Republicans are really opposed to government-funded abortions. But the dirty little secret is that Republican leadership is blocking my amendment to defund Planned Parenthood... The public has long known that the Democrats are the abortion party. Now the public will know that many Republicans just pay lip service to pro-life issues...

Christian conservatives need to realize that the Republican Party has been marketing itself as pro-life ever since *Roe*, but it was a Republican-appointed Court that gave us *Roe*, and the Court has been dominated by Republican appointees ever since. Christian conservatives celebrated Trump's appointment of Brett Kavanaugh to the Court, but Kavanaugh was on the record describing *Roe* as "settled law," and saying he believed women and teenage girls "have a right to abortion." Those who were jubilant over Kavanaugh were mistakenly convinced that a particular nominee's approval would somehow tip the balance of power on the Supreme Court and finally abolish abortion.

I know what you are thinking. *But they did abolish abortion! They overturned* Roe.

The *Dobbs* Opinion

On 24 June 2022, in *Dobbs v. Jackson Women's Health Organization* (*Dobbs*), the Court finally acknowledged the proper authority and jurisdiction of the States, which is spelled out in the Tenth Amendment to the Constitution of the U.S. The majority opinion of the Court states: "The Constitution does not prohibit the citizens of each State from regulating or prohibiting abortion. *Roe* and *Casey* arrogated that authority. We now overrule those decisions and return that authority to the people and their elected representatives."

Hurray! The Hydra was slain. We chopped off its head. In ancient Israel every fiftieth year was known as a "Jubilee." Jubilee was a year of rest and recovery for the people and the land. Debts were cancelled and slaves set free. Property was restored and there was no sowing or commercial reaping. We suffered under *Roe* for forty-nine years, but thanks to the *Dobbs* opinion, thousands of preborn human beings would be saved and enjoy a year of Jubilee. Even in the pro-abortion, blue State of Wisconsin, Planned Parenthood ceased child sacrifice.

While everyone was celebrating this momentous opinion, some of us were wondering why the Court suddenly reversed *Roe*. Given the Court's past history of protecting and expanding abortion, and given the left-leaning ideology of most of its justices, what was Hydra up to?

It is easy to focus on the part of the *Dobbs* opinion that mentions "prohibiting abortion," but it also mentions the "regulating" of abortion, which is exactly what all fifty States had been doing since 1973. The overturning of *Roe* did not overturn forty-nine years' worth of state laws which had created a thriving abortion industry in every State in the union. Many activists fail to see that while the PLM was focused on the Supreme Court of the United States for all those decades, every state and federal court in the judicial system was being taken over by progressive judges who supported abortion. Judges and justices across the U.S. had been upholding abortion for forty-nine years. What would they do now?

Even more concerning about the *Dobbs* opinion is its silence in regard to the rights to life and equal protection. The Fifth and Fourteenth Amendments stipulate that no life can be taken without first being found guilty by due process of law, and the Fourteenth Amendment requires every innocent life be given equal protection of the laws within a State. The Court should have said that all elective abortion is unconstitutional per the Fifth and Fourteenth Amendments. The Court should have explained that the Mississippi Gestational Age Act was unconstitutional because it does not provide equal protection of the law to preborn humans who have not attained the arbitrary age of fifteen weeks. The Court should have advised all States to criminalize all elective abortions.

Consider sexual assault, for example. The penalties a guilty person might face vary from State to State, but within each State, it is always a crime for anyone who commits the act, regardless of the age of the victim. The state law gives equal protection against sexual violence. In contrast, abortion laws which protect only humans of a certain age, or which grant blanket immunity to mothers and accomplices, are discriminatory and do not provide equal protection. In order for an abortion law to provide equal protection, and thus be constitutional, it must criminalize all elective abortion, regardless of the victim's age, and it must apply to anyone involved in that criminal act.

These twin constitutional pillars of a right to life and equal protection are grounded in a biblical understanding of God's nature. God does not show partiality or favoritism (Lev. 19:15; Deut. 10:17-18; Rom. 2:11); therefore, neither should our laws.

By remaining silent on the rights to life and equal protection, and by indicating that the States may continue regulating abortion, the Hydra had just sprouted fifty healthy heads which are even now asserting *Roe*-like rule in each and every State. It has already begun.

For example, Wisconsin's Jubilee was short-lived. The reversal of *Roe* did not reverse all the state statutes enacted by the PLM over the years to legalize and regulate abortion in Wisconsin. Therefore, all it took was an opinion from a Dane County circuit judge, bolstered by a pro-abortion state attorney general, for the Planned Parenthood death camps in Madison and Milwaukee to resume committing murder by abortion on 18 September 2023.

But Wisconsin is a liberal blue State, some might reason. Surely, things are different in conservative red States like Oklahoma. Oklahoma, the most pro-life State in the union, did enact a trigger law prior to the *Dobbs* opinion, so when *Roe* was overturned, the State had two relevant statutes. The first is 21 O.S. § 21-861, which reads:

> Every person who administers to any woman, or who prescribes for any woman, or advises or procures any woman to take any medicine, drug or substance, or uses or employs any instrument, or other means whatever, with intent thereby to procure the miscarriage of such woman, unless the same is necessary to preserve her life, shall be guilty of a felony….

The second statute is 63 O.S. § 63-1-733, which reads: "No woman shall perform or induce an abortion upon herself, except under the supervision of a duly licensed physician."

These two statutes together sound like they would criminalize all elective abortions, and they would, if enforced and adjudicated by normal citizens in the ways they were obviously intended when originally written and enacted. Unfortunately, on 21 March 2023, the Supreme Court of the State of Oklahoma (SCOTSOO) issued an opinion (case no. 120543) to codify new interpretations of the Oklahoma Constitution and statutes, intending to dramatically broaden and permit murder by abortion.

First, in a very twisted trick of interpretation, SCOTSOO supposedly found a right to abortion in Article 2 Section 2 of the Oklahoma Constitution which provides: "All persons have the inherent right to life, liberty, the pursuit of happiness, and the enjoyment of the gains of their own industry."

Note this crazy analysis of the court: "We hold that the Oklahoma Constitution [Article 2 Section 2] creates an inherent right of a pregnant woman to terminate a pregnancy when necessary to preserve her life." Justice Combs later explains that the constitutional right to life and liberty "would include a right to privacy and personal autonomy." And of course they view abortion as a private and personal matter.

Furthermore, they reinterpreted the phrase "to preserve her life" to no longer mean to save her life in a medical emergency. Note the strained and contrived way in which they arbitrarily define *preserve her life*:

> We would define this inherent right to mean: a woman has an inherent right to choose to terminate her pregnancy if at any point in the pregnancy, the woman's physician has determined to a reasonable degree of medical certainty or probability that the continuation of the pregnancy will endanger the woman's life due to the pregnancy itself or due to a medical condition that the woman is either currently suffering from or likely to suffer from during the pregnancy. Absolute certainty is not required...

Remember the doctor's note in high school that was a free pass for tardiness and absence? A woman now needs no more than a doctor's note that she is acting to "preserve her life" to literally get away with murder. With this opinion SCOTSOO foretold how they would adjudicate abortion cases in Oklahoma: they will throw out any case against her or her doctor. This opinion was clearly designed to open the bloody floodgates in Oklahoma.

Oklahoma Chief Justice Kane, in his well-written dissent, said:

> [T]he majority engages in legal contortions...by fashioning Oklahoma Constitutional precepts of abortion law that simply do not exist. There is no expressed or implied right to abortion enshrined in the Oklahoma Constitution. In interpreting our Constitution, this Court must guard against the innate human temptation to confuse what is provided in the Oklahoma Constitution with what one wishes were provided.

SCOTSOO took its cue from the previous forty-nine years of successful judicial overreach by the Court. It appears that these justices have reasoned that if the Court could get away with bullying hundreds of millions across the union for five decades, surely they could get away with bullying less than four million here in Oklahoma. Now, doing their best imitation of the Court in 1973, they are establishing their own *Roe*-like rule, and they are counting on Oklahomans and our elected magistrates to behave as they have in the past, to continue bowing down and obeying immoral and unconstitutional court opinions.

These are just two examples, one from a liberal progressive State and one from a conservative State, but it is playing out similarly across the union. Even in the reddest of red States, justices act with outrageous impunity and will continue to do so. They are part of the Hydra, alive and well after all.

Roe and *Casey* are not dead. They are being instituted and upheld in a variety of wicked ways throughout the States. Long before *Dobbs*, the path had been fully prepared for abortion to continue under court protection within the States. The Hydra was more than willing for the *Roe* head to be cut off. The fight is right back where it started: when courts decide, babies die. As of this writing, there are no pro-life red States in contrast to pro-choice blue States. There are only pro-abortion States where the amount of regulation of the industry varies by degree.

Playboy

We believe another reason the Court overturned *Roe* was because the timing was right with the abortion industry, which was fully prepared to make the transition to a new age of private, prevalent child sacrifice. Technology, practices, and procedures had already advanced to a point that even without *Roe* the industry would survive and thrive.

Self-induced chemical abortions are now the rule, the new normal. Chemical abortion (also called medical abortion, at-home abortion, self-managed abortion, and pill abortion) is when the mother takes powerful drugs (typically Mifepristone and Misoprostol) to cause the death and expulsion of her baby. As of 2020 the Guttmacher Institute, the research arm of Planned Parenthood, reported that over half of all abortions were already being administered chemically. That means the abortion industry was prepared and ready to launch a program of full-scale, do-it-yourself, mail-order abortions. With no overhead for offices and staff, the advent of telehealth, and no in-person office visits, the abortion industry will ramp up and scale up operations. The total number of abortions will increase, even while the number of surgical abortions in red States decreases. Furthermore, self-induced abortions are either specifically protected by pro-life laws, or these types of killings are not being prosecuted by district attorneys or attorneys general. Women who have no fear of prosecution can easily and freely buy pills and share abortion advice online. To better understand the current transition in the abortion industry, consider the historical transition of the pornography (porn) industry.

Playboy magazine sold more than seven million copies per month at its peak! It averaged more than five million copies per month throughout the 1970s and into the 80s. Many of us grew up in that era and remember how we did not talk about porn. It was kept out of the public eye by pro-family regulations on the industry. Pornographic magazines were kept covered and concealed behind counters. Video tapes were sold outside of city limits at seedy storefronts. It could not be sold to minors. Consumers had to seek it out and ask for it.

Playboy's circulation dwindled over the years, eventually falling to only four hundred thousand per month in 2017, and it went out of print in the spring of 2020. Competing magazines such as *Penthouse* and *Hustler* have followed the pattern. Pro-family politicians could look at these statistics and claim, "Clearly, our pro-family regulations have ended the consumption of porn in the U.S.," but does anyone seriously believe that the consumption of porn has decreased?

We are in the midst of a similar transition in the abortion industry. Pro-life politicians tell voters that their new regulations have ended abortion in conservative States, but in reality their new laws have only removed the most obvious and easily tracked murders from public retail space. They are actually aiding and abetting the abortion industry in its transition to a new era of more private and pervasive child sacrifice. The closing of a few porn publishing houses, or, in this case abortion death camps, is the wrong measure of success.

Pro-life legislators seem satisfied with the transition from doctor-administered to mommy-administered murders, and the average voter in red States already believes that abortion has been abolished and the battle is over. If we allow Republican leaders to get away with it now, then the new normal will become entrenched. At-home abortions will replace surgery-center abortions, while voters naively bask in false victory and celebrate the politicians who drove the bloodshed out of sight and out of mind.

These are the results of having no other gods before the judiciary, of believing and acting as if court opinions are the law of the land and that magistrates must unconditionally obey all court opinions. It is time to answer these lies.

The Rule of Law

The Latin phrase *lex rex* is translated *law is king*. Today we refer to the *rule of law*. This concept has been the foundation of western civil law for centuries, but what does it mean?

First, we do not have a *who* at the top, we have a *what*. We are not ruled by a person, but by the law itself. The law is king. This is meant to protect us from being tyrannized and enslaved by our political leaders. Under the rule of law, every person is subject to the law equally, including our presidents, governors, judges, and legislators.

Second, if the law is king, then how is the law established? In our representative republic, our constitutions spell out how law is established in the federal and state jurisdictions. At the federal level, neither the President nor the judiciary makes law. Only the Congress does, and those laws must directly pertain to the seventeen powers granted to the federal government by the States. The President's job is to execute the laws of the Congress, and the federal courts are to settle disputes between parties arising from those laws. So, the proper way to establish law in our union is through our elected representatives in Congress. We have parallel structures and responsibilities in each of our States.

Third, if the law is king, how do we ensure the law is just and not tyrannical, as humans tend to become? Law must have a legitimate basis other than the will of the majority, the whim of a president, or the agenda of a judge. There must be an external standard to protect the people from tyranny.

The Founders believed that civil law should be based on what they called *natural law*, as it was defined by Blackstone, who acknowledged that man is a creature and subject to his maker's will. "This will of his Maker is called the law of nature..." Blackstone said. He goes on to say, "No human laws should be suffered to contradict these." James Wilson, a signer of the Constitution and original member of the Court said,

> It should always be remembered that this law, natural or revealed, made for men or for nations, flows from the same Divine source: it is the law of God... Human law must rest its authority ultimately upon the authority of that law which is divine.

Alexander Hamilton, also a signer of the Constitution and author of the Federalist Papers, said that the law "dictated by God Himself is, of course, superior in obligation to any other. It is binding over all the globe in all countries, and at all times. No human laws are of any validity if contrary to this." It is evident that our Founders believed civil law should be based on God's natural law, not on the desires of the majority or the fancies of judges.

These days, however, we labor under the misconception that civil law can be codified by the small band of unelected lawyers at the Court. In *Roe v. Wade* the Court violated the rule of law in three ways. The justices set themselves up as king, they established new law improperly, and they violated natural law.

To those readers who think that the Court can rightly establish law through their opinions, consider this example. What if the Court found a constitutional right to rape? What would we do if that opinion became the basis for public policy, if it became the "law of the land?" Would we allow rape clinics to open in our neighborhoods where men could safely and legally take innocent little girls—little girls who would come out abused and scarred for life? This sequence of events may seem impossible, but we all know parents and grandparents who felt the same way about abortion in 1973.

Hierarchy of Law

We have established that we are supposed to be ruled by just law properly enacted by legislative bodies. In our representative republic, we are surrounded by layers of jurisdictions, from God all the way down to dogcatcher. With overlapping and competing authorities, the question often arises: to whom must we submit when conflicts and confusion arise? These conflicts are more easily sorted out when we consider the concept of hierarchy.

The highest law and greatest authority is God himself. According to his character and naturally revealed law, it is wrong to kill innocent human beings. This natural law is above all others, so even if our earthly constitutions and statutes allowed murder by abortion, every earthly magistrate would still be under divine obligation to protect innocent preborn humans from destruction in his jurisdiction.

The next highest law in the U.S., which trumps all others where it speaks and has proper jurisdiction, is the U.S. Constitution, which we pointed out above enshrines God's human rights to life and equal protection in Amendments V and XIV. Per the Fourteenth Amendment: "Nor shall any State deprive any person of life, liberty, or property, without due process of law; nor deny to any person within its jurisdiction the equal protection of the laws." Therefore, any laws in any State that permit abortion are *prima facie* unconstitutional, and no magistrate is duty bound to enforce them.

The next highest laws in our republic are the state constitutions, each one of which states something like: "No person of this State shall be deprived of life, liberty, or property except by the due course of the law." Every single state constitution, echoing Amendment V of the U.S. Constitution, properly recognizes and prescribes the right to life. The Oklahoma Constitution, in Article 2 Section 2, explicitly states "All persons have the inherent right to life…"

As you can see, abortion already violates the higher laws: God's law that we shall not murder, the U.S. Constitution's guarantees of the right to life and equal protection, state constitutional guarantees of the right to life, and even state homicide codes. It is not until we drill down to pro-life statutes in state health and safety codes that we find legal permission to murder preborn humans by abortion. It is in these codes that the PLM obeyed and worshipped the Court and carried out the Court's sacrificial prescription.

Not all laws are equal in status. When there is a contradiction in the statutes, executives should uphold the higher laws and treat the contradictory lower laws as null and void. Upholding a higher law may require breaking a lower one. Yeshua taught the hierarchy of law and demonstrated it by healing on the Sabbath. Note his rhetorical question to the magistrates: "Which is lawful on the Sabbath: to do good or to do evil, to save life or to kill?" (Mark 3:4).

Imagine someone walks along the fence of a private swimming pool. The sign on the gate reads, "No Trespassing." What if a toddler falls into the pool and is drowning? A higher law demands that the lower law be broken to save the life of that child. In American jurisprudence the savior of the child would be vindicated for trespassing based on the "necessity defense."

At some point local magistrates will have to block or cross the abortionist's property line to uphold the higher laws. They may have to trespass to save a neighbor. Should the Allies in 1944 have waited at the border for a German court order to enter? No. The Allies were trespassing at Auschwitz.

Magistrates in every branch of state and federal government already have the moral duty and legal authority of the higher laws to immediately abolish murder by abortion.

Court Opinions Are Not Law

Politicians like to equivocate on abortion in order to mislead their constituents and to provide cover for their cowardice or for their continuation of wicked policies which benefit them and keep them in office. For example, in a press release dated 21 February 2019, the then-leader of the Oklahoma Senate, Greg Treat, said, "*Roe*...and [*Casey*] are horrible *decisions* of the U.S. Supreme Court. But I respect the *rule of law*, and the U.S. *Constitution*..." (emphasis added).

In this statement, Sen. Treat speaks as if the Court's "decisions" are the same thing as the "rule of law" and the "Constitution." This is a very clear example of equivocation to deceive voters into believing that court opinions are equal to the Constitution. He is attempting to hide behind the Constitution, while actually upholding an immoral and unconstitutional court opinion.

In another clear example of worshipping the judiciary, on 26 April 2021, Oklahoma Governor Kevin Stitt signaled that when it comes to murder by abortion, he will passively obey any judge's opinion on the matter. After signing three pro-life bills, the governor said to the media, "We signed three [pro-life] bills today. We'll let the courts work out if any of those get overturned."

Both of these statements are typical of pro-life politicians and reflect the dominant view that all magistrates must submit to court opinions as if they were the law of the land. Rather than rejecting false gods and unconstitutional court opinions, magistrates empower them through obedience and continue to play politics with dead babies.

Three Coequal Branches of Government?

Civil authority in our representative republic is divided among the executive, legislative, and judicial branches of government. We hear a mantra from every public school teacher and every politician that we have "three coequal branches of government," but our federal republic was not set up that way. Even if this myth were true, the executive and legislative branches currently let the judicial branch rule over them. But legally, the judiciary is subject to the legislative branch at both the state and federal levels. Each branch has its own duties which do not overlap with the other branches, and the only sense in which they are coequal is in their common duty to uphold our state and federal constitutions.

The U.S. Constitution, in Article III Section 2, stipulates, "The supreme Court shall have appellate Jurisdiction, both as to Law and Fact, with such Exceptions, and under such Regulations as the Congress shall make." Did you catch that? Congress can completely remove the Court's legal right to adjudicate certain issues and regulate how they operate. There is no equality between the two institutions. Congress should dominate the Court.

Based on this constitutional authority that Congress has over the Court, Representative Ron Paul from Texas authored the Sanctity of Life Act which simply said, "The Supreme Court shall not have jurisdiction to review [any abortion-related case]." He ran this same legislation for eight years in a row, from 2005 through 2012, but it never received even a committee hearing, and no grassroots activists like our readers ever heard about it. What does that tell you about the PLM?

Tyranny or Idolatry?

No court and no justice can truly be called a tyrant. You may not like the opinion of a justice, but you need not fear that he will personally try to enforce it. Justices have no enforcement power, no guns or handcuffs, so they cannot be true tyrants. Tyrants have armies or secret police to enforce their dictates. Whatever power justices have is gifted to them by voluntary worship and obedience. The problem we face from the judiciary is not their tyranny, but the idolatry of the PLM, the idolatry of all the other magistrates and pro-life people.

The Canaanite god Molech had no enforcement power either. His earthly priests prescribed human sacrifice, but the priests did not come to steal the sacrifices. People voluntarily offered up their own children to be burned.

To illustrate the point, consider the Blinking Red Hand. I was standing at the corner of Alamo Plaza and East Crockett Street in San Antonio, Texas. Twelve people stood in a herd waiting to cross the street, but they refused to go. Why? Because a blinking red hand told them not to.

The silence as they waited was pierced by a rhythmic BOOP, BOOP, BOOP, as the red hand flashed. Why was it so quiet between the beeps? Where was all the traffic? I looked to the north and saw not a single car for two hundred yards, but I did see an orange and white barricade. I looked to the south and saw not a single motorist. The road was completely deserted, but blocks away I could make out police cars and barricades. The road was closed, yet these people continued to stand on the corner for nearly two minutes, gaping at a beeping, blinking, red hand telling them to "Stay!"

What an amazing phenomenon. These people were perfectly willing to blindly, unquestioningly follow a symbol of authority, no matter how unreasonable or unjustified. What is stopping magistrates from abolishing abortion? Nothing but blind obedience to the Blinking Red Hand of an unelected lawyer sporting a black robe and wielding a gavel.

Later that day I circled back to the crosswalk where a new group of sheep was huddled before the Blinking Red Hand.

"Hey!" I hollered to get their attention. "Y'all can go on across. The road is closed." One lady finally looked up the street and stepped out in faith. The rest followed.

If the judiciary is not supreme, if its opinions are immoral and unlawful, if its enforcement power is nothing more than a blinking red hand, then how should we reorder our lives and work in accord with the truth? What should we do to uphold the true rule of law?

The Doctrine of the Lesser Magistrates

In 2015 one of our OC-PAC members handed me the book *The Doctrine of the Lesser Magistrates* by Matthew J. Trewhella. The historical standard has always been that when an earthly authority commands that which God forbids, or forbids that which God commands, we are to obey God rather than mankind.

The Doctrine shows that resistance to tyranny through local magistrates is an ancient tradition and a godly principle, one that Christians formalized and embedded into the political institutions of western civilization. Simply put, this Judeo-Christian doctrine is the duty of local authorities to oppose and resist laws or edicts from other authorities that contravene the law of God. Local authorities are to protect the lives, liberty, and property of those who reside within their jurisdictions against other rogue authorities.

Notice how this principle emerges from what Ezekiel prophesied to the kingdom of Judah (emphasis added):

> Her magistrates are like wolves tearing their prey; they shed blood and kill people to make unjust gain. Her prophets whitewash these deeds for them by false visions and lying divinations. They say, "This is what the Lord Yehovah says" when Yehovah has not spoken. The people of the land practice extortion and commit robbery; they oppress the poor and needy and mistreat the foreigner, denying them justice. *"I looked for someone among them who would build up the wall and stand before me in the gap* on behalf of the land so I would not have to destroy it, but I found no one. So I will pour out my wrath on them and consume them with my fiery anger, bringing down on their own heads all they have done, declares the Lord Yehovah." (Ezek. 22:27-31)

Yehovah is hoping someone will step in to correct the lawlessness of the magistrates so that he will not have to punish Judah. Who will step in to save preborn humans from lawless judges and protect our States from the wrath of God? Will it be a sheriff, a legislator, a governor? If no one steps into the gap, will God punish us? Are we already under his judgment?

The Doctrine is so profound in its application to upholding the rule of law that it is easily one of the most important books written in this generation. We have purchased and distributed hundreds of copies. In 2015 we gave a copy to every sitting Republican legislator in our State, and we give copies to all of our students, year in and year out. At only sixty-nine pages, *The Doctrine* is easily consumed on a Saturday morning over a pot of coffee.

How will we restore the rule of law in our States? The answer is: by practicing the doctrine of the lesser magistrates, which will remind justices that their power is limited, that they are accountable to other magistrates, to the Constitution, and to the Ultimate Authority.

Regardless of what any court says, legislators should attempt to criminalize abortion so that perpetrators can more easily be prosecuted. They should bring articles of impeachment for neglect of duty or gross partiality against any justice who tries to protect abortion. Regardless of what any court says, district attorneys and attorneys general should arrest those involved in committing murder by abortion and build cases under state homicide codes. They should argue that any existing statutes that permit or protect the practice of abortion are immoral and unconstitutional, therefore null and void. Like the Allies at Auschwitz, the governor and state police should shut down death camps.

True, local magistrates will be loath to stick their necks out. That is why we, as the people of God, must plead our case and assure our support. Our role is to rally around our local magistrates to encourage them to take a stand. We must educate and instruct them in their moral and legal duty to ignore immoral and unconstitutional court opinions.

In the movie *A Few Good Men*, two Marines, Harold Dawson and Louden Downey, accidentally kill their fellow Marine William Santiago while carrying out a questionable order called a "Code Red" from a superior officer. At the trial the two are found guilty of conduct unbecoming an officer and are dishonorably discharged from the Marines. Since he was following an order, Downey is dismayed by the verdict and cries out,

"I don't understand…he ordered the Code Red! What did we do wrong? We did nothing wrong!"

"Yeah, we did," Dawson responds. "We were supposed to fight for people who couldn't fight for themselves. We were supposed to fight for Willie."

At the final judgment, which magistrates will have fought for the preborn Williams? Which will be found guilty and dishonorably discharged…forever? Obeying unjust orders is never an excuse.

11

VICTIMS OR CRIMINALS?

Yes. Some women who choose to kill their babies are victims. Others are criminals. Unfortunately, most magistrates and activists in the PLM either reject or ignore the second category, choosing instead to classify all women who abort as victims and to follow the second Corrupt Commandment: "Thou shalt not punish the woman."

This flawed ideology, like the worship of the judiciary, is a major reason why, even after *Dobbs* overturned *Roe*, the practice of modern-day child sacrifice continues throughout all the States. In this chapter we will take a closer look at the innocence or culpability of women who choose to abort, explore how the second Corrupt Commandment has influenced pro-life laws both pre-*Dobbs* and post-*Roe*, and attempt to outline a just public policy that accounts for both guilt and innocence, justice and mercy.

Back in 2019, my friend Richard, who is an evangelical Christian conservative, shocked me by publishing an article about abortion subtitled, "Making Victims into Criminals." His claim was that with rare exceptions, women who get abortions are victims, not criminals.

Josh Brahm is the president of Equal Rights Institute, an East Coast pro-life organization. He is a personal friend and colleague. We have spent hours together discussing how to be better apologists and evangelists. I appreciate his work and the lives that it has saved, but I strongly disagree with the statement he posted around

Thanksgiving 2023 in which he asked, "Should women be prosecuted for illegal abortions?" This was his answer, in part:

> We do not believe that women should be prosecuted for abortion, because the state of public thought about abortion precludes us from assuming women understand what they are doing in an abortion…
>
> It will take many years to undo the misinformation, propaganda, and deception of the last 50 years.
>
> And so, while a minority of women might have full moral culpability for abortion…most women don't. It makes no sense to advocate for prosecution when only a tiny minority could be found guilty, and the rest would be unjustly dragged through our criminal justice system.

It might be argued that in the 1970s a majority of people believed that early in pregnancy there was nothing but a clump of cells that had the potential to become a human. In those days, the use of ultrasound in obstetrics was not yet a common practice. Similarly, in the mid-twentieth century people mistakenly believed that smoking cigarettes was not actually harmful.

On the other hand, even in the early days of *Roe v. Wade*, it could be argued that claiming victimhood was little more than a rationalization of the guilty, a self-defense mechanism that would allow those who purchased abortions to somehow live with themselves. We have received numerous notes and testimonies over the years from men and women who say they knew they were committing murder, but they did it anyway because it was legal and no one tried to stop them. For example, Jessika writes:

> Before I had my baby murdered in an abortion, I knew what I was doing. I cried thinking of it, but I feared losing my youth, my freedom, angering my parents, and on and on. Sadly, I chose to have that innocent baby murdered… Now I will proclaim the truth without holding back. Lying and coddling these parents does nothing good for them. The truth hurts, but it can also set them free.

Even if it were true that a majority of abortion buyers in the early days were naïve victims, it has certainly not been true in recent decades. Volunteers with organizations like Love of Truth Ministries, Missionaries to the Preborn, Abolitionist Societies, Operation Save America, and this ministry have interposed regularly for years in front of abortion facilities across the union. They report that the vast majority of abortion buyers, men and women alike, are hardened and know exactly what they are doing. Those purchasing abortions routinely hurl curses and insults at those who would help them and their preborn children. Just like with cigarettes, people now know better. After decades of beautiful ultrasound images, and with easy internet accessibility to the latest information, the miracle of life in the womb is common knowledge.

In the many years that we have stood at the gates of Molech, and of all those we have witnessed go up to the altar, I believe only a small percentage were truly victims. They were obviously young and under the control of an older handler, often a hardened boyfriend, parent, or grandparent directing the steps of a scared child. A few times I was certain that the woman was drugged and being trafficked for sex. Those times we turned in a description and license plate to law enforcement. But these are the rare exceptions. The website notavictim.org is a repository of compelling evidence that the vast majority of those who go up to the altar of Molech know exactly what they are doing.

The truth is that abortion providers are meeting a demand. The parents and grandparents of an unwanted child seek out an abortionist and pay him to murder their child. Or, as is the case now in conservative States, they seek out and purchase a chemical murder weapon. Sometimes other family members, friends, or a boyfriend encourage the scheme. In any other crime we would recognize these participants as accomplices.

In their history we read that the Israelites made their sons and daughters "pass through the fire" of Molech (2 Kgs. 16:3, 17:17, 21:6, 23:10; 2 Chr. 33:6; Jer. 32:35; Ezek. 20:26, 20:31, 23:37). Yehovah calls this practice of child sacrifice "evil" and an "abomination." In fact, it "provoked him to anger" and was a primary cause of God's judgment and wrath upon their nation. Dare we call these Israelite parents victims?

Today we see people in various states of heart and mind coming before the abortionist's altar of Molech to "slaughter God's children" (Ezek. 16:21). Some are in denial. Some are hardhearted, scared, evil, and twisted. Perhaps some have even been victimized. Regardless of their situations, we must not use their various mental and emotional states to justify their actions or excuse the heinous practice of legal child sacrifice. Therefore, like Josh, we still must consider how we will respond to those women who choose to kill their children by abortion.

In *Ethics*, Dietrich Bonhoeffer writes:

> Destruction of the embryo in the mother's womb is a violation of the right to live which God has bestowed… A great many different motives may lead to an action of this kind… All of these considerations must no doubt have a quite decisive influence on our personal and pastoral attitude towards the person concerned, but they cannot in any way alter the fact of murder.

Here Bonhoeffer eloquently differentiates our two responses to abortion. On the one hand, we respond with pastoral care for the person who is suffering the hardships of fear, abuse, and poverty. We boldly preach to the victims and perpetrators the good news that they can be forgiven for the sin of abortion and be reconciled to Yehovah.

Our culture says guilt is bad and we should avoid it. We have lost the gift of shame. The constant refrain is, "It's okay, you didn't do anything wrong." This leads to cognitive and emotional dissonance because the conscience knows abortion is wrong. Yehovah never says we should avoid acknowledging guilt. On the contrary, God encourages us to confess our sins and own our guilt. He says if we will humble ourselves and repent, then he will lift us up, and we will be reconciled to him (Jas. 4:9-10; Prov. 14:9). To ignore our guilt is to allow a dirty wound to fester. Responding to guilt with confession and repentance is to cleanse the wound and invite the Father's healing. The truth may hurt like hell, but it is actually the pain of hell being removed from us.

Yet even in the light of pastoral care for people in difficult circumstances, we must still recognize the sin of abortion as a criminal act of murder. Because every human being is intrinsically valuable, and because justice must be served, it is morally incumbent upon those living in proximity to investigate every homicide and prosecute the appropriate parties. What district attorney would prosecute a naïve, thirteen-year-old girl who was abused and coerced? But the attacker, family members, friends, and doctor who victimized her and murdered her baby should certainly be held accountable for their actions. And should a victim mistakenly be prosecuted, I believe we can trust a jury of our peers to extend mercy when appropriate and to establish justice for preborn humans in cases of murder by abortion.

Josh and those who share his point of view believe that rather than prosecuting abortion, we should address it primarily through social support and education (more on that below). Teaching in schools and person-to-person among family, friends, and Facebook connections is bound to change some hearts and save some lives, but ultimately it will not transform our broader culture of death.

The greatest teacher and behavior-modifier of the broader culture is the law. For example, the most effective way to keep people from speeding on the highway is not funding an educational billboard campaign about the dangers of speeding; we keep people from speeding by posting the law and issuing citations. Likewise, when it comes to abortion, social support and education are of some value, but to effectively save the most lives possible, we must outlaw abortion and prosecute transgressors of the law.

This is a matter of principle, not practicality. The number of cases should not be considered in the question of whether or not to prosecute. In fact, it would be a mistake to assume we would see thousands of expensive, tedious, and heart-wrenching trials. It would take only a few marquee cases, over a few weeks or months— not years—for everyone everywhere to get the message that they cannot get away with murder by abortion. Again, the law is the most powerful and effective teacher we have for effecting immediate and broad change of public behavior. Besides, the fundamental duty of government is to protect the lives of those living in its jurisdiction.

Summarizing thus far, *some* of those who get abortions are victims, but this should not be our default assumption, and it certainly should not be an excuse to keep criminal behavior legal or to refuse to prosecute those who knew what they were doing and did it anyway. It is a grossly bad argument to say that because some percentage of people did not know they were sinning or breaking the law, we should not prosecute those who did know. How dare we refuse to grant justice to innocent human beings because it might be financially or emotionally challenging to prosecute cases? In fact, protecting women from prosecution removes the greatest teacher and cultural tool for change at our disposal. It further entrenches our culture of death and contributes to the victimization of women.

Pro-life License to Kill

Pro-life politicians have no trouble imagining abortion doctors as evil creatures with yellow eyes crouching in alleyways waiting to snatch pregnant women and murder their babies against their wills. They see every pregnant woman as a victim. Let us look at how this fantasy has played out in pro-life policy prior to *Dobbs* and since *Roe*.

Conditions on the ground in the States are changing rapidly. Some of the laws we will use as examples in the next few sections may no longer be in force, or were not fully enacted. Some are simply not being enforced. Still, they each illustrate the attitude and approach of magistrates in the PLM.

Pro-life Policy Pre-*Dobbs*

In the Oklahoma Unborn Child Protection from Dismemberment Abortion Act, we find, "No woman upon whom an abortion is performed or attempted to be performed shall be thereby liable for performing or attempting to perform a dismemberment abortion" (63 OK Stat § 1-737.9).

In the Prenatal Nondiscrimination Act of 2016 (HB 3128), we find the mother directly referred to as a victim: "Any woman upon whom an abortion in violation of this act is performed or attempted is entitled to all rights, protections and notifications afforded to crime victims under the Oklahoma Victim's Rights Act."

I completely missed this trend when I first started reviewing pro-life legislation years ago, but once I saw it, I went back and found loopholes like these in nearly every pro-life law in every pro-life

State, going back for years. Pro-lifers were content to go after the abortionist in some way, but those same regulatory laws directly protected the woman.

Pro-life Policy Post-*Roe*

Right after *Roe* was overturned, pro-lifers in red States were granted a clean slate, a chance to start over and to enact moral and constitutional laws that would completely abolish abortion. But would they? Most pro-life States did a good job of shutting down the physical death camps, but the old view of women as victims was still at work. As they had done before, pro-lifers began enacting laws to protect women who wanted to murder their own children themselves. We will recount what happened in Oklahoma, but keep in mind that the other pro-life States have followed similar paths.

With the overturn of *Roe*, Oklahoma's pro-life trigger law went into effect. It immediately made it a criminal offense for any doctor to perform an abortion. However, under the trigger law and two other newly enacted pro-life laws, all women of childbearing age were completely free to pull the trigger on their own preborn babies by various chemical and abortion pill methods without risk of investigation, prosecution, or criminality—no legal consequences whatsoever.

Ignoring the moral and constitutional principles of a right to life and equal protection, pro-life politicians specifically granted blanket immunity to women committing murder by abortion at any time during their pregnancies. Senate Bill 612 said: "This [act] does not: a. authorize the charging or conviction of a woman with any criminal offense in the death of her own unborn child…"

At a pro-life signing ceremony with Oklahoma's pro-life Governor Kevin Stitt, his pro-life Attorney General John O'Connor bragged about the gaping loophole when he said, "What I love about this one is that there is not a punishment in it for the mother…" At another press conference with Governor Stitt celebrating the reversal of *Roe*, the attorney general reiterated, "In the Oklahoma law there is no punishment for the mother." He would later claim that "the womb is now…the safest place for a child to be."

How can the womb be safe for a preborn child when the State had just allowed every new mother to go shopping for potions, pills, and poisons, and specifically granted them the license to murder their own preborn children legally? The abortion pill had become a State-sanctioned coat hanger. They can easily obtain instructions online from hundreds of websites, and the means are delivered within hours right to their front doors next to their Amazon packages. These types of murders have become the new normal.

Private data collected by a Christian pregnancy clinic in Oklahoma showed a 306% increase in online inquiries during the summer months following the release of the *Dobbs* opinion. Furthermore, whereas keyword searches had been predominantly for "abortion clinics," there was a pronounced increase in searches for "abortion pills." Volunteers at the clinic reported receiving calls asking, "How do I get the abortion pill?" and "Do you have the abortion pill?" Some callers reported they had taken abortion pills and were experiencing complications. Some women shared that they had obtained pills from other States, on the streets, and even by mail from India. Several pro-life news outlets reported a 500% increase in emergency room visits related to "miscarriage." These visits are actually women checking themselves in after taking abortion pills.

The abortion industry has not been shut down; it has merely changed how it does business. The data, the trends, and the current laws all indicate that the number of abortions committed in Oklahoma will remain similar to past levels and will likely continue rising. At the same time, our politicians will pretend that there is nothing to see here. This is the same approach being followed in red States across the Union.

One wonders, would we allow these politicians to get away with this kind of injustice if the victims were born children? Recall the story of Andrea Yates, who drowned her children in the bathtub because she was depressed, or Darlie Routier who stabbed her son to death with a kitchen knife because of financial trouble, or Dena Schlosser who hacked off the arms of her eleven-month-old daughter Margaret. In these cases the women were found either guilty of murder or to be insane. We would never default to the position that all women should be granted authorization to murder their children, so long as those children were delivered through the birth canal. Yet, currently, the opposite is true. Republican magistrates across the States have specifically granted women the legal right to murder their children, so long as those children have not passed through the birth canal.

The *license to kill* is defined as the official sanction by a government to initiate the use of lethal force in the delivery of their objectives. As noted earlier, pro-life Republicans were satisfied with the transition from doctor-administered to mommy-administered murders, and they enacted the legislation paving the way for the abortion industry to make a smooth transition.

I answered the work phone on Sunday afternoon 24 July 2022. "My friend bought the abortion pill. She used it to murder her baby; then she delivered her victim, her own child, into the toilet," said "Johannah," a student at Oklahoma State University (OSU).

Whoa! I was accustomed to hearing about abortions, but this one was like a gut punch after all the work we had done throughout the lead-up to *Dobbs* to warn pro-lifers what would happen with the license to kill.

According to the Guttmacher Institute, over ninety percent of abortions are committed within the first trimester of pregnancy. We know that abortion pills are effective well beyond the first trimester. That meant that stories like this one from OSU were going to be repeated thousands of times per year in my State and throughout the pro-life States following a similar policy of immunity for women. This was no longer hypothetical. This was real. It had arrived, and it was legal.

Three days after receiving this phone call, I attended a luncheon where Governor Stitt was the speaker. During his presentation the governor falsely announced that "abortion is illegal in the State of Oklahoma." He also thanked the legislators who brought him that legislation and called them "amazing." After the meeting, I shared the OSU story with the governor, making it clear to him that the killing was legal, and asking him to call for closing the loophole. The governor grimaced and thanked me for the information, but he did not indicate he would do anything.

The following year, Oklahoma State Senator Warren Hamilton, an abolitionist, authored a bill to remove the legal protection of women who personally commit murder by abortion. On 3 February 2023 a KOCO reporter asked Governor Kevin Stitt about Sen. Hamilton's bill to revoke the license to kill. When asked if he would sign such a bill, Governor Stitt said, "No, we're not going to punish women in the State of Oklahoma. That's preposterous."

Then Sen. Hamilton requested an official legal opinion from the new attorney general to clarify whether or not women who abort their own babies could be charged with a crime. On 21 November 2023 Oklahoma Attorney General Gentner Drummond issued his opinion:

> Oklahoma law does not allow the punishment of pregnant women attempting an abortion, self-induced or otherwise. The Legislature has repeatedly made this clear in statutory text, and just last year [via its abortion trigger law], repealed the one law that would have expressly allowed such a prosecution.

Perhaps if we put the pregnant woman in a different context, the license to kill would suddenly make sense:

- "You may not own a slave in this State, unless you are a pregnant woman."
- "You may not poison a secret lover in this State, unless you are a pregnant woman."
- "You may not torture puppies in this State, unless you are a pregnant woman."

No. It is still absurd. With the overturn of *Roe*, the PLM was given a chance to start over and get it right. So far, politicians, lobbyists, and the biggest influencers in the PLM have rebuilt on the old paradigm of regulating the industry and always treating women as victims. This approach plays right into the hands of the abortion industry which has been transitioning to privately and personally administered abortions that cut out the hired hit man.

With their gestational age acts, heartbeat bills, and licenses to kill, pro-lifers continue to deny the right to life and equal protection of the law, to deny justice to the preborn. Pro-lifers have addressed abortion with superficial policies as if there were no serious problem. They cry "Victory!" and "Peace!" when there is no peace (Jer. 6.14). "Woe to magistrates who enact unjust laws and keep issuing unfair orders!" (Isa. 10:1).

PLM Sticking with the Corrupt Commandment

After the *Dobbs* opinion, Abby Johnson, Lila Rose, and other well-known pro-lifers released a "Joint Statement for Building a Post-Roe Future" (Joint Statement). Regarding women who carry unwanted preborn babies, they state:

> [S]upport from non-profits will not be enough. State and federal governments must take action to eliminate or reduce the significant economic and social pressures that we know drive women to seek abortion in the first place.

While the Joint Statement sounds compassionate and winsome, let us examine the three major underlying assumptions that are highly debatable and with which other pro-lifers and abolitionists disagree. They are:

1. A lack of resources causes people to sin.
2. Resources are not available.
3. Government should provide resources.

The first debate is over the cause of sin. Why do some individuals steal, kill, and destroy? Theologians and philosophers have argued the question for millennia. Do people sin because of something internal or external?

If sin is of internal origin, then it must be generated from something like human nature, depravity, or free will. According to this view, circumstances are only influencers, not determiners.

If sin is of external origin, then it must be generated from something circumstantial like poverty, physical or mental abuse, deprivation, or trauma. According to this view, circumstances are more than influencers; they shape humans to the point of irresistible outcomes.

While this may be an oversimplification of the debate, it does present the basic position of the opposing views. It is important to clarify the assumptions and implications of each view because they affect our response to sin and abortion policy.

Those who believe circumstances "drive women to seek abortion" tend to be less willing to criminalize abortion. Instead, they seek to meet the needs of pregnant women in desperate situations, to ensure that they are not abused, that they have adequate food, shelter, healthcare, and self-actualization. They imply that women only get abortions because they are victims on some level. If we just cared more for women with unwanted preborn children, then they would not kill those children.

Those who believe in an internal locus of sin freely admit that circumstances are influencers. They, too, are helping women with the needs just mentioned. However, it is a false dichotomy to assume that a woman will either keep a child when resources are adequate or kill a child when resources are lacking. If that were true, why do we hear of victims of starvation sharing their last crust of bread? It is insulting to needy women to assume that they are immoral. Their moral quality is not equal to their subtotal of resources. They are not a byproduct of environmental factors, fated to be bullied by difficulties into committing heinous acts. On the contrary, they are made in the image of Yehovah, the one true God, and should be given the credit, value, and respect they deserve as fellow image-bearers. We should place faith in all women, as free moral agents, to choose to do right and work hard to make the best of a situation, even in less than ideal circumstances.

That is why we should not allow neediness to excuse or justify behaviors that ought to be criminal. The law exists to set expectations and uphold a standard worthy of human dignity. Because humans sometimes choose to sin, regardless of circumstances, the law must hold accountable those whose sins destroy innocent lives. We must criminalize the act of abortion itself.

The second debate is over the supposed lack of resources. Regardless of the cause of sin, believers agree that we do have an obligation to help fellow humans in desperate situations. We are commanded to love our neighbors, and we are given examples of self-sacrificing love that provides the basics for those in need, even when those people are religious, political, or cultural enemies.

In fact, in places like Oklahoma and Texas, Christians have been doing a good job of helping mothers in tough situations. They have been investing in and building up pregnancy resource centers for fifty years, and now these centers are proving more useful than ever before. Every major city has at least one, and often multiple, centers. Resources are abundant.

Many different kinds of pregnancy-related resources are available through various faith-based, not-for-profit organizations: counseling, parenting classes, healthcare, adoption, baby items, housing, career counseling, and halfway houses for those in codependent or abusive relationships. They serve pregnant women, mothers of young children, fathers, adoptive parents, and even those who have lost a child. One such charity has food pantries stocked with vegetables and gives out diapers, wipes, and other baby items. Another teaches weekly parenting classes in English and Spanish, covering topics like appropriate feeding, potty training, and positive discipline. At one residential facility, women have immediate access to impromptu counseling of all kinds, from crash courses in conflict resolution, to help soothing a colicky baby, to professional counseling sessions on setting life goals and transitioning to self-sufficiency.

Note that this infrastructure described above has been established by private funding. Only in recent years has the State gotten involved, which brings us to a third debatable assumption in the Joint Statement, that "State and federal governments must take action" to provide resources.

Again, Christians and others already provide these services. And now, whether or not we believe it is a proper function of government, States are getting involved in a big way. Here are two examples among many. In 2005 Texas enacted the Alternatives to Abortion program. For fiscal year 2024, Texas budgeted $70 million per year on pregnancy-related resources across the State. The State of Oklahoma passed a similar program called the Choosing Childbirth Act, and for fiscal year 2024, it budgeted $2.9 million per year for pregnancy resources—a healthy amount in such a small State with under four million residents. The funds go to the aforementioned types of privately operated charities. The good news is that with or without the State, God's people continue the good work of providing abundant resources to mothers in need. The people of God love their neighbors, born and preborn.

Many good people have cosigned the Joint Statement because they are focused on helping those in need, which is a worthy goal. While the Joint Statement sounds compassionate and winsome, its underlying assumptions and final implication make it divisive and problematic. The concern is with the promulgation of the false assumptions that (1) a lack of resources causes abortion, (2) resources are not available, and (3) that government should be the primary provider of support. One final concern is the unwritten but implied conclusion that individual women should not be held accountable for aborting their children—that a woman's volition is in the hands of politicians and that government is somehow to blame.

Justice and Mercy

In conclusion, we have seen how the false ideology of victimhood influences magistrates in pro-life States to grant legal licenses to women to commit murder by abortion, a policy that is morally indefensible. Sin is neither caused nor cured by external circumstances alone. Even when material support and assistance are available, some women still choose to murder their children. That is why fear of the law is essential to protect innocent preborn humans.

We must insist on personal accountability for the shedding of innocent blood. Before mercy can be extended, we must first administer justice. Justice is the road to mercy, although for those who lack humility and repentance, justice is an end in itself. It is not an either-or proposition; God expects and demands both mercy *and* justice (Amos 5:12; Zech. 7:9-10; Mic. 6:8; Luke 11:42).

Truth and Love

One of our ministry's core values is "truth and love." We have pledged that we will not sacrifice the truth to preserve people's feelings, and that we will not sacrifice people's feelings by the manner in which we share the truth. This value is paramount as we face a mixed audience of victims and criminals. Paul had this to say to the Ephesians (emphasis added):

> Then we will no longer be infants, tossed back and forth by the waves, and blown here and there by every wind of teaching and by the cunning and craftiness of people in their deceitful scheming. Instead, *speaking the truth in love*, we will grow to become in every respect the mature body of him who is the head, that is, the Savior. From him the whole body, joined and held together by every supporting ligament, grows and builds itself up in love, as each part does its work. (Eph. 4:14-16)

Notice that our action is "to speak." He did not say to hide the truth, sugarcoat the truth, ignore the truth, put off telling the truth, or keep silent lest we offend. We really do not have these other options. We must not be silent in our families, in our schools, or in the Church. We must speak to our friends, to the guilty, and to magistrates. If we do not love people enough to tell them the truth, then we do not truly love them. Later in the letter, Paul goes on to say, "Have nothing to do with the fruitless deeds of darkness, but rather expose them" (Eph. 5:11).

The first comment from the critic will be, "But it must be spoken in love!" Well, of course. If we use hateful words when sharing the truth, then we might as well hate those whom we seek to serve and save. The danger in our current culture is that we might use the fear of being perceived as unloving as an excuse to say nothing at all. It is all too common to be concerned about what other people think of us and use their possible reactions as an excuse not to teach and warn about the dangers of sin. That kind of silence is not Christian love.

We are called upon to speak, to say that which is true. We must verbally agree with Yehovah, his law, and his just character, and we must do so with a spirit of care and concern for our fellow image-bearers of God.

12

Pro-life v. Abolition

Imagine you set out from Washington, D.C., with the intent to drive west to Los Angeles. If you find yourself driving through Philadelphia, that would be good evidence that you were driving in the wrong direction. At this point you need to repent. So, you say to your wife and kids, "I'm really sorry about this. It was an honest mistake. I thought I was going in the right direction." Then you continue driving on up to New York City. Have you really repented?

Repentance is defined as a complete change of direction that involves a conscious turning away from attitudes, thoughts, and actions that violate God's law and an intentional turning toward thoughts and actions that please God. Modern believers often miss two essential points. First, repentance involves a demonstrable change in behavior. One's observable actions are different and opposite to what they were before. Second, repentance is inseparably linked to forgiveness. A quick review of scripture will demonstrate these connections.

First, repentance involves a demonstrable change in direction. Notice the prominent components of action in these verses:

- Recently you repented and *did what is right* in my sight. (Jer. 34:15)
- Repent! *Turn* from your idols and *renounce* all your detestable *practices*! (Ezek. 14:6)

- I preached that they should repent and *turn* to God and *demonstrate* their repentance by their *deeds*. (Acts 26:20)
- *Produce fruit* in keeping with repentance. (Matt. 3:8; Luke 3:8)

Second, repentance is inseparably linked to forgiveness:

- Repentance for the *forgiveness* of sins will be preached in his name. (Luke 24:47)
- Repent then…so that your *sins may be wiped out*. (Acts 3:19)
- God exalted him…that he might bring Israel to repentance and *forgive* their sins. (Acts 5:31)
- Repent of this wickedness and pray to the Lord in the hope that he may *forgive* you. (Acts 8:22)
- Godly sorrow brings repentance that leads to *salvation*. (2 Cor. 7:10)
- Repent and be baptized, every one of you, in the name of Jesus the Anointed One for the *forgiveness* of your sins. (Acts 2:38)

As I mentioned at the end of "Pro-choice Is Pro-life," 2015 was a year of rude awakenings, and I had begun to think in terms of political repentance. How should we reorder our political lives and work in light of magistrates and a PLM who had gone over to the dark side? This would require a change in attitude and actions, not only on my own part, but on the part of anti-abortion activists everywhere.

You may be tempted to think that the following history is irrelevant at best and tedious at worst. However, these stories of political repentance are crucial to understanding our way forward in a post-*Roe* United States. The principles learned through these experiences, and at great cost, should be applied even now in pro-life red States, and especially in pro-abortion blue States, so please bear with me for the next few chapters.

An Attitude Adjustment

In 2011 I was conducting training and outreach at the University of Oklahoma where I met some students who were wearing black wristbands marked with the word "Abolitionist." They were inspired by historical characters such as William Wilberforce and

William Lloyd Garrison, who made it their life's work to abolish the slave trade and slavery itself. In the eighteenth and nineteenth centuries, too many Christians had made their peace with slavery and were a big reason why the institution continued. Garrison called Christians to repent of their hypocrisy and complacency over slavery. He argued that slavery could not be defeated by regulating it. Rather, it must be completely abolished. I was immediately taken with the apt comparison of modern anti-abortion activism to the historical abolitionist movement. It was then that I began to think of myself as an abolitionist. I tried using the term a few times, but it seemed to confuse pro-lifers and took too long to explain. So I set it aside for the sake of efficiency.

Then, in 2014-2015, I met the political players on the dark side of the PLM and experienced their complacency, corruption, and compromise, which we outlined in the Ten Corrupt Commandments over the previous three chapters. They either had no hope of abolishing abortion or were not truly opposed to abortion. With each new disappointment and defeat at the hands of the PLM, that abolitionist comparison kept coming back to my mind.

At the time I was writing a weekly policy update and sending it out to several thousand conservatives. In the process of trying to communicate the truth about the PLM to average citizens, most of whom identified as pro-life, it became necessary to constantly use quotation marks around pro-life. Every time I mentioned a particular politician, policy, or lobbyist on the dark side, I had to use another *"pro-life."* My emails and newsletters were littered with them. It was cumbersome, awkward, and to some, confusing.

It was no good calling myself pro-life or talking about pro-life politicians any longer because the term had become meaningless in the context of politics. Pro-life policies were just another gate that opened into State-sponsored and regulated abortion. I decided that for the sake of clarity it was time to dust off the word abolition. By incorporating its use I was able to write about policies of the PLM versus abolitionist policies, and the common reader soon understood the obvious difference. My attitude of repentance was thus demonstrated in that I now called myself an abolitionist, and so did the members and supporters of our political action committee and ministry supporters.

Pro-life v. Abolition

About this time I came across a piece of artwork that was hugely helpful in clarifying the differences between the PLM and the abolitionist movement. Imagine a pen and ink drawing of a mature oak tree. The leaves are dense, and the branches are many. The trunk is massive, and the roots go down and down. As you look more closely, you notice a pattern in the branches. They spell out the word MURDER, and as you peer in, you see writing on the branches. Each branch has a label: *chemical, Plan B, RU-486, surgical, dilation & curettage, dismemberment, suction aspiration, partial birth, IUDs.*

This is the mighty abortion tree, the tree of child sacrifice. The roots are similarly labeled: *personal peace & affluence, lust, pornography, sexual immorality.* Like the branches above, the roots below spell out a word: SIN.

This tree was drawn by T. Russell Hunter, a historian, abolitionist, and an amazing graphic artist. It has been featured in abolitionist leaflets, pamphlets, and even campaign literature. Abolitionists have made the argument that politicians are only willing to nip at the ends of the branches, to prune the tree a little. When you prune a healthy tree, it grows back even stronger and denser, and this is what the PLM has done with the abortion industry. Each new little regulation further strengthens and entrenches the overall industry.

The PLM had fallen victim to the Hegelian dialectic. Pro-lifers were told that they could never truly abolish abortion because of *Roe* and *Casey*; they could only regulate it. Each new regulation was a further compromise, and the industry grew and grew. A mighty, thriving abortion industry grew up under the regulation of the PLM, with healthy branches in every major city. Its support network, its roots, still run deep in our sinful culture of death. Planned Parenthood's 2020 annual report showed a net worth of $2,341,200,000.

In the *Roe* era, pro-life politicians told us we must support incremental laws which regulated abortion in order to save as many babies as we could. They further argued that if we would just keep passing regulations, then eventually that strategy would completely end abortion. History has proved that concept to be a lie.

Passing regulations is only another form of crony capitalism. The biggest providers in any industry thrive in a government-controlled environment as they become proficient at regulatory compliance. Smaller temples go out of business, while Planned Parenthood builds newer, bigger, shinier altars. Regulating abortion enables the richest providers to become richer and more successful at providing their sinister service. Under new and existing regulatory schemes in 2016, two new abortion death camps opened in my State. I will share more about what we witnessed and experienced there in the chapter "Be Present."

Furthermore, pro-life regulatory proposals have always been the enemy of truly good legislative proposals to abolish abortion. Weak, feel-good bills function as stumbling blocks to legislators who can no longer see the right thing to do. They will always choose the easier of two options. The compromise bills get in the way of what is needed and necessary. Therefore, the blame for allowing the genocide of abortion to continue lies directly with those pro-life politicians who refuse to support total abolition and instead support only incremental bills of regulation.

In contrast to using pruning shears to lightly snip the branches of the abortion tree through regulations, abolitionists believe that we should take an ax and lay it to the root. We should chop down the tree by immediately criminalizing all abortion, leaving no stump to grow back. The two competing philosophies might be compared like this:

- The PLM advocates for incremental policy change, while abolitionists want to abolish abortion immediately. Notice how incremental changes never really change anything.
- The PLM tries only to regulate abortion (pruning). Abolitionists try to criminalize abortion (chop it down).
- The PLM treats abortion as medical care, which is a choice. Abolitionists treat abortion as murder, which is a crime and a sin.

- The PLM is content to compromise and carve out exceptions which become the rule. Abolitionists refuse to compromise. There should be no exceptions for murder.
- The stated goal of the PLM is to reduce abortions. The goal of abolitionists is to abolish abortion by establishing justice.
- The strategy of the PLM mocks God, our constitutions, and the rule of law. Abolitionists wish to obey God, uphold our constitutions, and uphold the true rule of law.

Pragmatism v. Principle

What we observe here are two radically different approaches. Pro-lifers are guided purely by pragmatism, while abolitionists are focused on principle. Every time the PLM promotes a new pro-life scheme, it uses a utilitarian argument to justify it. Utility means something is useful, and because utility can be measured any way the measurer decides, one can justify anything using utilitarian arguments. Two common questions of utility often posed by pro-lifers are: "Will the judiciary allow this bill to stand?" and, "Hypothetically, how many lives might be saved?"

Absent from their argument are words like proper and improper, right and wrong, just and fair. You see, measuring the worth of a proposal based on its likelihood to survive the courts and its hypothetical chance to save a percentage of lives is grabbing the wrong measuring stick. We should not ask if a pro-life bill might have some possible utility; we should ask if it is proper and principled. But to answer that question requires grabbing the right measuring stick; it requires a moral measure. Using a moral measure reveals that the State should not sanction any murder by abortion, and any proposal that does sanction some murders is inherently immoral and unjust. It is time to put away the utilitarian ruler and to grab the moral measure which comes from the Rightful Ruler (Amos 7:7-8).

From 1973-2022 the PLM was unsuccessful at outlawing abortion. Legislative efforts prior to *Dobbs* focused on incremental regulation of abortion and on education. Some of these types of regulatory bills might, under the best of circumstances, have saved a few lives (although it would be hard to prove), but the practice of abortion itself remained legal and condoned by the State. Where there is a market, someone will comply with State regulations to provide the service.

In contrast, efforts to protect all human beings equally under the law were nonexistent prior to 2016. When the movement to abolish abortion finally hit the political scene in 2016, those principled proposals were dealt death blows by the PLM's cozy arrangement between the Republican establishment and pro-life lobbyists.

Those few well-meaning legislators and lobbyists in the PLM who did hate abortion and want to end it simply refused to realize that their pragmatic strategy had proven a failure. They were like a team of talented athletes who kept losing by executing the wrong game plan; they had fallen into a comfortable pattern of losing.

This dichotomy plays itself out in a nearly perfect parallel in the story of Hebrew slavery in Egypt, which teaches that Yehovah demands justice, not compromise with evil. True leadership is not knowing when to compromise, but knowing when NOT to compromise.

Pharaoh v. Moses

In the story of Moses before Pharaoh, imagine Pharaoh as the typical pro-life politician in the PLM and Moses as the uncompromising abolitionist. The text we add in italics typifies what these characters might say in the context of abortion, rather than slavery.

Moses delivers his message to Pharaoh: "Thus says Yehovah, 'Let my people go!'"

But Pharaoh responds, "Why are you distracting the people from their work?" *We have to figure out how to give teachers a pay increase and balance the budget. We can't be distracted by social issues right now.*

So, Yehovah punishes Egypt with a few plagues, which puts Pharaoh in a mood to compromise. He offers to let the people take some time off work, but they must stay in Egypt. *We will take a day off to commemorate Rose Day at the capitol. We will celebrate our pro-life victories, then we'll get back to work.*

Moses refuses the deal, so Pharaoh counters with another offer. The people may travel, but not very far. *You can go on a pro-life holiday to the March for Life.*

Again, Moses refuses the deal, and after several more plagues, Pharaoh shifts from deals to paying lip service only. With each plague he promises to let the people go if only the plagues will stop, but each time he breaks his word and will not let them go. *I promise! I'll author any bill you like!*

Finally, after more plagues, Pharaoh is again ready to compromise. He understands that the key to keeping the Hebrews in slavery is an incremental approach. So, Pharaoh offers to let the men go, but the women and children must remain. *He offers the Abolitionist a ban on aborting those preborn humans who have been diagnosed with Down Syndrome or who have detectable heartbeats.*

But Moses knows better than to compromise with evil, so he rejects the scheme: "We shall go with our young and our old; with our sons and our daughters, with our flocks and our herds we shall go."

Outraged by the principled consistency of Moses, Pharaoh drives him out, and Egypt is plagued again. Then, exasperated by three days of total darkness, Pharaoh offers a new deal. The people may go, but their animals must remain.

Not willing to go against God's command, Moses replies, "Not a single hoof will be left behind." *Not a single preborn child of any age or level of development will be sacrificed.*

So, Pharaoh drives Moses out once again and threatens to kill him. The story resolves itself when God's judgments of economic destruction, disease, and death become so great that Pharaoh can no longer tolerate the presence of Hebrew slaves. Finally, he does what he should have been done from the start—he abolishes Hebrew slavery.

When pro-life politicians act like Pharaoh, when they simply pay lip service to ending abortion or offer incremental schemes, they are keeping murder by abortion entrenched and protected. Even post-*Roe*, pro-life politicians keep refusing to abolish abortion and drive abolitionists from the capitol. How will this story resolve itself?

When the State goes bankrupt and can no longer fund NBA basketball? When there is a drag queen in charge of every elementary school? When the dollar is so devalued that no one can buy bread? When the body count of preborn babies reaches another million?

In 2016 we were asking if the judgments upon us had become great enough, if we had sacrificed enough of our preborn neighbors to satisfy the obdurate hearts of the pro-life politicians in our state capitol. The answer was no. We were nowhere near the end of the Moses-Pharaoh saga. We were only at the beginning.

Veritas Vignettes

I teach a four-hour college course on the topic "Pro-life v. Abolition." The following comments are from graduating seniors who took the course.

> I'm still processing what you told us about the lies we have been told for forty-seven years... Learning that elected officials and pro-life organizations...are really just interested in regulating abortion, not ending it, has blown me away. I can never call myself pro-life again. I am an Abolitionist. And I intend to join the battle. - *Bonnie*

> I understand now that we can't wait for the culture to change, but that we must be the ones that change the culture... We must change the law. We must be a voice, we must keep pushing and demand our leaders to do the right thing, the just thing. We must demand complete abolition and hold our government officials accountable. Abortion is UNCONSTITUTIONAL! ALL persons have the inherent right to life. -*Tammy*

> This class had so much information. I was completely ignorant of the fact that abortion is actually unconstitutional. I wasn't aware of all the legal and strategic lies that I had believed. I didn't realize that our states could begin the process of abolishing abortion...

How deceived we have been by...only regulating abortion instead of doing away with it. -*Nancy*

Thank you for arranging this outstanding training... I have been overwhelmed and discouraged for a very long time... Now I actually have hope and intend to get involved...but so few appreciate that we must approach this as Abolitionists, not status-quo Pro-Lifers." -*Mrs. DeMartini*

I understand now that regulating abortion does nothing except allow the slaughter to continue, legally. If we truly want to see an end to abortion, then we can no longer go after it bit-by-bit with any kind of regulations. We need to be abolitionists and take the whole issue head on, starting at the local and state level. Change begins where you are and where you can be most effective. -*Vanessa*

I am reminded that...Paul stated, "Brethren, I do not want you to be ignorant..." I have learned a tremendous amount from this class... I was ignorant of...the endless cycle of financially supporting pro-life organizations...voting for pro-life candidates, and seeing little if any results. This cycle has been perpetuated for forty-seven years... I repent, change my way of thinking, and I change where I sow into the kingdom of God to stop the unlawful practice of killing innocent preborn children. I now consider myself an abolitionist." -*David*

13

Political Repentance: The Legislature

As the story of Moses before Pharaoh illustrates, we could no longer compromise and support the Orwellian bills of the PLM. Our attitude was changing, and we were willing to say, "Thus says Yehovah, *abolish abortion!*" Now we needed practical action to demonstrate true repentance. We had to work toward abolishing abortion. So, in the summer of 2015 we began building a network of support that would help us apply pressure at the state capitol, and at the start of 2016 we began to see "fruit in keeping with repentance."

An Action Adjustment

Paul Blair, a local pastor at an independent Baptist church and former Chicago Bear with a charismatic personality, had taken over the leadership of Reclaiming America for Christ, the ministry started by Dr. D. James Kennedy. Dan Fisher, a local evangelical pastor serving in the State House of Representatives, was sick and tired of the state legislature enacting symbolism over substance. That year we had a handful of legislators who were advocates for state sovereignty, a reality enshrined in the Ninth and Tenth Amendments to the U.S. Constitution. Mat Staver, chairman of Liberty Counsel, was also consulting with our cadre. Together we hatched a plan to go after the licenses of abortion doctors.

The licensing bill (Senate Bill 1552) said that performance of an abortion by a physician constituted unprofessional conduct and would prohibit the physician from obtaining or renewing a license to practice medicine. The bill attempted to work within the PLM's accepted constraints of constitutional interpretation, relying on the strength of the Ninth and Tenth Amendments and upon previous opinions of the Court that the States can direct their own regulatory agencies without federal interference. We felt there was at least a chance that the federal courts and SCOTUS would leave it alone, and Liberty Council was standing by to defend the law if we got it passed.

We called our project "Protect Life OK." We hired staff, started an online petition (which was signed by more than 20,000 people, including almost 1,000 pastors), and began building momentum going into the 2016 legislative session. Everything we did centered on activating grassroots pro-lifers to help educate every pro-life legislator about the power of the State to revoke doctors' licenses. Our coalition was able to gain an audience with then Governor Mary Fallin who promised to sign the bill if it made it to her desk.

All of these activities were different from anything tried before. They were outside the box and encouraging. They were the first faltering steps of pro-lifers trying to repent politically. However, I had a lingering concern. Although SB 1552 in and of itself was a proper application of licensing law, it did not attack *Roe* and *Casey* head-on. It was an attempt to dance around the Court and work within the rules that the Court had told us to play by. Furthermore, by not criminalizing abortion itself, it communicated implicitly that the State still did not view abortion as a truly serious offense. Consequently, I decided to recruit a legislator to author a bill that would directly criminalize abortion.

The obvious choice was State Senator Joseph Silk, a serious Christian, homeschool father, and outspoken champion of state sovereignty. OC-PAC had just named him "Freshman Legislator of the Year," so we already had a bit of a relationship. At the time Sen. Silk was sponsoring a heartbeat bill, so I asked him in his office why he would discriminate against very young humans whose heartbeats were hard to find. That was all it took. The proverbial lightbulb clicked on, and I was nearly blinded by the light reflecting off Silk's beautiful bald head.

Senator Silk amended his heartbeat bill (SB 1118) so that it would establish justice for those being deprived of life without due process of law. The bill's new language proposed to classify abortion as first-degree murder. Silk was asking the State of Oklahoma to unabashedly defy the Court. We knew SB 1118 would bring Oklahoma law into conflict with the *Roe* and *Casey* opinions, but more importantly, we knew that it would comply with the higher laws of the U.S. Constitution and the law of God. It was time for the lesser magistrates to do their duty. Senate Bill 1118 became the first truly righteous bill to abolish abortion in any State of the union.

The Ground War

Early in February we hosted Matt Trewhella, author of *The Doctrine of the Lesser Magistrates*, to assist us with outreach and education across the State. We began with an address to sixty-five patriot pastors, encouraging them to lead their congregations into political action. We then spoke at a Christian leadership conference where Trewhella addressed the problem of pietism and the proper role of Christians in civil government, using abortion to illustrate his points.

The week culminated at the annual banquet of OC-PAC where Trewhella delivered a charge to our State's most conservative legislators. His message to them was a reminder of the historical standard that when any authority commands that which God forbids, or forbids that which God commands, we are to obey God rather than mankind. He reminded them that as God's ministers of justice, they were to apply this standard not only personally, but also in their roles as civil magistrates.

The message of the entire week was that the magistrates of the State would be on solid legal ground to defy the Court, and that they were all duty bound to uphold the laws of God as they are set forth in the Oklahoma and U.S. Constitutions. All of this activity was strategically planned to prepare the hearts and minds of pro-life legislators to advance the abortion-as-murder bill (SB 1118) and the licensing bill (SB 1552) through the long legislative process.

Dead Rose Day

Sponsored by the Southern Baptist Church and the Catholic Church, Rose Day at the Oklahoma State Capitol has been a tradition since 1992. Pro-life advocates from around the State flood the halls of the capitol building at the beginning of each new legislative session to present their legislators with fresh, vibrant roses and ask them to remember the rights of the preborn. The atmosphere has always reminded me of a Christian pep rally, a celebration of past PLM victories and victories to come. The event culminates with a rally in the House chamber. Notable keynote speakers of the past have included Abby Johnson, Alveda King, and Lila Rose.

Fresh off the realization that legislators were going to continue doing what they had always done and giving us what we had always gotten—dead babies—I decided to stage a counter outreach event. We called it "Dead Rose Day."

Former state legislator Porter Davis, a personal friend, owned a flower business. A few weeks before Rose Day, he donated hundreds of perfect, long-stemmed, red roses. Each one was exquisite. I spread them out on the floor of my garage and cracked the door to let in a week of winter. They withered and became spotted with rot. Another friend of mine, Ken, who owns a graphic design business had hundreds of cards printed to distribute to the legislators and to the pro-lifers who would visit the capitol on Rose Day. Here is the verbiage from that card:

> **May these dead roses remind you of the nearly 6,000 innocent babies who were lost to abortion last year in Oklahoma.**

> For twenty-five years citizens of Oklahoma have been delivering vibrant roses to these offices, asking their legislators to remember the rights of unborn children. After twenty-five years, this pro-life strategy is not working. Therefore, this year our message is different. How can we celebrate life when all around us is DEATH?

Criminal and civil law are in the hands of the state, not the federal government. There is bloodguilt on the Oklahoma Capitol. But the good news is you have the power to cleanse it this session by stopping abortion in Oklahoma.

Legally, you can. Morally, you must! Will you?

These symbols caused no small stir, and the confusion on the faces of legislators and rally attendees was apparent. Their traditional pro-life ideas were coming into conflict with the ideas of abolition for the first time. What began with just a few humble servants attempting to stand in the gap ballooned into a volunteer team of over fifty by the day of the event. Pastor Matt Trewhella went from office to office with me, explaining the doctrine of the lesser magistrates to our state legislators.

The Campaign Continues

Later in the session, we combined forces with several volunteers from Missionaries to the Preborn and about one hundred seventy-five members of Abolitionist Societies to stage protests, petition, distribute pamphlets, and call on our state magistrates at the capitol to repent of forty-three years of idolatry to the Court and state-sanctioned child sacrifice. Within a week, abolitionists collected nearly 10,000 signatures demanding the total and immediate abolition of abortion in Oklahoma. This was in addition to the signatures already gathered by Protect Life OK. The synergy of different activist groups coming together was incredible. We were joined later by even more volunteers from county-level grassroots organizations as we attempted to influence every legislator at the capitol to abolish abortion.

Legislative Shenanigans

With so much public support and pressure calling for the abolition of abortion, how would our proposed legislation fare? What would be the fallout of our ground war? Need we remind you about the kings of the capitol and the practical impotence of individual legislators?

Senator Silk's SB 1118 (abortion-as-murder bill) made it out of committee by one vote in mid-February, but as the details became more public, the negative political pressure began to mount. Senate leadership refused to schedule a hearing of SB 1118 on the Senate floor. Although Sen. Silk gathered signatures of other senators requesting the bill to be heard, all was for naught. The majority of the Republican caucus wanted to continue claiming they were pro-life without actually calling abortion murder or standing up to the Court. The voices of average Oklahomans and the voices of their elected senators were no match for the single voice of the Senate pro tem. The first state bill to abolish abortion had been aborted.

Senate Bill 1552 (the licensing bill) moved quietly out of Senate and House committees, but heavy artillery was brought out on Thursday, 21 April 2016, when the Oklahoma House of Representatives met in session for over thirteen hours, finishing at 11:05 p.m. With each new measure that reached the floor, the length of debate became longer. It was incredible how long the progressives could stretch the debate over painfully simple bills. One of the longest debates was over whether or not a person needed a license from the State to shoot feral hogs. It was clear that these long debates had little to do with discovering the right thing to do on any issue. Instead, it appeared to be a tactic to prolong the day and run out the clock on SB 1552.

The licensing bill likely would not have received a hearing at all if it had not been for the hard work of Representative David Brumbaugh who rallied a slight majority of House Republicans to demand a hearing. He was aided by thousands of calls, emails, and visits from grassroots activists.

Finally, long after the average citizen had had his dinner and settled down to late-night TV, the debate on SB 1552 began. We watched from the gallery above. Besides grandstanding, the opponents also piled on silly motions, amendments, and amendments to amendments. It was like watching a bunch of fifth graders call each other names without using vulgar words, although it came close a few times. Democrat Rep. Jason Dunnington sounded like an obnoxious bell, tolling over and over that the bill was "unconstitutional." A lie oft-repeated is believed, so repeat it he did. Of course, licensing is an internal function of the State; therefore, the Legislature's effort to properly deny licensing to abortion doctors was perfectly constitutional.

Democrat Rep. Emily Virgin tried to add the silliest amendment of the day on to SB 1552, calling for doctors to lose their medical licenses for performing vasectomies. All five silly amendments to the bill were defeated. After much tedious and illogical grandstanding by Virgin and Dunnington, the measure passed 59-9, while thirty-three representatives snuck out of the chamber so as not to go on record. The bill still needed final approval by the Senate before it could go to Governor Fallin.

Oddly enough, on the day after Senate leadership cowered from calling abortion murder and aborted SB 1118, they scheduled a hearing for SB 1552. Why would this incredibly liberal body do such a thing? Frankly, we had not expected them to hear it at all. First, we knew that Senate leadership was worried about the marketing aspect. The pro tem and floor leader had no desire to come under tremendous national scrutiny. Most of the senators did not want to be called religious hicks by the rest of the States.

Second, most of the pro-life senators were not really pro-life. As we mentioned before, most of them really believed, but were politically unwilling to say, that abortion is a necessary evil or even a woman's right.

Thirdly, the Senate simply had no stomach for a direct conflict with the federal government, specifically the Court. Nearly every senator, except for the author of the bill, believed that abortion was constitutional because the Court had said so. Therefore, they were unwilling to say by word or with a vote that the U.S. Supreme Court was wrong.

Of course, this was precisely what needed to happen. The supreme law of the land is not the Court's interpretation of the U.S. Constitution; it is the written Constitution aligned with God's natural law. So, I still struggled to understand why the Senate had scheduled a hearing of SB 1552. Perhaps it was because it appeared more nuanced and reasonable. There was no mention of murder; therefore, it was less intimidating and dodged the immediate marketing problem. A doctor who performed an abortion would receive only a comparative slap on the wrist. He might lose his license and have to move to another State to perform abortions, but he would not have to face any real justice. Or, perhaps it was because at first glance it appeared constitutional, even in leadership's skewed view of constitutionality. Licensing is clearly within the jurisdiction of the State. Nevertheless, the hearing was scheduled, and our supporters were elated. We rallied the troops and prepared ourselves for another brutal day of stall tactics and parliamentarian tricks in a war of attrition.

On Thursday morning, 19 May 2016, members of Oklahomans United for Life prayed with the author of SB 1552. Shortly after prayer, I settled into the Senate gallery with my friends and young children to observe what we anticipated to be a heated debate over SB 1552. To my surprise, the bill was announced during the day and on time. There were no questions; there was no debate. We had an uneasy feeling that something was wrong. The vote was called, and the abortion advocates registered their nays. Likewise, the pro-lifers registered their yeas. The yea tally slowed as it approached twenty-five, the number needed for passage. Finally, the total reached the magic number, and then it raced up to thirty-three as the closet abortion supporters jumped on the wagon. The final tally was 33-12. It was over in minutes. It was too easy. The fix was in.

Our fears were confirmed when pro-life Republican Governor Mary Fallin, who had promised to sign the bill, immediately vetoed the bill. Again, this was the governor who campaigned her whole career, spanning decades, as a pro-life Republican. But when a regulatory licensing bill that might have closed down death camps and set up a much-needed challenge to *Roe* hit her desk, the sheepskin was off. We saw the wolf underneath. How many more magistrates in the PLM are just like Bloody Mary Fallin, but stay under cover? Now we understood why SB 1552 had passed easily out of the Senate. The governor must have agreed to take the fall. She was already term-limited and at the end of her state political career. She had nothing to lose, but every senator of the State could now brag to their constituents that they had voted pro-life, while keeping their precious football game going.

After the governor's veto, the only hope of enacting the licensing bill and setting up a possible battle between the State and the federal government lay in a veto override. To override the veto would require a two-thirds majority vote in both legislative bodies, beginning with the Senate. There were two major obstacles to the override. The first obstacle was the number of votes needed: thirty-two. We knew that that number would be impossible to get, since some of the previous yea votes were not authentic, but politically expedient.

Second, Senate leadership had no interest in overriding the veto. The Senate pro tem and the floor leader work to protect the majority of the caucus who wanted to keep using preborn babies as political footballs. The Oklahoma Constitution requires a vetoed bill to be reconsidered, so in an unlawful move to protect their interests, Senate leadership instead adjourned for the year with unfinished business still on the agenda. They simply ran away.

Government Games

From the summer of 2015 to the spring of 2016, grassroots organizations that were part of trying to make Oklahoma ground zero in the abortion battle had spent hundreds of thousands of dollars. We had spent tens of thousands of work hours to raise the awareness and support of pro-life citizens around the State and beyond. We had convinced tens of thousands of believers that their calls, emails, and personal visits would make a difference, that their elected legislators would respond and establish justice. We had held rallies. We had waged a day-by-day and week-by-week ground war in and around the capitol to educate and cajole our elected officials to abolish abortion. Our prophetic voices had been loud, brave, and impossible to ignore.

In response, the legislature had kept abortion legal, sent us packing, and got themselves re-elected. We had spent a huge amount of time, energy, and money to mobilize the power and authority of the State to save our preborn neighbors from slaughter. How could they have done this to us? The answer is government games. Two in particular are very effective. The first is the Government Toddler Toy, and the second is Rock, Paper, Scissors.

Remember the interactive toys for young children that teach them fine motor skills? The toddler toy presents a series of buttons, switches, dials, and doors for children to manipulate. When they push a button, a door might pop open to reveal a funny animal, object, or character. When they pull a lever, a bell might ping! Every action is rewarded. They feel productive and proud of themselves for having made something happen. *Look what I did! I made it do something. I am winning the game.*

Our government is set up like a giant toddler toy with lots of fun-looking options. For example, you can write a letter, make a phone call, or send an impassioned email. You might even personally visit your representative. These actions on your part bring about reactions. You pull a government lever, and a light goes on. You get a nice return email. You receive a signed letter on gold-embossed letterhead. You get invited to an insider's meet-and-greet. During a personal visit your representative shakes your hand warmly and tells you all about the church he attends faithfully back home. Maybe he even offers to let you pray over him.

We get excited when government responds to our efforts, so we continue feverishly to operate the "controls" of the State. We return to the control bank of government and continue vigorously pushing, pulling, and poking, believing the government apparatus is responding to our commands. In reality nothing has happened beyond receiving a few temporarily gratifying lights, pings, and pops. Did you actually make a difference? Does the policy ever actually change? Or have you just been playing with the big government toddler toy designed to keep you busy and distracted as new death camps continue to open?

There's a second game that magistrates like for more advanced players: Rock, Paper, Scissors. For example, suppose you want to support Sen. Silk's bill to classify abortion as first-degree homicide, so you ask the pro tem of the Senate to the hear the bill.

"Well," he responds, "we have certain rules, procedures, and protocols here, so you will need to go take this up with the floor leader, who is responsible to get bills put on the agenda. Thanks for bringing this to my attention. Good luck, and God be with you."

So, you go meet with the floor leader who says, "I'll tell you what, you need to take this up with the committee chairman. He needs to submit an official request for a hearing. We just have too many bills to automatically schedule them all."

Then the chairman tells you, "Yeah, that bill qualifies for a hearing, so I don't understand why they aren't scheduling it. We can't get anything heard without the support of leadership, so you'd better ask the pro tem to make it a priority."

You call the rock, you email the paper, and you visit the scissors, but no matter what you try your efforts are covered, cut, or smashed, and you never win. They will play all day, and they actually like the game. It protects them from controversial policies, it gives them plausible deniability, and it hides their inaction and lack of character behind other members, leadership, and the rules.

Most activists will not make it all the way through this process, and those that do will not bother a second time once they figure out that they are getting played in an unwinnable game. Furthermore, this happens at every level, so it is a lot more complex than even Rock, Paper, Scissors, Spock, Lizard. Not only do they point from office to office, they also point to other branches of government, and then state magistrates point to the federal government, and the feds point back down to the States. Your issue always seems to be somebody else's problem, responsibility, and job, but you find that everybody's job is nobody's job.

The Aftermath

In the end, our magistrates, like Pharaoh, refused to repent. At this point I knew we would never pass a bill of abolition in a legislative body. It was like herding cats. They would never all go the same way at the same time, and they had no true desire to do so. There were too many magistrates to blame, so the blame would stick to no one. They could point fingers, hide behind one another, and play games. No one would know. No one would care. Nobody even knew who they were. They knew they could get away with it, and there was nothing we could do about it. Right before the next election, individual legislators would still be able to brag about their pro-life voting record, and the majority of uninformed voters would never know better.

The State Legislature had survived its first brush with abolition. They had ensured abortion would stay legal, kept the game going, and preserved their cozy arrangement. They had maintained the status quo and proven themselves faithful to their god SCOTUS.

On or about 12 September 2016, Trust Women South Wind Women's Center opened a brand new altar of child sacrifice in Oklahoma City. They had been waiting to make sure that SB 1118 and SB 1552 were defeated. According to a press release from South Wind, they estimated 1,500 to 2,000 "patients" would be seen in the first year.

Over the next many years, all the way up to the *Dobbs* opinion, we witnessed the "Running of the Bills." Every year, Senator Silk or Senator Hamilton, our great abolitionist senators, would file a bill to defy SCOTUS and completely abolish abortion, but every year the bill would be ignored or quickly and quietly voted down in committee by establishment pro-life Republicans.

What We Learned

We had made a huge strategic error. Pharaoh was one man who wielded a tremendous amount of power and authority. We had approached our state legislature as if it had a single mind, like Pharaoh. We focused on a collective and hardly gave a thought to the governor. We just assumed the governor was with us. There is that word again: *assume*. But we never stopped to consider why the governor was not out with us leading the charge, making speeches, or applying political pressure to legislative leaders. The governor was completely missing in action, and we missed the significance.

This experience with the legislature and the governor opened my eyes yet again. I could see clearly the political theater being produced for the pro-life masses. The pro-life legislative process is like a football season with its regular games, playoffs, and Super Bowl. No one pays much attention early on, but as pro-life bills make their way through the process, pro-life news services begin to report on pending legislation. As the bills advance closer to the Super Bowl of the governor's desk, the excitement ramps up and fans become frenzied. When a bill is signed, pro-lifers cry, "Touchdown! We win!" This cozy arrangement of the PLM does not care if we call ourselves pro-life or abolitionist. It cares not if the bills are compromised, pragmatic, or principled. The pro-life political machine is prepared to weed out, amend, ignore, or defeat any bill that might upset the status quo.

I learned that without executive leadership, the legislative process is nothing more than posturing and political theater. Fortunately, I was not the only one who allowed himself to accept this reality. In the aftermath of the 2016 legislative session, Pastor and State Representative Dan Fisher said, "We have got to get a governor!"

14

BEARING THE SWORD: THE EXECUTIVE

But if you do wrong, be afraid, for magistrates do not bear the sword for no reason. They are God's servants, agents of wrath to bring punishment on the wrongdoer. (Rom. 13:4)

A white sedan with the state seal of Oklahoma on its side crept up to the gate of the abortion death camp. My heart beat with excitement. Was the State here to shut it down? I flagged down the driver and was rewarded with a lowered window.

"Who are you with?" I blurted out. "Are you here to see if they are in violation of anything so we can shut them down and save lives?"

"No!" came the reply. "I'm with SoonerCare, and I help them stay in compliance and stay open. We don't want them closed."

You can imagine my anger and disappointment. SoonerCare is administered by the Oklahoma Health Care Authority, an agency of the executive branch, which answers to the governor of the State. According to the state website, SoonerCare provides "family planning" and healthcare to pregnant women. Here was a glaring example of how the abortion industry had become entrenched and protected by legislative regulations and executive agencies of the State.

This same death camp was one of the ones that opened its gates in 2016 immediately following our crushing defeat at the hands of Governor Mary Fallin, a pro-life Republican. We had learned a very important, expensive, and painful lesson, and our paradigm was shifting again.

Shell Game

Remember the shell game at the carnival? In the traditional version, a pea is hidden under one of three walnut half-shells. After the shells have been shuffled around, the mark attempts to choose the shell containing the pea. Pretend that the shells represent the executive, legislative, and judicial branches of government. The pea is the abolition of abortion. What happens?

We keep getting played by the pro-life carnival hucksters. The game is a con that keeps us looking under the wrong shell. While the typical pro-life advocate naively looks to courts and legislatures to do something, executives get a free pass for doing nothing and even allowing agencies under their direction to actively support murder by abortion. As we have demonstrated in previous chapters, abolition is not under the court shell. Likewise, because of the Ten Corrupt Commandments, abolition is not under the legislative shell. Legislators keep writing the wrong laws, there is no accountability, and no matter what law they write, they have no power to enforce it. What about the executive shell? That is our point: **No one ever picks the executive shell!**

In our representative republic, the three branches of government are charged with upholding the rule of law. Each branch has its designated task, which is different from the task of the other branches. The only sense in which the branches are equal is in their duty to uphold the rule of law, which we have seen means operating within the confines of God's natural hierarchy of law.

The legislative branch codifies statutes, which must be in accord with the law of God and our state and federal constitutions. The tools of legislators are pen and paper because they write laws.

The judicial branch resolves disputes between parties, but again, in accord with natural law and our constitutions. Judges wear black robes and carry gavels to symbolize their judgment.

Finally, the executive branch administers, executes, and enforces the laws of the land. Executive officers make use of jails, handcuffs, and weapons. Executive magistrates often sport badges and other symbols of authority. Like the crown in ancient times, these symbols communicate to civilians that these officers have the literal, physical power to uphold the law.

The thesis of this chapter is that the abolition-of-abortion-pea is under the executive shell. While legislative bodies ought to bring state statutes into compliance with God's law and our constitutions, keep in mind that the legislature of a State cannot abolish abortion without enforcement from the executive branch. Conversely, executives could nearly force the abolition of abortion through leadership and action. In this chapter we will explore why that is true and how we should reorder our political strategies and activism based on that truth. We will outline a righteous, biblical plan to abolish abortion, even in a post-*Roe* era in blue States.

Biblical Examples of the Executive

Recall that during a dark period of Israel's history, the people were sacrificing their children to false gods. Yehovah, the one true God, calls this practice "evil" and an "abomination." It "provoked him to anger" and was a primary cause of his judgment and wrath upon their nation. But then Josiah, a young boy, became king (2 Kgs. 22-23; 2 Chr. 34). He followed the example of King David and sought the ways of Yehovah. He gained knowledge and wisdom as he grew into a man. After studying the law and his duty to uphold it, he began his campaign to immediately abolish idolatry throughout the land. At that time idolatry was practiced through detestable religious rites, including homosexual intercourse and child sacrifice (2 Kgs. 23:7, 10).

Once Josiah made up his mind to change public policy, he followed a simple two-step process to abolish child sacrifice. First, he exercised leadership by announcing and explaining the new policy to the people. Second, he enforced the new policy. Simple. Say it, and do it.

After Josiah decided to enforce the law of God, he informed the elders, priests, and prophets. They brought together all the people, and Josiah "read in their hearing all the words of the Book of the

Covenant" (2 Kgs. 23:2). The "book of the covenant" was the legal agreement between Yehovah and the Hebrew people, which defined them as a nation. It was, in other words, what we would call a constitution.

Governor Nehemiah would later follow this example when he rebuilt Judah after Babylonian captivity. Nehemiah brought all the people together before a giant stage, a bully pulpit, where he, along with a team of prophets and priests, taught them the law of God and instructed them to celebrate the law and dedicate themselves to it. The chapter ends with all the people rejoicing "because they now understood the words that had been made known to them" (Neh. 8:12).

The next thing Josiah did was enforce the law. He tore down all the high places of idol worship and child sacrifice, and he punished those practicing idolatry. "Furthermore, Josiah got rid of...the household gods, the idols and all the other detestable things seen in Judah and Jerusalem. This he did to fulfill the requirements of the law" (2 Kgs. 23:24). Note that his policies were not applied only to public high altars—think abortion death camps. He even forbade household idolatry—think private, home-based child sacrifice by abortion pills. In the same way, the king of Nineveh led his State to repent in response to Jonah's prophetic message (Jonah 3). The king issued an executive order directing all citizens to "Call urgently on God. Let them give up their evil ways and their violence." That story ends with, "When God saw what they did and how they turned from their evil ways, he relented and did not bring on them the destruction he had threatened."

Josiah did not obey the priests of Molech the way our governors obey the justices of SCOTUS. He did not simply regulate child sacrifice the way our legislatures and governors do. For example, he could have banned the sacrifice of children over a certain age or banned the sacrifice of children upon altars uninspected and unlicensed by the kingdom. Strategically, he did not choose to launch an education campaign alone and trust that it would change the behavior of the people. Josiah did not wait for a mandate from the majority. He did not send out pollsters to determine whether the priests of Yehovah outnumbered the priests of Ashtoreth, Chemosh, and Molech (2 Kgs. 23:13). He did not wait for the people to speak through public referendums, rallies, marches, or even personal righteousness and repentance. He did not wait for positive public opinion polls. In short, **Josiah did not wait for his culture to change; rather, Josiah changed his culture.** At the end of his story, we read, "Neither before nor after Josiah was there a king like him who turned to Yehovah with all his heart and with all his soul and with all his strength, in accordance with all the Law of Moses" (2 Kgs. 23:25).

Josiah was successful for the following four reasons: (1) he had appropriate authority, (2) he took personal responsibility, (3) he exercised leadership, and (4) he acted decisively.

First, Josiah was king. He was in a recognized position of authority (Rom. 13:4) which was respected morally, culturally, and legally. Remember those adult Christian students I polled? I asked them to give me three names. Not one student could name a personal city, state, or federal legislator. About half could name an NBA basketball player on their hometown team. But in the final category, every single student, one hundred percent, could name the governor of the State. In modern times, the governor may not wear a crown or wield a sword, but he is still recognized as the top authority. Under his command are state police and other agents of the executive branch who do carry sidearms, handcuffs, and other instruments of law enforcement. The people recognize the authority of law enforcement, and they know the chief executive by name.

Second, Josiah took personal responsibility. An inherent benefit of having a single individual in charge is that he cannot hide in the anonymity of the collective. We have already seen that within a collective like a legislature, a legislator can hide and do nothing without consequence. President Harry Truman famously said, "The President, whoever he is, has to decide. He can't pass the buck to anybody." In fact, Truman kept a sign on his desk in his White House office that read, "The BUCK STOPS here!" The buck has always stopped with the chief executive. Incidentally, that sign was made in 1945 at the federal prison in El Reno, Oklahoma, near where I presently live.

Third, Josiah's authority and responsibility gave him the opportunity to lead. When he spoke, the people listened. When he directed, his subordinates obeyed. When he took action, the people took note. Remember, Josiah directed the other collective governing bodies—the elders, priests, and prophets—to help him gather and instruct the people. Governors in our States have similar leadership opportunities. When they call a press conference, the media shows up and reports what they say. The sound of the shepherd's voice causes the sheep to follow. Unfortunately, our governors have been completely silent about the ongoing genocide of abortion in their States. Rather than calling for the abolition of abortion and teaching other magistrates and the people how it could be accomplished, the extent of their "leadership" has been limited to labeling themselves "pro-life" in speeches and campaign literature and either signing or vetoing pro-life legislation.

Finally, Josiah took decisive action. Lip service was not good enough. Claiming to be pro-life and voting for a pro-life elder and priest were not going to get the job done. He fired the unconstitutional bureaucrats (perverse priests hired by corrupt kings) and directed executive officers under his command to literally tear down, burn, pulverize, and scatter the ashes of idols and their detestable altars of child sacrifice (2 Kgs. 23:5-6). The abolition of idolatry and child sacrifice was not carried out by the elders, priests, or prophets. In other words, it was not carried out by the other collective branches of government, but by the individual chief executive. Josiah recognized what our governors and other executive officers ought to recognize: that if they do nothing, they have innocent blood on their hands.

The Silver Bullet

Now that we have a biblical model from which to work, we can begin to look at how chief executives in our system of government could abolish modern-day child sacrifice. In our system of government, only the executive can take action. When you are unarmed and under physical attack, do you want a statute, a gavel, or a gun? The legislature cannot protect you with a piece of paper. A court cannot save you with its opinion. You need an executive officer with authority and the will to use his gun and handcuffs in your defense. The motto of many police departments is "To protect and serve." Only executives can stop the bloodshed, and the chief executive in each of our States is the governor.

According to folklore, a bullet cast from silver can kill a werewolf. Consequently, the silver bullet has become a metaphor for a simple, almost magical, solution to a difficult problem. Everyone is looking for a gadget or a gimmick—something no one else has thought of—a pro-life trick or legal loophole through which to save babies. But we cannot trick evil. There is no magic. There is only the righteous executive magistrate willing to enforce the law.

Imagine an individual who is righteous, courageous, and wise, who knows we should abolish abortion, knows how it could be done, and would be willing to do it, but who has no authority. Now imagine an individual who has the moral and legal authority, duty, and power to abolish abortion—a governor—but who has either made his peace with the practice or lacks the know-how and the courage to abolish it. The silver bullet is formed when these two individuals become one person. Either the righteous wise man gains the authority to abolish abortion, or the person who possesses the authority to abolish abortion becomes convinced that he can and should abolish it.

There is no gadget or gimmick. It takes righteousness, justice, and courage from the top. Godly governors matter. As we have seen, righteous leaders can restore righteous culture. When it comes to the abolition of abortion, a righteous governor would teach and explain that abortion violates natural law, our constitutions, and our homicide codes. Then he would direct those executive officers under his authority to enforce the law and fire those who are unwilling. Laws do not enforce themselves, and any new laws restricting or criminalizing abortion are toothless without a chief executive to enforce them. There is no sneaking in the side door. Our governors will have to kick down the front door in an all-out assault. And if the governor is the silver bullet, then we have to get a governor.

A Campaign for Governor

We will not get a governor unless the people of God expect and demand one. We are the furnace that forges the silver bullet. Once again, we must walk in that prophetic role of taking the word of God to the magistrate. We fan the flame of conviction. God pours melted hearts into molds of courage. But prophesy, beg, and cajole as we may, Governor Fallin refused to repent. She was slated to leave office in January 2019. That meant that we needed a candidate and a campaign to run from 2017-2018.

Dan Fisher, a pastor at an independent Baptist church, served in the Oklahoma Legislature from 2012 to 2016. He witnessed firsthand the dark side of the political PLM at the state capitol. His many attempts to expose corruption and gamesmanship caused one Republican leader to call him "The Moral Conscience of the House." That experience converted him to an abolitionist and was a major influence in his decision to pour himself out in an effort to become the silver bullet that would make Oklahoma the union's first abortion-free State. We launched his gubernatorial campaign in the summer of 2017 and ran hard until the race ended at the primary election on 26 June 2018.

Dan's campaign platform was radically different from almost every other candidate for high office. Typically, candidates try to stay away from controversial issues and avoid discussing details of policy proposals. Doing exactly the opposite, Dan's number one issue and claim to fame was that he would abolish abortion or go down trying. Echoing freedom fighters of old, he liked to say on the campaign trail, "I'd rather die on my feet than live on my knees!"

I was privileged to be a part of Dan's team, helping to write campaign material, and introducing Dan at rallies and events around the State. We truly believed that if enough believers took a few minutes to comprehend Dan's plan, he would have a long shot to win the election. See if you agree. Here is an excerpt from Dan's widely distributed ASAP campaign pamphlet:

WHOM WILL YOU SERVE?
GOD OR GOVERNMENT

According to God, proper government protects:
Life, Liberty, Property

Our government is prone to steal, kill, and destroy.
But Dan Fisher is running for governor to stop the killing by
Abolishing Abortion,

halt the destruction of liberty by asserting
State Sovereignty,

and fight the theft by
Auditing Everything.

Dan Fisher's mission is to restore
Proper Government.

My first act as governor will be to restore the God-given right to life. To fulfill this sacred duty, I pledge to:

1. Call an emergency special session of the Oklahoma Legislature to criminalize abortion as murder and to remove abortion from the jurisdiction of Oklahoma courts.
2. Instruct law enforcement officials to immediately close every abortion facility in Oklahoma in accordance with their sworn oaths of office.
3. Ignore all court orders...and advise Oklahoma officials to ignore any federal court summons.
4. Call upon President Trump to stand with Oklahoma, as we peacefully resolve this matter of jurisdiction.
5. Call for judicial reforms which would remove the power of judicial review from the courts.
6. Call upon Christians in Oklahoma to practice pure and undefiled religion (James 1:27), assisting mothers and fathers who would have formerly sought abortion.

The campaign strategy was to get word to every conservative Christian in the State that if we elected former Representative and Pastor Dan Fisher, then Governor Fisher would abolish abortion and make Oklahoma the first abortion-free State. Dan explained it like this:

> In Oklahoma, we have 3.9 million citizens, and 1.3 million (1/3) claim to be evangelical Christians. If the Church rises up in this primary election, I could be the Republican nominee for governor. This is the opportunity we've all been praying about for years—

not electing me—but returning our State to godly, moral principles.

Funding was the most immediate obstacle we faced. Dan was not a millionaire like the other leading candidates. In fact, his campaign spent well under one million dollars, while his leading competitors spent multiple millions. How would we reach our audience of evangelical Christians without the resources to buy advertising and mail hundreds of thousands of campaign flyers to our likely voters?

One option was to use social media, and we had a fantastically talented team in that department. Dan always had a great following on social media. For example, one of his early campaign videos surpassed 250,000 views in just twenty-four hours and kept zooming up from there. Subsequent ads also performed well and were widely shared. The trouble was, these interactions were not necessarily with registered Republicans in Oklahoma who were likely to vote. They were various people who liked or hated Dan's message and just enjoyed the political spectacle. We still needed to reach our target audience.

Our other strategy was to mobilize grassroots activists as volunteers to fan out across the State and find our voters face-to-face. Since the vast majority of evangelical Christians meet together in local churches on Sunday mornings, we knew right where we could find them. We decided to send delegations of Christians to each church that had a building in a town. We had a giant map, the size of an eight-foot wall, and each town was assigned to volunteers living in the area. Early on we had traveling teams until we could find local volunteers. I remember a few Sunday mornings when the coffee splashed from my mug as we bumped down potholed gravel roads in southeastern Oklahoma to visit rural churches among the chicken farms.

Megan was our volunteer coordinator. She was high-energy, incredibly organized, detail-oriented, and driven. Her permanent smile, which took up half her glowing face, made you want to do anything she asked. When she asked you to distribute three hundred pamphlets to Christians in a town, you did not let her down, and you went the extra mile, literally, to surpass your goal. And that is exactly what I, my children, and hundreds of volunteers like us did in the many months leading up to the election. Once the operation was ramped up, we were distributing over ten thousand pamphlets each Sunday morning. We felt like the soldiers of whom Herodotus said, "These are stopped neither by snow nor rain nor heat nor darkness from accomplishing their appointed course with all speed." All told, we put pamphlets like the one above into the hands of more than one hundred fifty thousand believers across the State.

The reception from our fellow believers as we met them and talked with them in church parking lots was warm and enthusiastic. The overwhelming majority of believers who received and read the pamphlet were thrilled and excited. At one church in Mustang, the parking lot security guard enjoyed reading the pamphlet and gave me a $100 donation to buy more. At another church in Blanchard, the security guard accompanied me around the parking lot while I distributed hundreds of flyers to members and left them on their cars. Several times I was asked to come in and make an announcement or distribute pamphlets inside the building. I remember one pastor of a small church in western Oklahoma took the opportunity of my visit to tell the congregation from the pulpit about Dan's campaign and asked them to join him in voting for Dan.

Our hopes and enthusiasm ran high throughout the spring. We could have reached thousands more likely voters if it had not been for one glaring problem: the leaders of the earthly church kingdoms.

The warmth of the reception was inversely proportional to the size of the congregation. The smaller churches with fewer members tended to welcome us warmly. But the bigger the church, the colder the attitudes and actions of the leaders and gatekeepers. We were berated, bullied, badgered, criticized, run off, and threatened with arrest. Our pamphlets were often stolen and destroyed by church deacons. The designated leaders seemed more interested in protecting the borders of their property than in welcoming and conversing with fellow citizens of the kingdom of heaven.

One pastor confronted a young female volunteer and told her that her distribution of the pamphlet was making people feel guilty about abortion and was worse than women choosing to abort. At one of the largest evangelical protestant churches in the State, one at which

Dan had previously spoken while he was a sitting state representative, we were rudely run off and our pamphlets were confiscated. The pastor later wrote Dan as follows:

> Our church policy does not permit any kind of promotion or endorsement of any political candidate. That is why our security did not allow your volunteers to put pamphlets on the cars in our parking lot. And we will not be able to have you come and speak at this time. I have a large number of Democrats, and church is not where we want any division.

Here again was the dark side of the PLM at work.

The Aftermath

On 26 June 2018 Oklahoma believers were given an opportunity to vote for the abolition of abortion. Dan Fisher, who stood firmly on a powerful platform based on God's law and our constitutions, received 35,818 votes. Three other candidates, a mayor of Oklahoma City, the lieutenant governor, and a rich business owner, offered mere slogans, yet they combined to receive 351,270 votes.

This election result revealed that the average self-identifying Christian was now only a nominal or cultural Christian. When presented with the opportunity to abolish murder by abortion and return to a godly rule of law, the vast majority of Christians said, *Yeah, but NBA basketball. Yeah, but top-ten state.*

This result also highlighted the disturbing condition of the churches in Oklahoma. Modern evangelical megachurches have become nothing more than corporate religious-service providers. They are like gas stations providing a commodity, where church shoppers choose the one that has the cleanest bathrooms and the least bad coffee. Rather than rallying congregants to abolish abortion, too many Christian leaders kept quiet, or worse, actively opposed the overtly Christian campaign, preferring instead not to risk losing numbers, nickels, and noses.

In a twisted merger of church and State, the dark forces of the Religious-Industrial Complex and political PLM had converged to defeat us. I was reminded of the false priests who had been appointed and propped up by the idolatrous kings of Judah in a kind of Hebrew 501c3 church scheme (2 Kgs. 23:5). As my friend Miles put it, "Pro-life politicians are getting away with murder, and megachurch pastors are covering it up."

Although he did not secure his party's nomination, Dan Fisher did accomplish an important prophetic task. He called the entire Christian community in the State to examine themselves and their congregations in light of God's expectations of his people. After the election, one Fisher supporter had this to say:

> I was in what I thought was a very conservative church, especially on pro-life issues. When my family heard about you and your message, we got excited. When I experienced our congregation's reaction to you and your message, it was very eye-opening to me. Please pray for me as I seek another church to attend. Their silence was extremely loud. I don't understand how a Christian and a Patriot could not have been excited about your candidacy for governor. I was unequally yoked. Thanks, for now I know!

We are seeing a broadening gap between two religious groups. The first group is the one that the world recognizes as the church, the denominations with all of their property, programs, and paid staff (see the chapter "Earthly Kingdoms"). The second group is the true Church, or what the scripture calls the "remnant." These are the individuals whom the Lord has added to his Church, who are salty and bright and who are recognized by their fruits.

Now, more than ever, the true Church must shine like a beacon to push back the threatening darkness. There are still tens of thousands of Christians in every State who have not bowed the knee to idols (1 Kgs. 19:18). They understand that godly governors matter and that we have a collective duty to establish justice for our preborn neighbors. The remnant is out there, and they need our help.

15

GRANT JUSTICE!

Although Dan Fisher did not win the election, his plan to abolish abortion was still right morally and legally. And while the element of defying SCOTUS is no longer needed now that *Roe* has been overturned, the same basic plan could work today for closing legal loopholes in red States and abolishing abortion in blue States. The governor leading and mobilizing other magistrates is still the key to success.

Prophesying to the Governor

It was time to follow the biblical model of prophesying to the king. Like Moses before Pharaoh, our job now became to say to our new governor, "Thus says Yehovah, 'Let my babies go!'" After the campaign I fleshed out Dan's plan, complete with additional tools that the governor could use, political analysis, and answers to objections, and turned it into a brief for the new governor. All we needed was an audience, but that would not be so easy.

Governor J. Kevin Stitt had just spent a year ignoring abortion and his abolitionist opponent. Although he had no answer, no plan, and no track record on abortion, simply claiming to be pro-life was good enough during his campaign. He did not need the issue of abortion to get elected, so why would he need to do more now? If we were going to convert our new governor to an abolitionist, if we were going to ask him to repent with us and adopt and implement a plan to abolish abortion, then we would have to find creative ways to get his attention.

In the following years of the new governor's tenure, we took advantage of every conceivable opportunity to educate him about his duty. We held conferences and rallies at the capitol. We called and emailed. We visited his office individually and en masse. We mailed letters and packets of information, and we spoke with him at his public appearances. He did not listen. He did not respond. He would not relent or repent.

The Alamo

The sixth of March is an inauspicious day in history. It marks the day in 1836 that the Alamo fell to General Santa Anna of Mexico. Twenty years later, also on March sixth, SCOTUS said that slaves should be treated as property, not people. While the day might be remembered as one of defeat, it was also a catalyst for victory. The rallying cry, "Remember the Alamo!" eventually propelled Texas to independence, and the *Dred Scott* opinion eventually led to the abolition of slavery. Both of these events were fresh in my mind in the spring of 2019 as our outreach team asked visitors to the Alamo to support "The Abolition of Abortion in Texas Act."

The small sign in my hands read, "ABORTION MUST BE ABOLISHED! WILL YOU HELP?" The Alamo security guard, crowned with a ten-gallon cowboy hat and sporting a five-point star badge, announced that the State of Texas had taken over the property on which I stood. He demanded that I remove myself down the street and over a railing to practice free speech…or go to jail.

I was stupefied. The Alamo is hallowed ground, the place where Texans fought to the death for liberty. It was here that Colonel William Travis had drawn his famous line in the dirt and challenged, "Every man who is determined to stay here and die with me come across this line." They courageously faced bullets and cannonballs. But now their armed descendants exhibited fear in the face of true words printed on the plastic sign I held!

In a bizarre reenactment of Col. Travis's call to arms, these modern-day guards of the Alamo did not invite me to cross a line in the dirt to stay and fight. Rather, they demanded that I cross an invisible property line to leave, to take my battle elsewhere. They would not permit me to speak freely on behalf of the victims of abortion with other Alamo visitors who were permitted to speak freely in support of Kansas Jayhawk basketball, GAP clothing, and the Rolling Stones.

These tyrannical officers illustrated the most immediate political reason that the abortion genocide continues unabated: the absence of executive leadership and action at every level, from local law enforcement all the way up to the governors of our States. We were fresh off a gubernatorial campaign that proved leaders these days are not chosen for their knowledge and wisdom (Deut. 1:13; Acts 6:3). Instead, they achieve office by spending more marketing dollars than their opponents in a popularity contest. All around us, executive magistrates either lack knowledge or reject knowledge, and the people blindly follow them right into the wrath and judgment of God (Hos. 4).

Bad executives keep drawing the wrong lines. They listen to SCOTUS or the will of the people; then they bark at us, "You're out of line! Get back in line!" We need executives who will draw the right lines, the righteous lines, and lead like Col. Travis, whose challenge only echoed what Joshua said: "Choose for yourselves this day whom you will serve...but as for me and my household, we will serve Yehovah" (Josh. 24.15) and what Moses said: "I have set before you life and death, blessings and curses. Now choose life" (Deut. 30:19) and what our Lord said: "Whoever wants to be my disciple must deny himself, take up his cross, and follow me" (Matt. 16:24; Mark 8:34).

It is time that we draw our own line in the dirt and make it clear to our magistrates that they must choose sides. They can side with the idols of the PLM and continue regulating and protecting murder by abortion, the same way that Israel's kings of old did with the false priests and prophets for profits, or they can side with abolitionists to restore the right to life and equal protection of the law, as King Josiah did. Modern abolitionists are drawing that line and are asking magistrates to cross over and lead with wisdom, direction, and courage.

While I stood up to the officer at the Alamo and explained his proper duty as a lesser magistrate, an observer in the crowd was excitedly taking notes. After the altercation concluded, Bob introduced himself and excitedly said he would like to join his forces with ours to bring about the abolition of abortion. We immediately made plans, and within a few weeks I was winging my way across the States to meet his personal friend Dr. Alan Keyes.

Alan Keyes and the Oath of Office

In 2000 I found myself wedged between my wife and my mom in a Del City auditorium. Thousands packed both the floor and the balcony. No seats were available, and listeners stood shoulder to shoulder, lining the red brick walls. It was a good thing the fire marshal did not swing by. We were so tightly packed that everyone's elbows overlapped his neighbor's, and each round of thunderous applause only deepened the bruising of the ribs from the previous round.

We were there to hear Dr. Alan Keyes, who was campaigning for President of the United States. This clear-thinking, articulate Harvard graduate had hit the political big time when President Ronald Reagan appointed him an Ambassador to the United Nations and later an Assistant Secretary of State. Keyes went on to host syndicated radio and television talk shows throughout the 90s and early 2000s in which he brilliantly espoused the principles of liberty and godly government.

Back in that auditorium in the spring of 2000, when Keyes called for the abolition of abortion, we once again raised the roof with our rib-bruising applause, whistles, hoots, and hollers. How was I to know that nineteen years later I would be sitting in his living room discussing a state-by-state strategy to abolish abortion. Keyes agreed that it was time for governors in every State to uphold their oaths before God to enforce the Constitution and abolish abortion.

Before commencing service, every executive magistrate is sworn in by taking an oath of office, which is typically required to be recorded with the Secretary of State. Here is a typical example based on the State of Texas:

I do solemnly swear (or affirm), that I will faithfully execute the duties of the office of [governor, attorney general, peace officer, etc.] and will to the best of my ability preserve, protect, and defend the Constitution and laws of the United States and of this State, so help me God.

These oaths are solemn promises, witnessed by God, to the citizens of the State. Executive magistrates swear before God to uphold our constitutions and the rule of law—not the will of the people, not the twisted interpretations of justices, and not the immoral and unconstitutional statutes of legislatures. If they are to be faithful to their oaths, they would not comply with any other magistrate or branch of government that legislates, opines, orders, or acts in violation of any state or federal constitution. Rather, they would defy them.

Under Nazi rule, the German church was told it must exclude Jewish Christians from the church. Many church leaders at the time decided to go along with the decree, reasoning that they should put up with it for the sake of the weaker believers. One pastor argued to Dietrich Bonhoeffer that they should join the German church in order to work against the Nazis from within. Bonhoeffer answered, "If you board the wrong train it is no use running along the corridor in the opposite direction."

Similarly, when it comes to stopping the evil of abortion, our executives and legislators have boarded the wrong train. Prior to the *Dobbs* opinion, every official abortion-related act taken by our state magistrates was an act of obeisance to the immoral and unconstitutional opinions of justices. Even now, in the post-*Roe* era, magistrates in blue States continue to regulate abortion as medical care, as SCOTUS encouraged them to do in *Dobbs*. In red States, magistrates have criminalized only a few doctors, while continuing to allow thousands of women to get away with murder. Every time our magistrates' inaction or actions fail to uphold God-given rights enshrined in the constitutions, they commit perjury.

But the loyalty oath is not just some archaic tradition, a mere formality to be filed and forgotten. It is time for us to take promises to God and each other seriously. Magistrates who violate their oaths are guilty, and they invite judgment upon themselves and their jurisdictions. In a show we did together, Dr. Keyes said the time was right to rethink our approach and go on the offensive. He explained, "All law enforcement officers…are sworn to uphold the Constitution, according to its terms. They are therefore duty bound to hold the [SCOTUS] decision in contempt and move without delay to end the wholesale atrocity it entails."

We planned for Keyes's staff to begin scheduling appointments for him with Republican governors of conservative States who might be open to the plan to abolish abortion through executive leadership and action. I would come back to Oklahoma to plan a series of events that might get the governor's attention. Then, Keyes would begin meeting with governors and would make his way to Oklahoma to join me for a meeting with Governor Stitt.

Once an ambassador of the United States to the United Nations, Alan Keyes would now hit the road as Ambassador of Abolition to the United States. He met personally with the governors of Kentucky and Tennessee, and then made his way to Oklahoma. We spent a week in grassroots activity, spreading the word that the governor could abolish abortion. Keyes was live on the radio during drive time. He recorded several hours of his national show, *Let's Talk America*, while he was here. He graciously recorded local podcasts and social media shows and attended a Tea Party meeting. He was the keynote speaker at a conference that was held in the exact same auditorium where he had campaigned for President back in 2000. That night he made the case that the PLM mistakenly focuses on the courts when it should focus on governors to provide equal protection. He reasoned that any governor who fails to immediately shut down "murder mills" is guilty of high crimes and should be booted from office. He explained that abortion is a "tool of totalitarians" and is ultimately about murdering any person inconvenient to the government. Finally, he argued that executive enforcement of constitutional law is the key to abolishing abortion.

A Plan for the Governor to Abolish Abortion

In the end, Oklahoma Governor Kevin Stitt refused to meet with Ambassador Keyes. We were relegated to making our presentation to a staffer. We covered all of the necessary presuppositions and then recommended a detailed, state-specific plan for the governor to abolish abortion.

The following outline is a generalized version of the briefing which can be used as a framework to build your own state-specific plan to abolish abortion in any State, red or blue. These are necessary presuppositions:

1) Every human being, regardless of his stage of development, is intrinsically valuable simply because he is a human being made in the image of God.

2) A unique human being comes into existence once the conception process is complete.

3) Innocent human beings have a God-given right to life, so killing them is murder.

4) Abortion is the killing of an innocent human being. Therefore, it is murder.

5) The primary purpose of government is to protect God-given rights.

6) Per the U.S. Constitution's guarantees of the right to life and equal protection of the laws recorded in the Fifth and Fourteenth Amendments, abortion is unconstitutional and unlawful.

7) Per the State Constitution's guarantee of the right to life, abortion is unconstitutional and unlawful.

8) Per homicide statutes of the State, abortion is criminal homicide.

9) Those statutes describing legal abortion conflict with higher laws. Not only are they immoral, but they are unconstitutional; therefore, they are null and void.

10) SCOTUS opinions such as *Roe v. Wade*, and now *Dobbs* in part, are in violation of the clear wording and meaning of the U.S. Constitution.

11) Executives have a duty to uphold the U.S. Constitution regardless of how other magistrates ignore or lie about the Constitution.

12) Higher even than constitutions, all men everywhere have a transcendent and moral duty to disregard and, where possible, resist an order from a fellow magistrate or superior to allow mass murder.

13) SCOTUS opinions which sanction the practice of abortion, even in limited and regulated ways, function like orders from SCOTUS to the various and united States to permit mass murder. Therefore, magistrates of the various and united States have a transcendent moral obligation to ignore and, where possible, resist genocidal applications of SCOTUS opinions.

14) All law enforcement personnel have a duty to protect innocent humans within their jurisdictions.

15) The governor of a State is the highest-ranking executive officer in that state.

16) The governor has a moral and legal duty to take executive action to protect and save innocent lives in his State.

Power of the Governor

Should the governor of your State accept the preceding presuppositions, he might be open to hearing more about what he could do specifically to abolish abortion. You might be able to move forward with explaining certain powers and tools that the governor could use. But first, a governor must decide whether or not he is willing to abolish abortion. The entire proposition comes down to a battle of wills. No matter what else happens with statutory legislation or the courts, ultimately the governor must be willing to follow through with his plan to abolish abortion, come what may. If he is unwilling, all other efforts are doomed to fail, and abortion will continue in the State until a future chief executive says, "No more!" Here are some of the powers that governors could exercise:

1) *Lead and Communicate*. This is the most important role a governor could fill as an abolitionist leader. The people are currently in the habit of abortion, a habit that can only be broken with decisive intervention. Constant, clear rhetoric from the governor could break the habit and lead the people in a new

direction. The governor must communicate, communicate, communicate.

Think in terms of Roosevelt's "fireside chats" where he took to the airwaves and spoke directly to the people. The governor could hold regular press conferences in which part of the messaging would be daily death counts and progress reports. He could open people's minds to a full comprehension of the genocide around them and create in them a deep feeling for the need to abolish abortion. If abolishing abortion were the governor's priority, it would soon become the people's priority. Guiding the people's thoughts and feelings with proactive assurances, messaging, and teaching would help them follow where the governor led.

2) *Recruit Support.* Leadership through communication goes beyond the people. An abolitionist governor could hold preliminary private meetings with other governors who might be friendly to abolishing abortion at the same time so that they might benefit from the strength of solidarity. Similarly, before launching a plan publicly, the governor could hold preliminary meetings with city, county, and state police to identify and solidify officers who were committed to the plan and would stand their ground. The governor could identify and communicate with sympathetic district attorneys and district judges. The governor could meet with pastors of his State to recruit spiritual and moral support.

3) *Launch.* Once the governor had formulated a specific plan, it would be time to start an all-out communication and marketing campaign. He could hold a press conference to announce the immediate abolition of abortion per the above premises and his executive oath of office. To prepare the people and set their expectations, he would:

- Explain the entire plan from start to finish.
- Announce the effective date of enforcement.
- Detail the specific actions of the executive officers under his authority.
- Outline the preferred method of filing a complaint by anyone who had evidence of murder by abortion, whether it was committed by a licensed physician or by parents privately.

- Assure the citizens that he was committed to moving forward.
- Repeat the plan and talking points until the people understood and supported it. It is just like getting elected.

4) *Lead the Legislature.* On top of executive power, governors also wield tremendous influence with the legislative bodies of their respective States. In fact, most governors possess the exact same power that any individual legislator possesses, but many times over. Consider, a legislator has only one power guaranteed to him. As we have seen, no single legislator has a guarantee that any of his proposals will be heard, unless he is the leader of the legislative body. But he is guaranteed the right to vote yea or nay on any piece of legislation being heard. A governor has this exact same power when legislation lands on his desk. He can vote yea by signing it, or nay by vetoing it, but in doing so, he has not voted just one time like the individual legislators who sent him the bill. His yea or nay is worth up to two-thirds of the total votes of the legislature, depending on the rules outlined in the constitution of the State. In Oklahoma, for example, the governor's veto has the same weight as ninety-nine votes in the legislature because the legislature would need at least one hundred votes to enact anything against the governor's wishes. He is an ever-present supermajority.

In some States, the governor has the power to put the legislature into special session and tell them what to consider. Oklahoma is one of those States. The governor could put legislators into a special session and demand a statutory change that would completely criminalize all elective abortion in the State so that district attorneys could more clearly and cleanly prosecute those who commit murder by abortion. The statutory change would not be absolutely necessary in order for executives to immediately stop the bloodshed, but it would be important to establish equal protection of the law all the way down to the statutory level. That consistency would assist prosecutors and lessen the likelihood of courts throwing out cases based on contradictory statutes. If necessary, a governor could even discipline an obstinate legislature. If they did not follow through with establishing equal protection under the statutes of the State, the governor could veto other high-profile and important measures until they did.

5) *Stop the Bloodshed*. On the first practicable date, the governor could order state police to descend upon all abortion death camps to set up barricades and prevent entry to any party other than the registered owner. He would instruct all law enforcement personnel to stand their ground, even in the face of unconstitutional court orders which might be forthcoming. He would refuse to back down or remove police, no matter what, until properties were sold, converted, or relet. If your State does not have state police under the command of the governor, then the governor could declare an emergency and mobilize the militia or National Guard of his State.

6) *Executive Orders*. The entire executive branch with its dozens of powerful agencies and thousands of personnel answers to the governor. You will have to research just how many options your governor has, but consider these examples of what the governor of Oklahoma could have done prior to the *Dobbs* opinion. These kinds of actions could be taken by a governor who is determined to lead his blue State in repentance. The Oklahoma governor could have issued executive orders to the Oklahoma Board of Medical Licensure and Supervision instructing them to revoke medical licenses of abortion doctors. He could have issued executive orders to the Oklahoma Department of Public Safety instructing them to blockade and shut down abortion death camps to prevent any further murder by abortion. These executive agencies answer to the governor. If they did not follow his orders, he could replace their agency heads with ones who would.

The governor could have declared the murder of preborn humans by abortion in Oklahoma to be an emergency, thus opening an even broader scope of executive orders. The Oklahoma governor is granted the authority to issue emergency executive orders by the Oklahoma Emergency Management Act of 2003. Some of his powers are outlined in 63 OK Stat § 63-683.8 and 63 OK Stat § 63-683.9. These orders have the same authority as statutory law. According to 63 OK Stat § 63-683.23 they are enforceable by the Department of Public Safety and the Oklahoma State Bureau of Investigation, and violators

> shall be deemed guilty of a misdemeanor, and shall, upon conviction thereof, be punished by imprisonment in the county jail for not more than six (6) months, or by

a fine of not more than Three Thousand Dollars ($3,000.00), or both. Each day of violation shall constitute a separate offense.

In a sad irony, Gov. Stitt did declare an emergency in Oklahoma and order abortion death camps closed (Fourth Amended Executive Order 2020-07 filed 24 March 2020), but it was for the wrong reason—a scare over coronavirus disease (COVID), and he refused to enforce his own order. His order said, "Medical providers in Oklahoma shall postpone all elective surgeries…," an order including abortions. Understandably, all major news agencies in the State and pro-life news sites across the country rushed to congratulate Gov. Stitt on his pro-life executive order. But it was only more PLM symbolism over substance.

Throughout the same week that Gov. Stitt's order was making pro-life headlines, I stood each day at the gates of death and watched hundreds of innocent preborn victims be led by their parents to their deaths. While witnessing the ongoing slaughter in person, I called the Oklahoma City Police Department. I read them the order and asked them to come enforce it, but Sgt. Clark said that they would not enforce the governor's order. Then I called the Department of Public Safety. They said they considered the order a "recommendation" and would not enforce it. Then I called the governor's office, and a spokeswoman for the governor confirmed that the order was legally binding, and to violate it would be a misdemeanor, but she also admitted that they were not expecting or seeking enforcement from any police or other executive officers. She said, "At this time we are hoping that people follow the honor system and abide by the executive order."

Given an incredible opportunity to learn about and implement the power of executive orders, magistrates on the dark side of the PLM squandered the gift. Thanks to Gov. Stitt, abortion death camps in Oklahoma stayed open throughout the COVID scare to assist thousands of parents from Oklahoma, Texas, and surrounding States in the murder of their preborn children.

Legally, governors have the power to declare an emergency, prohibit the sale of abortifacient drugs, and shut down abortion death camps, and they have the power to enforce these orders. Find out what specific powers your governor has under normal circumstances and during a declared emergency. The ongoing genocide of the preborn is certainly a moral, constitutional, legal, and humanitarian emergency of epic proportions.

7) *Prosecute.* The governor could coordinate with the attorney general or district attorney to press charges and prosecute cases that arise from new evidence received after the effective date of abolition. The prosecutor could assign cases to a sympathetic judge who would not dismiss the case.

8) *Reform Adoption and Foster Services.* The governor could direct the legislature to remove legal barriers, restrictions, regulations, and costs that hinder adoption and foster care. Currently, it is expensive and frustrating for middle-class Christians to practice properly the admonitions of James 1:27.

It is high time for governors and chief executives who have been bearing the sword in vain to take the needed and necessary role in leading the modern-day abolition movement. Only chief executives have the civil authority and duty to immediately stop the bloodshed. Their actions could drive the issue to a resolution and end the genocide of abortion.

What About the Courts?

The main objection to moving forward with an executive-driven plan like the one outlined here is the negative response of the courts. What if the State Supreme Court attempts to stay the governor's actions? There are several steps that the governor and executives could take to prepare for this eventuality.

First, the Governor should arrange with the attorney general or district attorney to try the first test case before a sympathetic judge. Obtaining a headline-grabbing and attention-getting conviction would go a long way toward teaching the public that abortion really was no longer a legal option. Should a higher judge attempt to vacate the conviction, the executive branch could ignore the judge and continue to enforce the law. Anyone who ignores God and the Constitution should be ignored. Executive officers could continue to blockade, make arrests, and bring charges, even if certain judges refused to hear cases.

Furthermore, most States have constitutional ways to remove contrary judges from office. Research the options in your State. For example, according to the Oklahoma Constitution, the State Supreme Court is not supreme. Article 7A § 1 provides for the "Removal of judges from office - Compulsory retirement - Causes." Note: "Cause for removal from office shall be: Gross neglect of duty, corruption in office…gross partiality in office, oppression in office; or other grounds as may be specified hereafter by the legislature." According to § 4, the process to remove a justice of the Supreme Court is begun via a simple petition filed by any of several parties, including the governor, attorney general, or by a resolution of the House of Representatives. Therefore, the governor could file a petition to remove from office any judge who dismisses an abortion case or call for his impeachment, citing "wilful [sic] neglect of duty, corruption in office" and "incompetency," or whatever reasons are given in the relevant state constitution.

In addition, any statutory language used by the legislature to abolish abortion should include a new section of law along these lines: "Any judge or court of this State that purports to enjoin, stay, overrule, or void any provision of this act shall be subject to removal from office per the power granted to the legislature by the State Constitution."

What if the People Will Not Follow?

Another objection we hear against an executive approach is that the people will not go along with it. We strongly disagree. While there is no guarantee, based on what we know of human nature and what we have witnessed with emergency executive orders during the COVID years, governors would likely be successful. But even if we assumed the worst, that the people would not go where the governor led, that would not mean it was the wrong thing to do. Let us examine some reasons for optimism.

First, it is axiomatic that collectively people conform. The prophets of old compared the people to sheep because people need to follow a leader, just like sheep follow a shepherd. Cultural currents already exist, sweeping people along. Leadership is the tiller that steers the boat in the current. Whoever is at the tiller determines what the mob does. We need righteous boat captains, shepherds, and governors. During the COVID years, executive shepherds issued orders that destroyed liberty, property, businesses, and ultimately lives, but, appropriate or not, moral or not, the people went right along with it. Those same executive shepherds could issue orders to abolish abortion, and the people would likewise go along. The time is now.

Second, people will acquiesce if they perceive that lives are at risk. They will vote for anything, do anything, follow anywhere, or allow anything, if they believe it will save lives, or if it is "for the children." They clearly believed that about COVID. If a chief executive were courageous enough to proclaim the truth of the abortion genocide and declare it the emergency that it is, the people would believe the governor's message. The time is now.

Third, people go along with just about anything if it does not affect them personally. "Oh, whatever… That doesn't affect my house, my car, my cell phone, or my Netflix," seems to be their attitude. Shutting down abortion death camps would not immediately affect enough people to cause dissent. Those who have participated at some level in the sin of abortion, and who are suffering the guilt and manifestations of physical, emotional, and spiritual death accompanying such sin, are not likely to rise up to prevent the abolition of abortion. The time is right now.

Fourth, executives need not fear the people's reactions. It takes an extraordinarily high level of wicked behavior from a magistrate to initiate an impeachment trial, much less a conviction or civil unrest. The time is right now.

Fifth, we are in a time of radical political change and economic chaos. The dollar is inflating, and nations are at war. Heads are spinning, and the people are not sure what to think about their futures. Now is the time for governors to ease the people's fears and shore up the foundations of society. And what is more foundational than respect for life and upholding the right to life? This would be firm footing at a time when the ground seems to be giving way. On top of all that, the people know that *Roe v. Wade* was overturned, but they do not fully understand the implications. Now is exactly the right time for governors across the union to tear down the altars, fire the false prophets and priests, and abolish child sacrifice in their States.

Ultimately, it will take a chief executive to abolish abortion, and if a governor is willing, there is nothing standing in his way—not the federal government, and not the people of his State. The lives of preborn humans are on the line, and the people will understand that if the governor communicates it clearly and with conviction. Abolishing abortion does not affect most people enough for them to oppose it in any meaningful way. And finally, the people's acquiescence to executive authority with COVID has proven beyond reasonable doubt that the people will go along with the governor's leadership.

A Model Letter

Calling our leaders to lead is the prophetic role of the people of God. Some might listen, while others will not. The king of Nineveh appears to have responded quickly to Jonah's warnings. Remember, within a matter of days he issued an executive order directing all citizens to "Call urgently on God. Let them give up their evil ways and their violence." King Nebuchadnezzar required more time and persuasion. He was warned by Daniel, his trusted counselor, but he had to eat grass before he humbled himself to obedience (Dan. 4:25-35). Unfortunately, most magistrates never listen to God's messengers at all, but our duty to instruct them remains. Here is a generalized model letter you could use in communications with your governor:

> Dear Governor, Abortion is the murder of preborn human beings. The purpose of government, as outlined by both our founding documents and the word of God, is to protect life, liberty, and property. According to God's law, it is wrong to kill innocent human beings. According to the Fourteenth Amendment to the U.S. Constitution, "Nor shall any State deprive any person of life, liberty, or property, without due process of law; nor deny to any person within its jurisdiction the equal protection of the laws." The same is recorded in our state constitution. Therefore, abortion is a violation of our highest laws and is unconstitutional.

I appeal to you, as the chief executive of the State, to abolish murder by abortion in our State. You not only have the moral duty before God to immediately stop the shedding of innocent blood in our State, but also have constitutional authority and specific legal powers which would allow you to lead the movement to abolish abortion literally and fully in our State. You may not think so, but in the eyes of God, protecting innocent preborn humans from murder is more important than balancing the budget, regulating marijuana, or increasing teacher salaries. You have the duty and the authority to stop the bloodshed. If you do not, you will approach God's throne one day as a leader whose hands are stained with innocent blood.

As head of the executive branch, which functions independently of the legislative and judicial branches, you have as much right and duty to act in accordance with the constitution as do legislators and judges. You need not wait for a court's permission to enforce constitutional protections. When God's law and our constitutions are disregarded by other magistrates, a governor's duty is not to bow down to them, but to resist them and uphold our constitutions to protect innocent lives.

Your leadership is paramount. As chief executive, you need no further authorization than your oath of office and our constitutions to proceed with a plan to abolish abortion. Furthermore, your leadership through executive action could stop the bloodshed and inspire such actions by other magistrates, saving countless lives throughout the land.

Governor, instruct the legislature of this State to abolish abortion in statute so that district attorneys can prosecute those who commit murder by abortion.

Governor, the law grants you the power to issue executive orders to the Medical Board, State Department of Health, Department of Public Safety, and the National Guard, among others. Command your executive agents to immediately stop the bloodshed. Instruct them to revoke medical licenses, shut down abortion death camps, and prevent any further murder by abortion. Executive agencies answer to you, Governor, and if they do not follow your orders, you can replace their heads with leaders who will.

You can be encouraged and emboldened that when Christians across the State hear that you are leading the charge to end this atrocity, they will rally to your aid. We will do everything within our power to support your leadership and action to abolish abortion in our State.

In conclusion, it is time for you to accept your God-given role in leading the modern-day abolition movement. Only chief executives have the civil authority and duty to immediately stop the bloodshed, thus driving the issue to a resolution and ending the genocide of abortion. Sincerely yours...

Craft a message in your own words. These are the main points: (1) It is your moral duty and legal responsibility to stop the bloodshed. (2) You must obey God, rather than mankind (even in the form of courts or legislators or other magistrates). (3) Abortion will continue without your executive leadership.

This message can be communicated not only in letters, but in emails, on social media, and in letters to the editor of local newspapers. Ask your church congregation to follow your example. Start a letter-writing campaign and send a delegation to deliver them to the governor's office in person. Request an appointment with the governor while you are there.

Other Executive Magistrates

While the governor is the highest-ranking executive in any State, other executive magistrates can implement the doctrine of the lesser magistrates due to the authority they possess within their jurisdictions. For example, city police chiefs and county sheriffs have also taken an oath of office and have the same duty to protect innocent lives and property. Regardless of what other branches of government and executive magistrates are doing, they also have the power to blockade death camps and make arrests.

On a crisp morning in March, some forty peaceful protestors gathered at the Trust Women abortion facility to interpose for innocent children being led to slaughter (Prov. 24:11). Rather than help the protestors defend innocent children from murder by abortion, Oklahoma City police officers completely ignored their oaths of office and instead sought to stop free speech and attempted to bully protestors into leaving the area. Unable to scare anyone off, Officer Smith resorted to cruising the area looking for an excuse to harass protestors with his power.

At the conclusion of the protest, I got out of my idling vehicle to gather signs from my friends. Obviously, I could not get in and out of my vehicle while wearing a seatbelt. Once I finished gathering signs, I buckled up and drove off. Officer Smith pulled me over a few blocks later and issued a ticket for a "seat belt violation." The traffic stop was obviously politically motivated harassment and had nothing to do with public safety. So, I wrote to Bill Citty, Chief of Oklahoma City police. Here are some lightly edited excerpts from my letter:

> I am registering this official complaint with you, hoping that you will correct and redirect those officers who oppress the innocent while protecting murderers just on the other side of a fence. Chief Citty, the idea that the Supreme Court of the United States must be obeyed when they issue immoral and lawless opinions is a fiction. Your duty, and that of your officers, per your oaths, is to uphold the Oklahoma Constitution and the Constitution of the United States, both of which clearly defend the right to life.

> Those executives, from governors and mayors, to police chiefs and officers, who uphold unjust and immoral court opinions are complicit in the court's rebellion against God. Chief Citty, you have a duty to interpose against this federal attack upon the preborn, not to accommodate it. As Chief of Police you possess lawful authority to uphold the law of God and the Constitution.

> When God's law is impugned by other government entities, like the courts, your duty is not to bow down to them, but to resist them. Your duty is to uphold the Constitution and to protect innocent lives. Please direct your officers who serve in the area of the abortion facility to block "clients" from entering the killing center to murder their children.

Letters and messaging like this ought to be flooding the offices of police chiefs and country sheriffs across the union. Some sheriffs already agree and apply the doctrine of the lesser magistrates in other areas of immoral and unconstitutional public policy. For example, Sheriff Richard Mack became famous when he refused to enforce unconstitutional federal gun regulations in his jurisdiction. Mack went on to found the Constitutional Sheriffs and Peace Officers Association (cspoa.org) which educates sheriffs and other peace officers on their duties as lesser magistrates. In his booklet *The Proper Role of Law Enforcement*, Mack writes:

> When we raise our right arm and promise to protect and defend the Constitution, does that oath mean only as far as my supervisor or the Supreme Court allow me to? Or does that oath essentially bestow a responsibility on me to know it, study it, cherish it and ultimately defend it even against a well-meaning but misdirected supervisor or judge? I do not pretend to have all the answers, but I do know the notion that cops should enforce all laws regardless of how abusive, immoral, or unconstitutional they are, is dangerous and destructive.

While police chiefs could establish abortion-free cities, and sheriffs could establish abortion-free counties, other executive magistrates could likewise exercise their legal authority to uphold the Constitution and save the lives of the preborn within their jurisdictions. Here are some examples:

- The head of the Department of Health and Human Services, or such agency as your State may have, could use health and safety regulations to shut down death camps and remove abortifacient drugs from pharmacy shelves.

- The head of the Board of Medical Licensure and Supervision, or such agency as your State may have, could revoke the medical licenses of doctors who perform abortions.
- The state or city agency in charge of business licensing could revoke the business licenses of abortion clinics.
- The state attorney general, or any of several district attorneys, could investigate and gather evidence, file charges under the State's homicide code, and prosecute those parents who commit murder by abortion and the doctors whom they hired to advise or assist them.

The Persistent Plea

> In a certain city there was a magistrate who neither feared God nor cared about public opinion. And there was a widow in that town who kept coming to him demanding, "Grant me justice against my adversary."
>
> For some time he refused. But finally he said to himself, "Even though I don't fear God or respect the people, because this widow is wearing me out, I will see that she gets justice, or there will be no end to her harassing me!" (Luke 18:2-5)

The Lord told this parable to illustrate that we should not cease to call upon the ultimate magistrate, God the Father, in prayer, to ask for vindication against our earthly enemies. But that does not mean the story might not be literally instructive as well.

If we want good government, then we must raise our expectations and demand better of our magistrates. We may have no more power than the widow who exercised a persistent demand, but exercise it we must. We cannot make our own cozy arrangement with unjust magistrates, who fear neither God nor a few conservative activists. Their initial denial may be expected, but ultimate success depends partly on our unrelenting cry, "Grant me justice!"

One skeptic commented, "Perhaps what you are wanting the governor to do is a bridge too far." At the present time, this appears to be true. Governors seem to be a long way from doing what is needed and necessary. They seem unable to see past the political cost of the bridge, much less actually building it and crossing over to an abortion-free State.

Nevertheless, we do not know what is tumbling around in the head and heart of a particular governor, especially if you fill him with an abundance of prophetic activity and messaging. He is more likely to build and cross that bridge if we continue casting a clear vision before him. The more he hears it, the more likely it is that his thinking will shift and his heart will melt. That is the reason we must continue with pointed and precise communications to the governor. Emails, newspaper articles, social media posts, conferences, rallies, marches, lobbying, and personal visits all educate and influence the governor.

Mobilize your state Republican Party or church denomination to officially adopt platforms or resolutions calling upon the governor to totally and immediately abolish abortion. Stage rallies in front of the governor's office and place of residence. Get creative. One prophet was known to wear clothes made of camel hair and eat locusts.

We need to teach and remind our governors that leading collective civil repentance to abate God's judgment is the role of chief executives. They must abolish child sacrifice within their jurisdictions, but this cannot happen without their leadership.

King Josiah used his executive authority to tear down places of child sacrifice and punish those who murdered innocent children. He did not wait for the culture to change; he changed the culture. He understood his duty to uphold righteous law and that the time for justice is always now! We need our governors and chief executives to follow Josiah's example.

We cannot wait for society to wake up. Society is a collective term, so it cannot wake up. Only individuals have thoughts, choices, and actions, and no individual wakes up without a nudge or a noise. This is the advantage of focusing efforts on the executive branch where we find individuals, as opposed to collectives. The governor, police chief, sheriff, attorney general, district attorney, agency head, etc. are each individuals who possess personal responsibility and authority to carry out actions that would uphold the rule of law and directly save lives. If you live in a blue State, you will not get a collection of motley legislators to agree to criminalize abortion. There is a reason we have a Commander-in-Chief, not a Council-in-Chief. State legislatures, which are rife with group-think and crowd-cowardice, do not historically provide effective leadership, but you might get an executive, pricked to the heart, to exercise his authority and bring the issue to a head. We need a top dog to lead the pack.

In summary, the governor has leadership power through the authority of his position, name recognition, and the bully pulpit. He has legislative power through calling special sessions and vetoing bills. He has enforcement power through state police, state agencies, and influence with the attorney general, district attorneys, and other law enforcement executives. As of this writing, no governor has exercised any of these powers in the pursuit of the abolition of abortion and in the defense of our preborn neighbors. Governors and executives have been bearing the sword in vain.

Most generations receive judgment for the wickedness they accept and condone, but every now and again, a generation will be led to repentance by a chief executive who is himself repentant. Be forewarned, the vast majority of magistrates will shun you, denigrate you, and give you the runaround. Just accept that, call them on it, and continue telling them the right things to do. Then you will have done your duty. The rest is between them and God. You will be in the good company of many other prophets who offered magistrates the opportunity to repent or perish.

16

WHY BOTHER?

In 1936 *The Atlantic Monthly* published an essay in which Albert Jay Nock gave us a pretty good paraphrase of the prophet Isaiah's depressing job description:

> In the year of Uzziah's death, the Lord commissioned the prophet to go out and warn the people of the wrath to come. "Tell them what a worthless lot they are." He said, "Tell them what is wrong, and why and what is going to happen unless they have a change of heart and straighten up. Don't mince matters. Make it clear that they are positively down to their last chance. Give it to them good and strong and keep on giving it to them. I suppose perhaps I ought to tell you," He added, "that it won't do any good. The official class and their intelligentsia will turn up their noses at you and the masses will not even listen. They will all keep on in their own ways until they carry everything down to destruction, and you will probably be lucky if you get out with your life."

The people's response to Isaiah's message is summarized in Isaiah 30:9-11:

> For they are a rebellious people, lying children, children unwilling to hear the instruction of Yehovah; who say...to the prophets, "Do not prophesy to us what is

right; speak to us smooth things, prophesy illusions...let us hear no more about the Holy One of Israel.

Isaiah was not the only prophet called to fight a seemingly losing battle. Jeremiah was told, "But you, dress yourself for work; arise, and say to them everything that I command you" (Jer. 1:17). So Jeremiah also had to teach and exhort, even though Yehovah warned him, "So you shall speak all these words to them, but they will not listen to you. You shall call to them, but they will not answer you" (Jer. 7:25-28).

Likewise, Ezekiel was told:

> Son of man, go to the house of Israel and speak with my words to them... But the house of Israel will not be willing to listen to you, for they are not willing to listen to me: because all the house of Israel have a hard head and a stubborn heart. (Ezek. 3:4-7)

Daniel mourned in Babylon, "We have not listened to your servants the prophets, who spoke in your name to our kings, our princes, and our ancestors, and to all the people of the land" (Dan. 9:6).

Habakkuk complained to God that his demands for justice were ignored, and he wondered why Yehovah allowed the unjust to continue in their wickedness: "Why do you make me look at injustice? Why do you tolerate wrongdoing? Destruction and violence are before me; there is strife, and conflict abounds. Therefore the law is paralyzed, and justice never prevails" (Hab. 1:3-4).

Even when God's own son, with miracle upon miracle, called the nation to repent, the political and religious leaders rejected his message, ignored his warnings, beat him, and crucified him.

In our day we write and call the governor, we visit legislators at the capitol, we beg our preachers, pastors, and priests to speak up; but our "kings and princes" and the intelligentsia follow the same old pattern, rejecting repentance, rejecting the administration of justice and mercy.

At first glance, this all seems depressing. It begs the question: *Why bother if they are not going to listen anyway?*

First, speaking the word of Yehovah is a command, not a suggestion. It is not optional; it is our sacred duty. Throughout scripture we find numerous moral duties for believers such as: "Speak up for those...," "Rescue those...," "Warn them for me...," "Go...," "Preach...," "Teach them everything...," "Baptize them...," and "Make disciples..."

Second, speaking the word of God encourages the remnant. Other believers are strengthened knowing they are not alone. Warning and teaching prepare us for future suffering and strengthen us for the rebuilding task that follows the destruction that attends judgment.

Third, speaking the word of God preserves innocence. Notice one of the reasons given that Ezekiel should speak up:

> [If] you do not warn him or speak out to dissuade him from his evil ways in order to save his life, that wicked person will die for his sin, and I will hold you accountable for his blood. But if you do warn the wicked person and he does not turn from his wickedness or from his evil ways, he will die for his sin; but you will have saved yourself. (Ezek. 3:17-19)

If we do not speak to magistrates who promote or permit wickedness, we share the blame for the wicked culture around us. If we do not warn individuals living in transgenderism, homosexuality, adultery, and other sinful lifestyles, we will also be accountable for their ultimate destruction. This is a grave responsibility.

Fourth, speaking the word of God saves. Emotionally, it may feel like we have zero success. But when the prophets were told that the people would not listen, it was a general principle, from a collective point of view. It is easy to look at our collective culture, at the masses heading for destruction, and feel overwhelmed.

We must remember that saving even one lost sheep out of one hundred is cause for great rejoicing (Luke 15:3-7). Charles MacKay said in *Extraordinary Popular Delusions and the Madness of Crowds*: "Men, it has been well said, think in herds; it will be seen that they go mad in herds, while they only recover their senses slowly, one by one."

This perspective can help immensely while exercising our prophetic role. Rather than thinking in terms of fighting a culture war, rather than expecting mass media to bring mass repentance, we should remember that we can reach individual lost sheep who need to be saved, both physically and spiritually. In our families and churches we should speak to our children, brothers and sisters, aunts and uncles, and friends who suffer from hidden sin and doubt. In our schools we should speak to board members, teachers, and students about what is true and right to learn and practice. At abortion death camps we should speak to would-be murderers and rescue those being led to the slaughter. At our capitols we should speak to our governors and representatives about administering justice.

In summary, we are called to join what appears to be a lost cause, to speak in the face of rejection. But perceived failure is not actual failure. God's accounts are not like human accounts. In fact, he is more like a gardener than a bookkeeper. The death of God's son on the cross looked like the end of Israel's hope, but that buried seed of presumed failure was the germ of Yehovah's salvation.

We must bury our ideas of success as we walk in obedience. We must speak, even when others do not listen. We must warn, even when they do not heed. We must encourage, even when the cause seems lost. Even if it appears our acts fall to the ground to be trampled, in time, these seeds of obedience will bring forth life.

17

BE PRESENT AT THE GATES OF DEATH

Rescue those who are led to death; spare those stumbling to the slaughter. (Prov. 24:11)

Speak up for those who have no voice; in the cause of those who are appointed to die. (Prov. 31:8)

The disciples were average citizens from small, conservative towns that had all the observable trappings of faithfulness—attendance at synagogue, keeping of Sabbath and holy days, and an absence of idol worship at temples to false gods. In fact, the Lord had to take his disciples on a multi-day mission trip through several towns to Caesarea Philippi, a Greek city, to show them physical idol worship at the Grotto of Pan (Matt. 16:13-20).

It was here that Yeshua explained his coming kingdom to the disciples. It was here that Simon confessed, "You are the Anointed One, the Son of the living God," and the Lord replied:

> Blessed are you, Simon son of Jonah, for this was not revealed to you by flesh and blood, but by my Father in heaven. And I tell you that you are the Rock, and upon this rock I will build my church, and the gates of Hades [death] will not prevail against it. (vv. 16-18)

When the Lord mentioned the "gates of Hades," it was not just a turn of phrase or literary allusion; it was a real place that bore that name right there at the Grotto of Pan. The headwaters of the Jordan

River sprang from a deep cave there in the grotto. The spring was so deep that the pagan population thought of it as a gateway to the underworld, the place of the dead and of evil spirits, called *Hades* in Greek. The cave was said to be the birthplace of the Greco-Roman god Pan, the god of fields, forests, flocks, and shepherds. Tradition held that Pan was able to travel to and from the place of the dead through the cave in the grotto, known as the "gates of Hades." Pagan worshipers made sacrifices to Pan at the mouth of the cave. They also committed detestable sex acts with male and female prostitutes as religious rites to the fertility gods.

But the Son of God had said that the gates of death would not prevail against the Church. And in his triumphal resurrection, it was the true Son of God, not Pan, who entered a cave to Hades and came back alive. He would later reveal to John, "I am the living one! I was dead, but now I am alive forever and ever, and I hold the key to death and Hades" (Rev. 1:18). Indeed, the Grotto of Pan and its temple complex were eventually destroyed by earthquakes, and the Church spread across the Greco-Roman world.

Like the first disciples, I never gave much thought to the high places of idol worship growing up. We had no altar of child sacrifice in our town, and even as an adult, the nearest abortion death camp was three towns and a long drive away. That all changed after our first failed attempt to abolish abortion. That year a new abortion facility opened in the next town over, just twenty-five minutes away. I suddenly became aware of what was happening in my own back yard. The Lord was leading me on a journey out of my comfort zone to the very gates of death. I wondered, *Who will tear them down?*

The Dark Side

Tina's children were grown, and she was looking to get involved in ministry. After attending one of our six-hour interactive workshops, she knew she had to do something, so she began going daily to the gates of death. She began studying what other ministers around the States had already been doing for decades and learning on-the-job the best ways to save lives and save souls in front of the abortion death camp.

The first couple of years were lonely. No one would help. We had assumed that with the majority of the city's population calling themselves Christian, and with dozens of churches within five minutes of the death camps, it would be easy to systematically recruit enough volunteers to cover the gates of death every business hour. No one volunteer would have to stand at the gates more than an hour or two per month if all the believers in the area took an active interest in addressing the evil in their own back yards. We asked for volunteers to help via social media, in emails, and at all of our workshops and seminars. From individuals, the typical responses were "I don't have time," or "That's not my calling," or "I support the pregnancy resource center instead."

Theological Social Distancing

We also heard excuses from corporate churches. We covered many of those in the chapter "Earthly Kingdoms." I met with the pastor of one local corporate church to request material support and volunteers to help at the gates of death which were less than a block from his congregation. He flatly refused to get involved and explained that his idea of outreach was to send a gift basket inside to the "healthcare workers."

One morning I was standing at the gates of death when a satirical headline from *The Babylon Bee* crossed my phone screen: "Oh No! The First Question at the Gates of Heaven is *Are You a Calvinist or an Arminian?*" After laughing really hard, my analytical mind began thinking about the false dichotomy this meme presented. These two views are not the only possible ways to reconcile the concepts of sovereignty, election, omniscience, and free will. Most controversies are the result of attempts to reconcile difficult concepts in scripture. One day we may learn that the authoritative answer to questions like these, more often than not, is "d.) None of the above."

It took me a while to figure it out, but part of what kept some churches from volunteering with us was their fixation on differences over church doctrines. Churches with competing ideologies, missions, strategies, and doctrines often do not play well together. One organization leader found out my eschatological view was different from his, so he called me a "damnable heretic" and refused to ever work with me again. Several pastors of reformed congregations who had partnered with us in the past to train and field evangelists cut all ties when they learned that I disagreed with John Calvin's doctrine of divine determinism.

When faced with tough theological questions, individual believers and groups of believers will handle the resulting differences in various ways. Some ignore the questions, change the subject, and move on to sports and the weather. Others view theological differences as an opportunity to do spiritual battle and eagerly jump into the fray with practiced rhetoric, ready to debate and conquer.

Conversely, others welcome such questions as an opportunity to adjust, clarify, and deepen their own understanding of truth. Their attitude is one of willingness to be molded by the truth, rather than forcing the truth into their own preconceived constructs. In addition, they seek to protect reputations and egos by pursuing discussions discreetly and privately, as Priscilla and Aquila did with Apollos (Acts 18:24-26).

However, too often we witness the kind of response that we call Theological Social Distancing, which manifests itself to varying degrees. Some feel that they cannot worship together. Others feel they cannot fellowship at all with those with whom they disagree. Still others choose not to participate in various kingdom endeavors based on who else is involved. For example, we know some believers who say they are against abortion, but they refuse to intervene at the gates of a death camp or attend anti-abortion events because they disagree with the ideologies or strategies of other believers involved.

Granted, some distancing may be warranted. We are not saying that every level of distancing is bad. But we find that those who refuse to co-labor in the work to abolish abortion tend to mostly ignore abortion. Here the problem is really about fighting an easier foe. Too many Christians find it easier to fight about scripture with other Christians than to go out and face the reality of children being killed right on the other side of a fence. This level of distancing is particularly saddening because it is a negative witness to new converts, and it removes Christian soldiers from the field. When Christians fail to oppose murder by abortion because of theological disagreements, are they perhaps "neglecting the weightier matters" (Matt. 23:23)?

How should we respond to such treatment and adversity? Should we pull back and disengage, or continue to recruit? It is helpful to remember what is at stake and allow that vision to inform our choices about how to reorder our lives and work. If someone told you that she could no longer be a mother right now for whatever reason, and she was going to go home and shoot her toddler in the head, how would you respond? Would you not personally attempt to intervene in some way? Realizing that no magistrate is exercising his duty and authority to place himself between would-be criminals and their preborn victims, should we not place ourselves in a position to intervene and recruit others to help us stand in the gap?

I will never forget the cartoon I saw in which new converts are sitting in a "Membership Class." The teacher is pointing to a giant family tree on the wall titled, "Churches & Christian Movements Throughout History." The tree begins at the cross in the first century and then grows thousands of branches over the centuries. The teacher points to one little branch among the thousands and tells the class, "So this is where our movement came along and finally got the Bible right." One of the students piously responds, "Jesus is so lucky to have us."

Theological Social Distancing is a real phenomenon, and it is part of the dark side of the PLM. You, too, will face it. I have personally disagreed with many a sidewalk minister, and many have disagreed with me, but I would rather we both be there, even if on different days or different sides of the street, than not be there at all. We have lives to save and souls to reconcile to the Father. We can work on the other family disagreements at another time and place.

A great example of the right attitude and approach is found in our friends at Sunnyside Baptist Church. They have faithfully joined the ministry at the gates of death in every possible way. They provide Bibles, gifts, financial support, volunteers, signs, literature, water, and even a closet to store outreach gear. This congregation of the Lord's Church has been a tremendous testimony to unity and faith in action.

The overwhelming lack of interest in and support for ministry at the gates of death was one dark side we experienced within the PLM. Then, another dark side enveloped us for a season.

Turf Warfare

When people did show up, it was often to get in the way and criticize. Catholics and those participating in 40 Days for Life often criticized us for trying to speak out and actively engage those entering the gates of death. They believed in the more passive approach of simply praying and keeping vigil.

There was a rift between those who offered the biblical good news of reconciliation first and those who offered material support first, often never getting to sharing the good news. One group from a pregnancy resource center criticized Tina for aggressively leading with the gospel. Then an abolitionist group criticized her for being too soft and not preaching a hellfire and brimstone message.

We were criticized for using signs that were too graphic. We were criticized for using signs not graphic enough.

We witnessed many different factions come and go in a strange type of turf warfare. Catholics with rosaries prayed on the street corner. Angry abolitionists yelled epithets on obnoxious bullhorns. Charismatics danced, sang, and blew shofars. Participants in 40 Days for Life would find a spot for an hour, then disappear until the following year.

Another huge rift we have witnessed is between those who work strictly within the bounds of state and federal statutes, versus those who personally, as civilians, defy immoral and unconstitutional statutes and get themselves arrested, fined, and jailed. I have personal friends who are currently facing financial ruin and years in jail because they sat themselves down in the driveway of an abortion death camp. Are these actions good or bad, right or wrong? I understand the arguments on both sides. I sympathize with those who are facing charges. I understand their choices to literally interpose, to live out the prophetic role of suffering servants, and to serve as real-life visual aids.

This book and this chapter is not about sorting out the disputes among believers, disputes that are ongoing and unfortunately often put an ugly face on Christianity through social media debates full of name-calling, bad logic, and poor hermeneutics. Rather, this chapter is about pointing out the darkness that prevails in the absence of those willing to be present. Not enough believers are willing to employ some method—even if controversial—of intervention, some attempt—even if denigrated by other believers—to rescue those being led to the slaughter. In my opinion, when it comes to life and death, it is better to do something than nothing.

A war is raging, not just against abortion, but within the ranks of believers. Be forewarned that you will suffer from friendly fire, but please do not let it deter you from getting involved. Despite the dark side of the PLM, our presence is a great light.

Be Present

At high places of child sacrifice, we witness women escorting their daughters in to murder their grandchildren. Three generations go in, but only two come out. We witness fathers too scared to exercise moral leadership. Drivers become accomplices because of a mistaken understanding of friendship. The sad part is that they all appear to know they are wrong—no eye contact, heads hung low, guilt written all over them. And then there are the employees.

"You are a disgrace to your church. You are a disgrace to God. You should have been an abortion." The security guard's bald head reflected the sun angrily at us. His eyes remained hidden behind dark sunglasses. "Do y'all like Marilyn Manson, cuz you're fixin' to listen to some death metal." He cranked up his truck stereo so loud that it was difficult to hear one another.

These kinds of experiences scare most believers away from standing at an abortion death camp. They are also afraid of not knowing what to say. But your simple presence, even without words, is powerful and important. Here is why.

Your presence outside the abortion facility directly saves lives. It is the single most detrimental thing to their business. Former abortion workers have reported that when five or more people gather outside a facility, a certain percentage of appointments become no-shows.

Your presence convicts others as you draw their attention to the evil being committed in their midst. These death camps are not side notes in a history textbook; they are real. Children are dying, and families are being wounded by their own wickedness. But how many citizens connect with this truth in a meaningful way? For most, murdered babies are emotionally little more than a statistic in their minds. We must be there to point to the death camps and tell others that the American genocide is real, that it is happening next door to where they shop, work, and worship. More citizens must viscerally connect with the truth that their government sanctions murder.

Your presence forces abortion workers to rethink what they are doing. If no one is out there, it must seem to the workers that the community has accepted what they are doing and appreciates their "service." When people are out there, it forces them to examine their lives and work.

Your presence forces customers to reconsider what they are buying. Beyond the mother, even the father, driver, friend, or other family members must rethink what they are doing when they walk or drive by your witness. They must ask themselves whether they are truly friends, or accomplices.

Your presence shatters the illusion of privacy and illuminates the darkness. They thought this was a private affair. If those who drive up to the altar face a crowd of witnesses at the gates, they have to consider whether they want to be seen. They might think, "Does someone here know me, or my mom, or my grandmother? Do I really want to be seen going in here?" Your presence may awaken the resounding voice of conscience.

Your presence forces law enforcement officers and executives to face their own hypocrisy. Sadly, security guards and law enforcement officers like the one quoted above cannot see that they are destroying the rule of law and bringing bloodguilt upon themselves. We are kind to the security guards and pray for them, but we also remind them of their culpability. Their job is to protect the innocent and to uphold the rule of law. Our best hope for abolition is for executives to take action to stop the bloodshed. Therefore, they cannot be left alone to become comfortable in their apathy and inaction. We do what we do because governors and sheriffs refuse to do their duty. One day a chief executive will allow his conscience to be pricked to the point of action. Until then, "Let us not become weary in doing good, for at the proper time we will reap a harvest if we do not give up" (Gal. 6:9).

Our physical presence at abortion death camps is a powerful mental, emotional, and spiritual blockade. It saves lives, and it teaches, rebukes, and exhorts. We strongly encourage you to join experienced ministers in your area who can guide your participation and help you be present with confidence. Remember that you will not be alone, for the Lord promised, "For where two or three gather in my name, I am there with them" (Matt. 18:20).

Abortion Intervention Ministry

While we eagerly pray, wait, and seek for an executive magistrate to finally abolish abortion in his jurisdiction, innocent blood continues to be shed at abortion death camps. We know that many believers are deeply grieved and want to rescue as many as they can, but they are typically not present at the gates of death. We believe that a major obstacle to participation is not knowing what to do or how to do it. Therefore, we developed our own training program, which we call Abortion Intervention Ministry (AIM).

AIM is an interactive workshop for those who have wanted to intervene and minister at abortion facilities but have been too nervous to get started, or who wanted some basic training first. AIM was built on the best practices of successful ministers from Sidewalk Advocates for Life, Equal Rights Institute, 40 Days for Life, Pro-Life Action League, Operation Save America, and other experienced abolitionists. Combining their input with our own volunteers' experiences, we developed a crash course that analyzes what, when, and how to say things. It recommends solutions to logistical problems. It models skills and offers role-playing exercises to immediately bring proficiency and build confidence. The interactive style allows participants to ask questions and workshop potential solutions with experienced ministers who will mentor them out on the sidewalk as they put their new skills into practice. AIM training gives believers the confidence to immediately go stand at the gates of death. They might simply observe and pray, or they might hold a sign, or they might even speak up and attempt to start a conversation. AIM was designed to quickly equip volunteers to be on site in short order, saving lives and saving souls the very next day. Following one of our AIM workshops, Rachel said:

> I am way more comfortable about the idea of ministering in this way. [AIM training] leaves nothing to guesswork. I like the explanations of the reasons why things are done certain ways. The presentation was NOT boring. I always felt if I did this I would be unarmed and alone, but this was very encouraging and made me feel this is doable.

Finally, Christians began to move from the pew to the pavement. We saw volunteers come and stay. The turf warfare dissipated, and we all began to settle into a rhythm.

When I arrived at the gates of death one Monday morning, it looked like a street festival was in full swing. A woman was strumming a guitar and singing. The nurses from the mobile ultrasound unit were putting out signs. Two gray-haired retired ladies held hands to pray. A local pastor was preaching on a boom box. Tina and Delilah offered gifts as they called clients to stop and listen. There were young and less young, experienced and more newly arrived. I recognized almost everyone present. I recognized believers who identify with Free Will Baptists, Southern Baptists, Charismatics, Reformed Baptists, house churches, Churches of Christ, and various other nondenominational groups. My heart was warmed by the unity of faith and purpose.

Although there will always be naysayers, be encouraged by this picture of unity. Across the States many Christians are choosing to co-labor in the work to abolish abortion. We are grateful for each and every one who can get beyond interpersonal and interdenominational debates to stand together with other believers to defend their preborn neighbors. We want to encourage you to stand with us. For some pointers on how to get started, see Appendix: Abortion Intervention Ministry.

Veritas Vignettes

Those who have never kept vigil at an abortion death camp may have trouble imagining the scene. They ask, *What goes on down there? What is it like?* In the following vignettes, we offer pictures of life at the gates of death.

The first thing to understand is that a typical day is depressing and uneventful. Depressing, because we witness client after client go in to murder their preborn babies. Uneventful, because other than clients coming and going, not much happens. After the thirty seconds it takes a pregnant woman to reach the door, the only audiences remaining are the drivers sitting in their cars for hours on end and the homeless who shuffle by to watch the show.

We stand at the gates, with arms outstretched, offering a gift bag as each car approaches. Once a woman or family exits the car, we begin to speak. Here is a transcript of an actual conversation I had with a couple crossing the parking lot. I began:

"You waited all this time to come. Just give me three more minutes. I'm a minister. Let me hear what your need is and pray with you. If you are here for some service, we can help you for free. That's what we do as Christians. There are free clinics less than two miles from here. It's not too late. Whatever you need; let me try to help you."

"Are you thirty to thirty-five years old?" the father asked.

"I'm a forty-six-year-old Christian. I don't know what your issue is, but just tell me about it, and let me see if I can find some way to help."

"It seems like you should have been here forty-six years ago."

"Why is that? Because you want me dead?"

"Yep."

"Dude, that's pretty perverted."

"I'm being honest."

"I care about human beings, whether you do or not. I think God does, too. That's why we have this conscience, this idea of right and wrong. I just hate to see people do stuff that they will regret for the rest of their lives, even if they are in denial." And then they were gone inside.

In the midst of reaching out to these women and men, vagabonds who shelter behind nearby gas stations stop to gawk. We give them snacks and toiletries to make their lives a little easier for a day. We lean against the fence with them, listening to their stories, connecting them to local resources, and sharing the biblical good news of reconciliation with their heavenly Father.

Now imagine a white Isuzu Rodeo and a black Dodge Charger parked side by side. They are across a parking lot about twenty yards away. The drivers, who are barely visible through darkly tinted windows, have hours to wait while their own children are being murdered by the hand that they hired. They are a captive audience, and so we speak to them. Talking to fences, gates, and car doors with a public address system often feels hopeless, but we know they can hear us loud and clear. Here is a transcript of exactly what I said:

"I hope you are hearing me because what I am telling you is the truth. Whether you are here to murder a child by abortion or not, that is how this place makes its money, and you need to have no part in that. Do not aid, abet, and support a wicked place that kills innocent children and has blood on their hands. By participating with them you have blood on your own hands.

"Why is your woman here today? Is it birth control? Is it hormones? Is it some sort of health checkup? Again, all of these things we can help you with for free.

"Is she here because she's thinking about killing your child she's carrying in the womb? You may have convinced yourself that what you are doing is for the greater good, because you can't support this child right now, but it's never the greater good to kill someone that you don't want, don't like, or fear. We have justified genocides, murder, holocausts, and all manner of wickedness by calling it the greater good. It never works in the eyes of God.

"You don't kill innocent people that you don't want. If you had a two year old that you couldn't support, you wouldn't shoot a hole in his head because you didn't want that child. You would find someone else to raise that child.

"You may have convinced yourself that this is not your decision, but her decision, but no, no, no; you crossed that line when you drove into this parking lot. You are an accomplice. You are affirming and supporting an act of murder. That's what you are contemplating here today, and you are just as guilty. If you willfully help someone rob the bank, even if you didn't go in and point the gun, you still do time. If you hire a hit man to kill somebody, you are the primary guilty party and get the death penalty before God at the final judgment. You need to think on that.

"Your conscience is not just some quirk of your body chemistry. That is God telling you that what you are doing is wrong. That's a warning that you need to stop and turn the other way, and I'm here to affirm that word from God right now that you have felt and been trying to rationalize away and deal with. It's not too late to change your mind right now."

A speech like this one brought two different men over to talk, and one of them began urging his girlfriend to come out. We do not mince words, because time is of the essence. We provide assistance for any need and a clear choice between life and death. All of this is delivered in a spirit of humility and grace.

During one stretch we saved seven babies in four months. The gospel is shared with everyone who stops for a conversation. Almost all allow us to teach them, comfort them, and pray for them. Some, who were already professed Christians, repent on the spot and restore their relationship with the Lord. Ashley, Nicole, Marvin, and Mandy all gave their lives to the Lord based on conversations with Tina at the gates of death, and I was able to baptize Jessica in Tina's pool. My friends David and Julie, who operate a mobile ultrasound unit, baptized a homeless woman in a nearby horse trough.

On Monday morning I was the first sidewalk minister to arrive at the abortion death camp. I was shocked to see eight cars occupied by escorts already in the parking lot. Every tag was from Texas. Over the next three hours, more than ten more couples arrived to murder preborn children, all from Texas. No one came over for an extended conversation that day.

On Tuesday morning the Texans came streaming in once again. With escorts waiting in their cars, I cranked up the PA system and said, "Welcome to the Sooner State, Texan. Shame on us for promoting this wicked interstate commerce." Immediately, a hard-looking young man with sharp tattoos, black cap, and black eyes jumped out of his nice ride and marched over to me outside the gate.

"Why you pickin' on me 'cause I'm from Texas?" he asked.

"Actually, you all are. Look at the plates," I said.

"Oh, I thought you was calling me out, so I wanted to come talk about this here. I spent four years in prison and had a lot of time to study the Bible. Where does it say you can't get no abortion?"

"Are you familiar with 'You shall not murder?'"

"Well, yeah, but...well, I dunno."

"You know this is wrong, don't you? Don't you know that you'll have to give an answer to God for this?"

"But God will forgive this, right?"

"I know that he can, but I also know that you cannot presume upon God's grace. It doesn't work that way. It's about being in a right relationship with God, about being humble and obedient before your Father. You can't just arrogantly commit mortal sins assuming God will overlook your attitude. That's like flipping God the bird. That's the very opposite of the humility that puts you in a position to be right with God, who, like a loving father, wants to forgive his child, but will not be mocked."

"Yeah, well, I just wanted to see what you thought."

He claimed to be just an Uber driver, but people claim a lot of things out there.

Back on the microphone, I spoke again to the men in the cars. I let them know that they, too, would feel the guilt of this day for the rest of their lives. I challenged them, asserting that they were not acting like real men. The next driver who came over was certainly feeling guilty.

"I just wanted to come over and straighten you out, because this doesn't have anything to do with me. I'm just being a friend and driving her here. It's her choice, not mine. I'm just supporting her."

He was defensive in front of other witnesses, so we walked to the corner store and talked privately while he purchased a cigarillo. There he calmed down enough to listen as I explained that a real friend would do everything in his power to stop a loved one from committing murder, and would certainly not participate. He again offered excuses, arguing that her father was paying for everything, and that all he was doing was driving. He kept saying, "It's not on me."

Finally, I explained one more time that by driving and offering "support" he was affirming her choice to murder and assisting her to do it. The only way he would be able to sleep with a clean conscience in the future was if he immediately did all he could to change the girl's mind and save the innocent child. He finally let the message penetrate. He urgently got his phone and rushed back into the compound. He said he would call me, but it had already been several hours. Probably too late, and I never heard from him again.

A twenty-three-year-old Asian man stopped at the gate as he was returning to pick up. It would be too late for him, as well. But as he talked, he did confess that his participation was sin and that he wanted to repent. Was he truly brokenhearted, or like the ex-convict was he arrogantly presuming? Only God knows, but we pray that some of these hearts are truly broken and will be drawn to the Father for reconciliation.

On Wednesday morning, as four Christians gathered in prayer at the death camp, something different happened. A woman from Fort Worth walked out of the gates.

"Hi. I'm Tatiana. I decided to keep my baby..."

She said it felt like the Holy Spirit was convicting her while she was sitting inside. She felt compelled to come out and share this with the team that had been praying for her. We connected Tatiana with Christians in Fort Worth who could encourage her and provide material support.

On a sweltering Friday in August, a middle-aged woman walked out of the front door of the abortion death camp. Tina beckoned to her.

"Ma'am, I can help you right now. What do you need?"

Crying, the woman responded, "What am I going to do? My daughter is pregnant. She can't drop out of school right now."

"I can help you. Go get her out of there and come talk to me. We have all the help you could need, and we'll work this out together. That's why I'm here."

In the next few moments, Tina burned up the cell towers making phone calls. Within minutes the mother and daughter came out together, and Tina drove with them to an impromptu meeting with a Christian adoption agent. She sat with them, offering comfort and praying over them. By the end of the meeting, the family knew they could not kill their baby, and the seventeen-year-old daughter had begun the adoption process.

Reflecting on that day, Tina said, "This is what makes life worth living! This is what God does when the body of Christ is available to help those who are in great need."

Jody was at the gate when a mother dropped off her daughter. As the mother waited in the parking lot, she began to look more and more distressed. Jody attempted to speak to her, but she could not get a conversation going. Eventually, the woman began crying and drove to a nearby fast-food restaurant. Jody followed her to see what was wrong and how she could help. There, she was able to sit and talk with the woman, offering friendship, material support, and prayer. The woman then retrieved her daughter from the abortion facility. This family agreed to attend church with Jody and let the congregation help them through the pregnancy.

One winter morning it was bitterly cold, and I was the only one standing at the gates. I held a clipboard and tried to look professional, like I belonged there—no easy task standing on the *outside* of the gates next to the street. Two Hispanic women walked up but suddenly halted at the sight of my neon green vest. They looked questioningly at me. I asked if they were there for an appointment. The elder of the two asked if I could speak Spanish.

"Un poquito," I said.

She spoke into her smartphone, then showed me the screen. It read: "My friend has an appointment at this pregnancy termination place."

I pointed across the street at the mobile pregnancy resource unit and motioned for them to follow me. A volunteer nurse welcomed them inside, and continuing to use the translation app, began to build a relationship. We learned that Fabiola was about nine weeks pregnant and abortion-minded. Her boyfriend did not want to support another child. We continued to offer help and shared materials from Focus on the Family. Fabiola finally agreed not to go through with the abortion.

Events like these do not come daily, but they do come. Perhaps one out of one hundred comes over for a conversation, but we know that finding even one lost sheep is cause for great rejoicing. How many more lost sheep could be rescued if more believers were willing to be present? We must train fellow servants to rescue our preborn neighbors at the gates of death.

18

WHAT CAN I DO?

I may never march in the infantry,
Ride in the cavalry,
Shoot the artillery;
I may never fly o'er the enemy,
But I'm in the Lord's army!
Yes, Sir!

Most books of this nature that identify problems often end with the same old worn-out plea: "Pray and give money to our ministry." Not this one. This chapter is not about you giving to our ministry; it is about you starting your own ministry. The goal of this chapter is to inspire you to go out and do more than you thought you could do, to be bold in ways that you have never been bold before, and to take others with you.

A spiritual war is raging all around us, and we are surrounded by death and destruction. Everywhere we turn we see people suffering from their own sinful choices or the choices of others. People are killing, stealing, and destroying minds, bodies, and souls. This war has many fronts—hunger, homelessness, addiction, sexual brokenness, and human trafficking—but we cannot fight on all of them. We cannot be in two places at once. To be present under a bridge feeding the homeless is to be absent from ministering in the prison. Each of us must consider our gifts and our calling. We may not be called to take every possible action, but we are called to action. Where will you fight? What are your orders?

For many of us, our orders have sent us to the abortion front, where the war is for the physical lives of our preborn neighbors and for the souls of those who condone and participate in murdering them. If your orders are to join us there, then this chapter will summarize some specific, real, effective, and meaningful ways to enlist and serve.

Nametags

If you attend a large church, the chances are there are many members whose faces you recognize, but you cannot call them by name. How well do you really know them? You know you know people when their names finally stick. We have all been to conferences where all the attendees wear nametags. This is a systematic attempt to help us feel more connected and get to know one another better. Some churches employ the use of nametags for the members or just for shepherds and greeters, which identify them by name and, if relevant, title.

Imagine visiting a church where a man named Jacob shakes your hand at the door and helps you find your coffee, class, and chair. If Jacob is wearing a nametag with his name and title—*JACOB, GREETER*—and he performs his duty well, you are likely to remember his name. If nothing else, you will remember that this man was a greeter.

Now imagine Jacob wears the nametag, but sits in his own class, minding his own business, and never greets anyone at the door. He might be wearing the name tag, but is he actually a greeter? No. He is claiming the name, but in vain. What makes Jacob a greeter is not the nametag, but the action of greeting people.

Similarly, we might ask, who is a believer, a disciple, a follower, a Christian? Is it those who simply wear the name? Or is it those who act in accordance with the name? Yeshua told his followers:

> You are the light of the world. A town built on a hill cannot be hidden. Neither do people light a lamp and put it under a bowl. Instead they put it on its stand, and it gives light to everyone in the house. In the same way,

let your light shine before others, that they may see your good works and glorify your Father in heaven. (Matt. 5:14-16)

What is the light of believers? Their light is their works, the things they do that the world can see. Nonbelievers will see your Christian acts of faith on the street, in the public marketplace, and in the state capitol halls engaging in conversation and ministering to people who have or are about to screw up their lives and need help and direction. These are the lights that can be seen and the works that demonstrate a living faith. This point is so important that one of the brothers of our Lord wrote extensively about it in a letter. Here is a condensed version of what he said on the subject:

What use is it if someone says he has faith, but he has no works? Can that faith save him?... I will show you my faith by my works... You foolish fellow, faith without works is useless... As a result of works, faith was perfected... You see that a person is justified by works and not by faith alone... As the body without the spirit is dead, so faith without works is dead. (Jas. 2:14-26)

These passages demonstrate that biblical faith is more than intellectual assent to a set of principles. Faith is belief conjoined with action. Those who wear a religious nametag claim to be in a reconciled relationship with their heavenly Father. But being in a right relationship takes proactive effort and work. One can wear a ring and call himself a husband, but being a good husband takes work. It requires daily acts of communication, nourishment, and protection. One can call himself a son or a daughter, but being a good child takes work. It requires daily acts of respect and obedience. If you truly love another, then you put work into that relationship every day in the things that you do to deepen and nourish the relationship so that it grows and thrives.

What if we apply this concept to our claim to be against abortion? What nametag are we wearing? Do we call ourselves pro-life? If so, how are we fighting abortion? What kinds of things have we been doing? These are typical examples:

1) Proudly call oneself pro-life.

2) Pray for an end to abortion during 40 Days for Life.
3) Wear pro-life T-shirts, display a pro-life bumper sticker, and post pro-life memes on Facebook.
4) Follow pro-life organizations on social media.
5) Watch pro-life videos, documentaries, and movies.
6) Attend the March for Life.
7) Donate to the local pregnancy resource center.
8) Donate to pro-life organizations and candidates.
9) Vote pro-life.

Are these actions good enough, or are they more akin to wearing a nametag? Is this type of faith alive or dead? These actions are not nothing. They are something. I do not intend to denigrate those who offer them as living sacrifices. I list them to illustrate that we have made a start, perhaps a start similar to having put on a nametag. But could we be more effective? Could our faith be more living? Perhaps, as the Lord suggested, these things are more like religious trappings such as church attendance or donating a tenth of our cooking spices. They may indicate that we have some head knowledge about the abortion issue, but are we in some respect still neglecting justice, mercy, and faithfulness? Are we still failing to do those things that would actually bring about the abolition of abortion (Matt. 23:23)?

If you have followed the evidence and arguments of this book, you know that mainstream pro-life ideas and actions have left tens of millions of dead and have not, even now in a post-*Roe* world, yielded even one abortion-free State. In fact, although well-intentioned, donating to some pro-life candidates and organizations has unwittingly helped protect and perpetuate the practice of abortion. It is no longer good enough to simply identify as pro-life and vote for self-proclaimed pro-life candidates. More is required. We must adopt abolitionist principles and move into the work of abolishing abortion.

Beyond the Nametag

A supporter of our ministry once emailed as follows:

> What do you feel is most needed? People getting involved politically? If so, what is the most effective position to place myself in? Or would it be best to just

try to get the word out to reach more people? Or do people like you need more financial support?

In other words, "What can I do?" There is much that believers can do, but first we need to understand that it goes beyond *can do* to *should do*. A better question is, "What *should* I be doing?" What are the ongoing duties and obligations of believers who are living in the midst of an abortion genocide?

We see two broad categories of activity. One category of activity is in the political realm of public policy. It might be summarized as our mission to magistrates, calling them prophetically to end the genocide and save masses of lives. The other category of activity is interpersonal. It includes the things that we do to save lives and save souls, one at a time. What should we be doing to influence our political leaders to abolish abortion? And until they do, what should we be doing personally to fight abortion?

The following recommendations do not address everything one could do, but they represent some of the most important priorities from the "should" list that have long been ignored or neglected by the vast majority of believers. These actions demonstrate our faith by our works and ensure that our light is shining on a hill for everyone in our cities and States to see. Many of these action items have been mentioned, illustrated, or explained along the way, but here is a convenient summary all in one place.

Public Policy

1) Teach others about good public policy. Understand and articulate the dark side of the PLM, its ideological errors, and its practical failures. For example, point out that political pro-lifers typically sacrifice equal protection for the preborn because they assume the victimhood of women.

2) Stop donating to establishment PLM organizations that uphold the Ten Corrupt Commandments. Proudly identify as an abolitionist instead.

3) Vote abolitionist. Promote, fund, and support abolitionist candidates instead of the compromised candidates of the PLM.

4) Embrace the prophetic mission to magistrates, the duty to call them to repent. Direct messages and influence at those with the moral duty and legal authority to protect innocent lives. Scrutinize, educate, and cajole magistrates.

5) Vet magistrates and candidates for office through cross-examination and observation of their performance. The Lord said, "By their fruit you will recognize them" (Matt. 7:16, 20). For too long candidates and magistrates have gotten a free pass by claiming to be pro-life. Stop believing their self-affixed pro-life nametags. Stop being bamboozled by those who talk about how their faith drives them, and instead ask them specifically where they are being driven. Ask specific, penetrating questions about what actions magistrates and candidates propose to take. Asking, "Are you pro-life?" is not helpful in the least.

Ask sitting and potential legislators, "Will you author legislation to provide equal protection of the law to all preborn humans?" Likewise, ask sitting and potential executives, "Will you act upon your oath before God to uphold our constitutions by immediately halting the bloodshed? Will you use your executive authority to lead the magistrates in other branches of government to abolish abortion and ignore immoral and unconstitutional court opinions?" This process and pressure might scare some magistrates into doing the right thing through fear of bad press, looking stupid or hypocritical, losing influence, or losing office. Or it might inspire magistrates to do the right thing by stirring their sense of duty and obligation.

6) Once magistrates and candidates reveal what they actually believe and will do or refuse to do, support the righteous ones and oppose the compromisers. Apply organized pressure through emails, letters, calls, visits, and political opponents.

7) Contact the governor routinely to demand his leadership in the abolition of abortion. The prophets of God were prolific writers. Jeremiah was well known among the kings of the land because he was constantly dropping them a line to remind them of what Yehovah the one true God expected and demanded of them as magistrates. Follow the examples of the prophets. Routinely write a physical letter to the governor, attorney general, and appropriate county sheriffs urging them to use executive authority and

leadership to abolish abortion in their jurisdictions. Many churches already have a card ministry in which members meet routinely to write cards of encouragement for those who are ill or who are celebrating milestones. It would be simple to add notes to executives like the ones modeled in the chapter "Grant Justice." Remind the governor and other executives that innocent babies are murdered by abortion every day in their jurisdictions and that it is morally incumbent upon them to stop the bloodshed.

8) Send a delegation to the office of the governor to deliver the letters in person. While there, request an appointment with the governor. This message can be communicated not only in letters, but in emails, on social media, and in letters to the editor of local newspapers.

9) Attend public meetings and gatherings where the governor will be present and seek an opportunity either in person or during public question and answer time to ask the governor to use his authority to abolish abortion. Again, the key to abolition lies in the executive branch. Without executive leadership, the legislative process is nothing more than posturing and political theater.

10) Expose any magistrate who does not respond positively to admonition and correction. Run, or recruit someone to run, against any such magistrate in the next election.

11) Prepare yourself with appropriate education, institutional knowledge, and experience. What kind of degrees and work prepare the way for future service as a legislator, agency head, district attorney, sheriff, or governor?

12) Learn about political campaigns by volunteering with a candidate, preferably an abolitionist. Working on any campaign will reveal the tricks of waging and winning a political war.

13) Launch your own campaign to convert or replace obdurate magistrates. We need righteous individuals to seek office. With believers as magistrates, we are in a better position to craft and uphold civil law that is based upon God's law. Of course, the presence of believers in official positions cannot guarantee the community's collective salvation ultimately, but their presence will help to preserve and protect that community in the here and now.

They will make that community safer and more righteous, a better place to live, and a better place to raise children. If we do not elect righteous leaders who will base civil laws on God's law, then we will get leaders who base our laws on the tyrannical will of the majority, on the pragmatic belief that the end justifies the means, and on political expediency, all of which lead to the loss of our property, our liberty, and even our lives. "When the righteous rule, the people rejoice, but when the wicked rule, the people groan" (Prov. 29:2).

14) Run for offices of all kinds, but especially executive offices. Political campaigns reach a much larger audience with their messages. The bigger the office, the bigger the megaphone. Statewide offices have the biggest reach, but even a county sheriff race reaches more eyes and ears than a lone evangelist at a street fair. Winning would be nice, but winning a political race is not necessary to win many people over to a godly perspective. When a candidate speaks, the media covers and multiplies his message, and people listen. By virtue of filing as a candidate and showing up with a message, you can play a major prophetic role and have a significant impact on your local culture.

15) Recruit others to join you in these acts of faith.

Personal Evangelism

Paul instructed the Colossian believers to "Walk in wisdom toward outsiders, making the best use of the time. Let your speech always be gracious, seasoned with salt, so that you may know how you ought to answer each person" (Col. 4:5-6; compare to 1 Pet. 3:15). With Paul's outline in mind, consider the following list of recommended action items:

1) Be proactive, not passive. Start conversations, rather than waiting for nonbelievers to approach you. This is good stewardship of time.

2) Be gracious. The message that a person is a sinner and not right with God is hard enough to hear without the Lord's ambassadors sharing it in an obnoxious manner. Ask honest questions, listen to understand others' points of view, and find common ground whenever possible.

3) Know how to answer each person and discuss abortion intelligently. Be prepared, trained in apologetics, to answer tough questions and give rational explanations in defense of the preborn and the Christian worldview. Evangelism should be interactive and tailored to individuals, not cookie-cutter. Too often, modern evangelists monologue without listening, or rely on ill-conceived, one-size-fits-all approaches. Be equipped to understand the questions and concerns of abortion advocates and nonbelievers. One option would be to invite United for Life to tailor a training workshop for your church, bible class, homeschool co-op, or club. Deb, one of our senior-level students at Charis Bible College, said:

> Years ago...I had several hours of training and read Christian materials relating to this subject. After completing [the United for Life] class, I realize how inept I actually was... This class helped me to see outside the proverbial abortion talking points and taught me how to engage in productive conversation with almost anyone... This course is a much-needed teaching tool, not just in a Christian school setting, but for churches and pro-life organizations. Understanding simple terminology and how and when to apply it is key to engaging others. The ultimate goal of...saving multiple innocent lives is too important for us not to be the most capable and skilled [ambassadors].

4) Engage in personal evangelism as often as possible. Discuss abortion with family, friends, classmates, church members, and co-hobbyists.

5) Here is an assignment to help you get started sooner rather than later. Write the names of three friends or family members. The first person should be someone with whom it would be easy to discuss the things you have learned in this book. The second person should be someone with whom it might be challenging to talk about abortion because she advocates for abortion, or because you do not know her views. The third person should be someone with whom it would be difficult to have a conversation, for whatever reason.

Your assignment is to talk to person number one within a week of finishing this book, and pray about numbers two and three.

Figure out when you can take fifteen minutes to start a conversation with person number one. Decide on a conversational approach. You might say, "I've been thinking about an issue that poses a challenge for Christians, and I want to get your opinion." Or, you might begin, "May I tell you about this book I just read."

Remember to practice good conversational skills by asking questions, listening, and finding common ground. Persons number two and three are up to you. Think about going the extra mile. Pray that they will be open to thinking differently about abortion. Ask the Father to grant you courage to speak to them and to grant you humility and grace in your speech.

6) Start a public space, evangelistic ministry. Public parks, universities, public roads, and street fairs are examples of public places where free speech is legally protected. Free speech includes the clothing we wear, signs we hold, and literature that we distribute. There are many ways to engage the individuals in your town in evangelistic conversations. One of the easiest ways is to conduct surveys. We would be happy to consult with you on how to stage effective evangelistic outreaches.

7) Volunteer with a local pregnancy resource center (PRC). Beware that there is yet another dark side of the PLM when it comes to PRCs. Many of them have decided to market themselves and operate like secular medical clinics. This of itself is not problematic, but in many cases, those PRCs have also chosen for strategic reasons not to openly share the gospel with clients on first visits. When and if they do share the gospel, it is strictly with the client's permission. I have friends and family members who have had to part ways with PRCs where they were not allowed to talk about abortion as a sin leading to spiritual death. This is something to research as you consider where, how, and with whom to volunteer and donate.

8) A PRC miles away from a killing center is of some value, but keep in mind that only a small percentage of abortion-minded women end up in a PRC, while the vast majority pass through the gates of death at the altar of child sacrifice. If those PRC volunteers and resources are not available where they are needed, consider converting and outfitting a bus, RV, or trailer as a mobile ultrasound unit, pregnancy resource center, or clinic staffed with registered

nurses, and licensed doctors and counselors. A mobile unit has the flexibility to go on location to the gates of death, to university campuses, or to other hot spots of opportunity to reach the lost. Follow our Lord's example who strategically went where the sinners were—a strategy for which he was criticized by other religious leaders (Matt. 9:10-11; Mark 2:15-16; Luke 5:30, 7:34, 15:1).

9) Attempt to intervene at abortion death camps. Recruit and prepare others to assist. Until executives exercise their duty to stop the bloodshed, someone must be there rescuing as many babies as possible. See the previous chapter "Be Present at the Gates of Death" and Appendix: Abortion Intervention Ministry.

10) Plan, encourage, and execute training for the younger members of your family and church. We do not wait until our kids are teenagers to train them to do basic math. Along the way they are learning addition, subtraction, and multiplication so that algebra comes easier when they get older. Similarly, if we want our family and friends to understand justice and mercy and be able to talk about these concepts and the actions that we should be taking to uphold justice and mercy, then we should start training them from a young age.

11) Bring a United for Life presentation, seminar, or outreach event to your community. From a brief crash course to a complete interactive workshop, we can customize a training program that will meet your needs. Our training in apologetics will prepare your group to give an answer that is "seasoned with salt." Our Abortion Intervention Ministry workshop will help you start a ministry at your local abortion death camp. We will be sensitive to your particular theological views and work within the framework of your faith tradition to train, encourage, and equip the saints in your congregation to join in the labor of saving preborn lives and evangelizing lost souls. One of our students named Carrie said:

> Another important aspect of the training was practice. We progressed from being given information to following examples on how to use it, to actually using it ourselves. This aspect really helped me gain confidence that I could be effective in conversing with others on the subject of abortion.

12) Recruit others to join you in these lifesaving spiritual acts of service.

Conclusion

One of my favorite college professors, Avon Malone, was fond of pithy sayings. He used to say, "Brethren and Sistren, we've got to stop sittin' on the premises and start standin' on the promises!" Or during football season he might say, "We need to break the holy huddle and run a play!" Professor Malone understood that church members are really good at seat work. From Sunday mornings, to retreats, conferences, and seminars, we love to go sit to learn.

There is a time for seat work, but we must not neglect the feet work. Transforming lives, whether it is others' or our own, occurs only when we are challenged by putting our learning into practice. Professional ball players study techniques on video and in the classroom, but studying all the tips and techniques will never transform the beginner into an effective player without the challenge of exercise and practice. At some point we must put down the Bible or the devotional handbook and go practice that which we have studied and profess to believe. As President Teddy Roosevelt said:

> It is not the critic who counts; not the man who points out how the strong man stumbles, or where the doer of deeds could have done them better. The credit belongs to the man who is actually in the arena, whose face is marred by dust and sweat and blood; who strives valiantly; who errs, who comes short again and again, because there is no effort without error and shortcoming; but who does actually strive to do the deeds; who knows great enthusiasms, the great devotions; who spends himself in a worthy cause; who at the best knows in the end the triumph of high achievement, and who at the worst, if he fails, at least fails while daring greatly, so that his place shall never be with those cold and timid souls who neither know victory nor defeat. ("Citizenship in a Republic" 23 April 1910)

Make a commitment to do something. It is easy to think that if you cannot give much, then you have nothing to give, or because you do not know what to do, then you should do nothing at all, but it is generally better to do something than nothing. It is better to do something and fail than not to do anything at all. If we were to ask Master Yoda about trying, he would answer, "Try not. Do, or do not. There is no try." Your first steps may be only studying, learning, and observing, but God can use what you might consider meager offerings. Remember the parable of the talents and the little boy with his loaves and fish. Bring what you have and let the Father multiply it.

If we are going to change the hearts and minds of the next generation about abortion, it will not come about through billboards, bumper stickers, and memes. Talking heads on television slinging slogans back and forth are not going to change minds or save lives. Change will come about because believers left the church building and took to the streets to engage this generation in true dialogue, one person at a time, and because they called upon our magistrates to grant justice to our preborn neighbors.

Steel yourself for the conflict that will come from the dark side of the PLM. You will disagree with every person and every organization about something. It might be eschatology, soteriology, theology, evangelistic strategies, political strategies, or all of them! Realize that these conflicts tend to divide and neutralize believers. Many Christians are guilty of focusing on debating the concepts of grace and faith at the expense of performing the acts of faith which should characterize Christian living. From the vantage point of outsiders looking in, should Christians be primarily characterized by statements of belief, or by their actions?

Similarly, when it comes to abortion, believers need to guard against losing too much time and energy fighting with fellow Christians over nuances of strategy and nomenclature. It is easy to focus on the differences, disagreements, and difficulties and allow them to become excuses for doing nothing, but that is the dark side. Turn to the light. Take control of your own attitude and actions. Decide to work with others, even when they are hard to work with. Be the person who will highlight the best in others and applaud their efforts, even if you believe you could do it better or the "right" way. Choose to do something in spite of what others will think or say about you. If you are serious about saving lives and saving souls, then you must go beyond debating. You must move to doing the specific work to abolish abortion. Regardless of your eschatological opinion, when you finally meet the Lord, will he find you faithful (Matt. 25:31; Mark 8:38; Luke 9:26, 18:8)?

In the face of threatening and bullying magistrates, never back down. In the face of critical pro-life friends, family members, and church leaders, never silence the truth. As the abolitionist writer William Lloyd Garrison said:

> I am aware that many object to the severity of my language; but is there not cause for severity? I *will* be as harsh as truth, and as uncompromising as justice. On this subject, I do not wish to think, or to speak, or write, with moderation. No! no! Tell a man whose house is on fire to give a moderate alarm; tell him to moderately rescue his wife from the hands of the ravisher; tell the mother to gradually extricate her babe from the fire into which it has fallen; — but urge me not to use moderation in a cause like the present. ("To the Public," *The Liberator*, 1 Jan. 1831)

Another brother of our Lord communicated a sense of urgency when he said, "Be merciful to those who doubt; rescue others by snatching them from the fire; and to others show mercy, mixed with fear, hating even the clothing stained by the flesh" (Jude 1:22-23).

The American house is engulfed in flames, and babies are cast into the fires of Molech. Now is the time for earnest action. How will you reorder your life and work to accord with the truths revealed in this book? Will you address the sin of abortion in your church congregation and with your family and friends? Will you rally to the state capitol to instruct your legislators to establish the right to life and equal protection of the law? Will you call upon your governor and chief executive officers to stop the bloodshed and end the genocide of abortion? Will you spend your time, talent, and treasure in pursuit of the abolition of abortion?

For some the fire alarm reverberates not only in their ears but also in their hearts. Are you one of them? If you hear and feel that sound, you now know what to do.

Appendix: Abortion Intervention Ministry

I do not claim to be an authoritative expert. I hope that my contribution here convinces you to do something. If that is being present at the gates of death, then I encourage you not to waste time. Whole books and courses teaching the skills of sidewalk ministry have been put together by faithful servants with decades of experience. We encourage you to read one or two, then digest the meat that agrees with you and spit out the bones. In the meantime, here are some practical pointers to help you get started.

Reconnaissance
1) Research your local abortion facility. What hours do they operate? What days do they commit abortion? Where is their property line? Where can you safely park your car?
2) Visit the facility a few times to meet regular protesters, sidewalk advocates, and other ministers who take a stand. Find a regular volunteer or group with whom you would feel comfortable associating and working.
3) Go take a stand and hold a sign for at least one hour. Do more if you can: speak out, distribute literature, or share the good news of reconciliation with passersby.

Planning and Tips

1) Do not dress oddly; dress like a normal person. Weirdness gets in the way of starting and continuing conversations. Do not be weird!
2) Go with an experienced mentor.
3) Strategically place various signs.
4) Offer gift bags.
5) Even nice words sound mean when you yell them, so if you choose to speak, we recommend an amplification device so that you can speak in a normal voice and not sound angry. Use a speaker system rather than a bullhorn which has no bass or mid-range, which makes your voice sound strident and mean.
6) Carry a recording device to document conversations with clients, security, staff, and law enforcement. This is for your own protection so that no one can claim later that you said or did something that you did not.
7) Carry a small notebook and pen. You will want to remember what happened and make notes about how to follow up with people, help them, and pray for them.
8) Be prepared with connections and contact information to various resources. We have a local resource guide with information on how to get help with everything from housing, food, addiction, professional counseling, pregnancy resources, healthcare, etc.

Attempt to Stop Clients

1) You and your partner should position yourselves on either side of the facility driveway.
2) Watch oncoming cars long before they reach the driveway. Anticipate their time of arrival.
3) Make and maintain eye contact with drivers.
4) When the car begins to turn in, throw up your hand and yell *Stop!*
5) You and your partner should offer highly visible gift bags.
6) Signal the occupants to roll down the window.

Talking Points for Clients

1) This gift is for you.

2) What brings you here today? We would like to help you right away.
3) We offer free healthcare and other services right over there.
4) Can we pray with you before you go in?
5) This is a wicked place that murders innocent babies. Please have nothing to do with them.
6) Abortion is never the answer; it can bring a lifetime of guilt and depression and even lead to suicide.
7) You will have to face God and answer for the murder of your child.
8) Use simple words. Less is more. Speak slowly. If they come over, get them talking, and listen.

Talking Points for Drivers

1) This is not over after today. Do you have abortion-recovery materials? You are going to need them. Come over and check out our resources.
2) Is this being a good friend?
3) Give other examples of where you would advise a friend against doing something stupid or immoral. Would not a true friend stop a murder?
4) Maybe you think you are not responsible, it is not your choice, or you have no influence. But you do have influence, and you should use it.
5) You, too, will have to face God.
6) You are just as guilty. You are an accessory. You are driving the getaway car.
7) This will haunt you. You will forever question yourself and this decision, asking, "Why didn't I try to stop her?"
8) It is not too late to show true friendship and courage.
9) You can save a life and maybe a soul today. Come on over, and we can talk about it. Maybe we can help you help her.
10) Use simple words. Less is more. Speak slowly. If they come over, get them talking, and listen.

About the Author

Since 2006 John Shipley Michener has spoken at hundreds of schools, churches, and community organizations on the topic of abortion. He has spent thousands of hours interacting with abortion advocates on university campuses and interposing at abortion facilities across the United States. As a professional educator, John's ministry has focused on getting believers out of their seats and into the streets to defend their preborn neighbors.

John is the past president of the Oklahoma Conservative Political Action Committee, is a newspaper columnist, and before becoming a full-time minister, he served in the administration of Oklahoma Christian University. He previously taught speech and debate.

John was raised in the Church of Christ tradition, and he is an ordained minister of the biblical good news of reconciliation. He has been active in home-based congregations of the Church for most of his adult life. He and his first wife Jayne, who is also his Chief Wife and only wife, have homeschooled their children.

Mr. Michener does not charge a fee for presentations, conferences, consultations, mentoring at outreach events, or customized, in-person training workshops. You may contact him at michenerjs@gmail.com. Learn more about United for Life training at UnitedforLife.us.

Made in the USA
Middletown, DE
02 September 2024